HOW DO YOU GET A WHALE IN VERMONT?

How Do You Get a Whale In Vermont?

The Unlikely Story of Vermont's Official State Fossil

Jeff L. Howe

How Do You Get a Whale in Vermont?

The Unlikely Story of Vermont's Official State Fossil
By Jeff L. Howe
Published by Little Big Trees Press
Strasburg, Pennsylvania, USA

Copyright ©2014 Jeffrey Howe
All rights reserved.

Regional map and cover design: Chalkley Matlack
Cover illustration and line drawings: Jeff L. Howe
Interior design: Davis Creative, www.daviscreative.com
Editing: Mary Ann Schlegel

Library of Congress Control Number: 201392220
ISBN: 978-0-9912853-0-3

ATTENTION CORPORATIONS, UNIVERSITIES, COLLEGES AND PROFESSIONAL ORGANIZATIONS: Quantity discounts are available on bulk purchases of this book for educational, gift purposes, or as premiums for increasing magazine subscriptions or renewals. Special books or book excerpts can also be created to fit specific needs. For information, please contact Little Big Trees Press, jefflhowe@verizon.net, jeff-howe.net.

Dedication

To Zadock Thompson, Vermont's greatest natural historian... and to George Perkins, Robert Trithart, Mary Ann Schlegel, Stephen Bechtel, Stephen Wright, Audrey Hunt, Mary Lighthall, the students of Charlotte Central, and anyone who has ever believed in "Charlotte."

CONTENTS

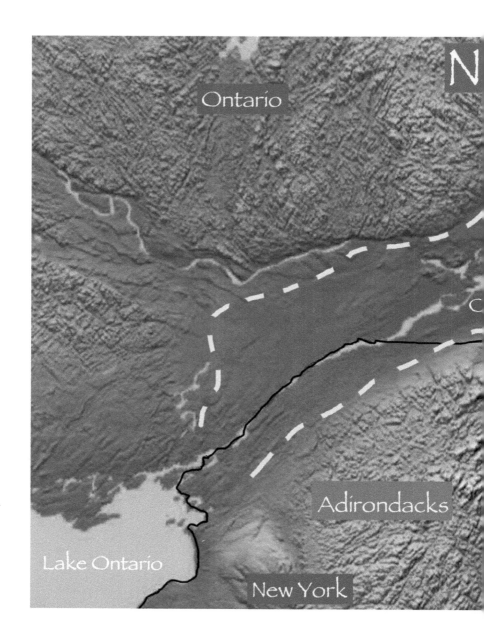

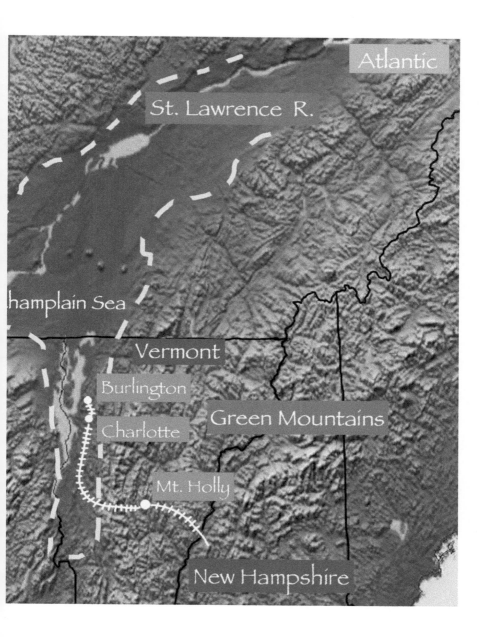

There is something fascinating about science.
One gets such wholesale returns of conjecture
out of such a trifling investment of fact.
                              – Mark Twain.
                        Life on the Mississippi

Introduction

If one sets their imagination free as they drive beneath the cool green August canopy of trees that line Greenbush Road near the base of Mt. Philo in rural western Vermont, it is not hard to envision the dappled submarine environment of a shallow ocean bay. The sun shining through the leaves resembles the rippling of light through the waves above. The fields in the distance become expanses of open water and the groups of scattered cows become schools of distant fish.

This leap of imagination is, in fact, not as drastic as it might at first seem. Approximately 11,000 years ago, Greenbush Road and the entire shore of Lake Champlain lay submerged beneath the cold marine waters of the Champlain Sea, an inland seascape that stretched from Vermont to Ottawa. Nearby Mt. Philo, which had itself been an island in an earlier and much more expansive freshwater lake, sat just above the shoreline, jutting out at times as a promontory. Spruce and pine dotted the surrounding land while herds of caribou and occasional mammoths foraged in the grasslands and bogs. The water was rich with plankton, shellfish and worms that fed schools of cod, capelin and sand lance that worked the shallows and salmon that plied the deeper waters of the sea. These fish in turn provided a plentiful food source for varieties of seals and small whales that frolicked in the cold, shallow, brackish waters fed by numerous streams rich with silt from the mountains.

This is the story of a remnant of that sea — a souvenir — and how it helped to shape the way we view Vermont's prehistoric past.

PART ONE

WIND, ICE AND BONES

1

The Wind and the Sea

It was almost cruel the way the wind blew. It gathered along the mountain ridges and spilled off the distant, retreating wall of glacial ice under its own weight before tumbling down the canyons and spreading out over the lowlands. Trapped between parallel ranges of mountains, the wind was amplified and focused. Without significant trees or vegetation to slow or soften it, it howled across the barren tundra raising clouds of fine dust and stinging crystals of ice, sandblasting everything in its path. And always it was bright – blindingly bright. The constant, penetrating dusty glare of sun reflecting off of ice, water and barren landscape was inescapable... even on days when thick grey clouds covered the skies.

The reigning land mammals – huge wooly mammoths, shaggy musk oxen and occasional herds of sturdy caribou simply turned their backs to the wind and resumed their endless forage through the barren lichens, mosses and stunted plants. Their thick coats and sturdy metabolisms were perfectly suited for the harsh tundra conditions. In temperatures that frequently plummeted fifty degrees below zero and beyond, they hunkered down in whatever shelter was available and waited it out.

Stretched along the horizon, at the foot of the mountains, lay a vast, gleaming, green-blue appendage of the North Atlantic Ocean – the southern arm of the Champlain Sea. It filled a large valley suspended between two ancient ranges of mountains and spilled out onto flat lands to the north and west. Recently, within geologic time, the valley had finally shed the overburden of a moving ice sheet nearly two miles thick. The constant weight of this ice was so great that it crushed the land down – pressing it and squeezing the water, the space, and the life right out of it. It pushed the land down below the level of the sea and held it there until the ice finally began to withdraw. When the glacial ice eventually retreated far enough north of the inlet, the ocean rushed in to fill the depression, creating a rich inland sea that stretched from New York to Quebec and from Ontario to Vermont. It was fed from the mountains and connected to the ocean through what is now known as the St. Lawrence River.

To the east rose a rugged mountain range that had originated nearly a half-billion years before from the muddy, compacted sediments of a long lost ocean. Known today as the Green Mountains, the range ran north and south along the entire eastern shore, forming an imposing barrier to travel from the rich river valleys to the east. And on the southern portion of the western shore rose the taller, older and more rugged Adirondacks – the remnants of even more ancient mountain building processes that pushed back over a billion years into the past.

To the south, the sea extended for over a hundred miles before tapering and ending. In a previous life, when the glacial ice extended this far south, the impounded water drained southward through the ancient drainage down the Hudson River Valley. But now the land was rebounding from the weight of the rapidly receding glaciers and the entire basin had tipped like a wine glass, sending its waters northward instead.

On its surface, blue-white icebergs floated like sailboats, 90% of their mass submerged beneath the waves. They were glacial offspring, calved from the remaining small alpine glaciers that still tumbled out of the mountains. As the wind blew across the surface of the water it raised frothy white caps that slapped against the ice and crashed upon the shore. The ceaseless waves created broad sandy beaches and crushed and recrushed the piles of marine shells into a fine calcareous ooze that trickled down into the beach sands and bound them together gently. From a distance, the water was a milky green-blue, as pale as sun-faded turquoise, from countless billions of microscopic silt grains that bounced the sun's rays back and forth in a spirited game of pinball. The silt poured into the sea from muddy rivers that originated as snow melt but quickly picked up their loads of sand, gravel and fluffy glacial rock flour as they scoured and eroded their way down through the frozen mountains.

In the water, life was abundant. Connected tenuously to the North Atlantic, the Champlain Sea was a microcosm of the great northern ocean, with the added advantage of productive shallows and protection from the deep. Into this inland sea migrated a wealth of marine species and communities. Plankton thrived on the rich nutrients, shell fish followed the plankton with herring and capelin close behind. Larger fish dined on herring and in turn were preyed upon by walrus and seals. Into this sea swam populations of small, white, singing whales with strange knobs on their heads. They played amongst the icebergs, hidden from the wind, feasting on the vast smorgasbord that surrounded them.

Above the water, the wind was relentless but reliable, and in the wind was routine. It blew so consistently that it was barely noticed. But eventually, even the tundra winds were forced from the lowlands and up and over the tops of the mountains by the force of the moving air behind. And as the wind was pushed ever-higher in elevation, it was stripped of any remaining moisture that it contained, coating the mountains with layer upon layer upon layer of fresh Vermont snow.

Nothing crosses the Green Mountains in the winter without paying a toll. The wind was no exception.

2

The Mt. Holly Mammoth and the Ice Age

The terrified mammoth screamed and bellowed inconsolably. Its flailing and splashing only caused more water to freeze on its thick mane, coating its nostrils and making the mammoth's eyelids heavy with ice. Every movement drew murky water beneath its wooly fur, forcing out the warm, thick air and replacing it with an icy, killing cold. The huge animal would hang on for days, alternating between thrashing wildly and resting in resignation. Initially the thrashing consumed the majority of its time and effort, but eventually exhaustion and defeat would hold sway.

The mammoth had been following the historical path of least resistance, journeying over a low, certain crossing of the southern end of the rugged Green Mountains which connected the great eastern river to the southern arm of the inland sea. It was the route that had been used by migrating herds for generations, since the leading edge of the huge wall of ice had ground to a halt and begun its northward retreat. The trail worked its way up out of the river valley to the east and penetrated the highest mountain ridge through a steep river gap. Near the summit, the trail crossed a low, flat hollow – a slightly protected depression that separated two parallel ridges. The ridges were low and the hollow was exposed but large rocks did offer modest protection from the killing winds that swept along the high ground. The site also offered fresh water and what scant vegetation that could be scraped from the rocks beneath the snow.

Just ahead (near a place that would eventually be named Mt. Holly) the trail dropped down along another river, this one draining westward towards the setting sun. It worked quickly out of the deep snow and into more forgiving terrain and more productive foraging. Eventually the trail spilled out along the shores of an inland arm of the sea. But these were the least of the mammoth's concerns. Its goal at the moment was simple survival.

The quagmire in which the mammoth struggled had likely begun as a kettle hole – a water-filled depression marking the spot where a giant glacial block of ice had melted. Originally buried in sand and mud by the retreating glaciers, the insulated block melted slowly, leaving a conical depression in the soil. Because the soil was thin and the bedrock so near to the surface, drainage was poor and the area retained water year-round. The brief summers had already filled it with clay and organic muck, and as plants began to colonize the edges, it would gradually become an acidic bog. Thousands of years in the future it would become a beaver pond, and after that, a spongy marsh. But the beaver and the marsh would first have to wait for the trees of the great southern forests to colonize and slowly overtake the barren tundra.

On this Pleistocene day the half frozen bog was covered with thin ice and the ice in turn by a dusting of wind-blown snow. A tiny underground spring brought up just enough subterranean warmth to prevent the ice at the middle of the bog from freezing completely.

Smelling water, the mammoth had approached cautiously. Its instincts, the product of a thousand generations, told it what to do. Gingerly it felt the ground for assurance, and found it. But the young mammoth was impatient. Mammoths spent up to 20 hours a day looking for food and it had had no water or food since entering the high country the day before. The faint scent of the sparse algae and matted plants beneath the thin veneer of snow was enticing, but the thick ice along the shoreline masked the delicacy of the ice at the bog's center. When the hungry mammoth reached the thin ice near the middle, it was plunged wildly and abruptly into the half-frozen muck and shoulder-deep water of the hole. The cold was immediate and terrifying.

"Sckloritich–glauk-ut" was the sound of mud suctioning and yielding to the massive, hair-matted body. *"Sckloritich-glauk-ut."* The mammoth's huge head reeled as the smell of rot and decay filled its sinuses and assaulted its brain. It was the terrifying smell of death.

Along the northern horizon, the mammoth could see the hulking wall of ice, so imposing that it created its own weather. What lay beyond was unrelenting ice and desolation. To a single mammoth the ice seemed stationary. Over a single lifetime, the ice never seemed to move.

In reality however, in Earth time, the wall of ice was in hasty retreat.

• • •

The Earth is an imperfect top, wobbling delicately as it spins on its axis. On a human scale this wobble is imperceptible, but over the course of 41,000 years, the pole scans an arc of greater than 45 degrees back and forth across the night sky. The North Star, reliable Polaris, is really only a momentary deer caught in the headlights of our wandering pole.

This imperfect wobbling creates an irregular orbit, varying from less than circular to strongly elliptical. In addition, the route our planet traces through space moves us in and out of clouds of dust and debris and in precarious gravitational alignments with other planets. The interplay of these variations and cycles, combined with the natural seasonal fluctuations that result from the northern hemisphere's tilt toward and away from the sun, produces progressive climate change that has been a part of the earth's history since shortly after its birth.

Ice Ages are one result of this give and take of energy. They are the complex, sum total, end-result of periodic decreased solar energy reaching portions of the Earth. Whether this results from the orbital cycles described above, from decreased activity on the sun or other reasons not yet discovered, is open to debate. We are only beginning to understand it.

The Ice Age that we are most familiar with, the one that ensnared the mammoth and the one that has been ebbing and flowing for nearly two and a half million years, is not the only ice age that has gripped our Earth. There is ample evidence — ancient striations and scratch marks in the rock, outwash plains and unconsolidated piles of drift — to indicate that ice ages have been part of the earth's history since shortly after it first cooled and formed a crust.

· · ·

Consider the view from the window nearest to where you now sit. If you live in a northern climate, you know that snow falls in the winter and can pile up outside, sometimes to great depths. On some occasions there may be great blizzards that dump snow by the foot, blocking the roads, canceling schools and sending everyone outside to shovel. On other occasions, it may become unusually warm for periods in mid-winter, melting the snow and causing water to run everywhere. But regardless of what the weather does on a day-to-day or week-by-week basis, you can be confident that by spring the snow will be gone, the sun will warm and another cycle of warmth and growth will begin. It has been that way all of your life. It is all that you know. But your own personal view of time is terribly short-sighted because even if you live to be 100 years old, you will have lived a mere *one forty-five millionth* of the age of the earth, or *one twenty-five thousandth* of the last ice age.

Now imagine what would happen outside that same window if conditions changed and following a winter of unusually heavy snows, spring came late and deep snows persisted into June. The Earth may be turned away from the sun at this particular time or excessive dust from volcanic activity elsewhere on the planet may diminish the amount of solar energy that reaches the surface. (A similar situation persisted in 1816 when the cataclysmic eruption of Mt. Tambora in Indonesia coincided with a historic low in solar activity. That year, 1816, is sometimes referred to as "the year without a summer.") The snow cover reflects the sun's rays and prevents the ground from thawing. The summer is unusually cold, and by autumn snow remains in the shadows, beneath bridges, and on the protected sides of houses and trees. Winter that year comes early and snow again piles up to uncommon depths. Once again, the spring fails to warm sufficiently to melt the snow and the next winter is begun with considerable snow on the ground. As this cycle continues, snow remains the entire year, and as the summer sun fails to melt away the accumulated snows of winter, the snow continues to increase in depth. Eventually, after many yearly cycles, the snow begins to compact under its own weight.

If you happened to be looking out your window onto the flat, featureless plains that surrounded the Hudson Bay a few million years ago, that is exactly what you would have seen. Within less than a lifetime, your house would become completely buried in snow, and would slowly be crushed by the accumulating weight. As the weight of the snow increased with depth, the ice at the bottom would begin to recrystallize into flat parallel sheets that slide upon one another. Eventually, you, your crushed house and your entire yard right down to bedrock would be slowly and inexorably moved down-gradient with the grinding, inching ice.

• • •

"Sckloritich-glauk-ut."

The mammoth had no way of knowing, nor did it care, that many years ago, the very spot where he was now mired had been over-run by a sheet of ice many thousands of feet thick. The ice had ground its way southward, smothering the landscape and gouging, scratching and polishing the bedrock as it went. The leading edge had traveled far beyond this spot, hundreds of miles to the south. At that point the physics that spawned the glacier and ran the engine could no longer be sustained, and the ice began wasting away. The leading edge retreated northward, melting and leaving behind a legacy of its furthest advance written in the rocky debris of Long Island and Cape Cod.

The mammoth had been bound for the productive, protected lowlands that surrounded the inland sea. In its haste it had strayed too far from the herd, and had taken a foolish chance. The mistake would be fatal. Now, almost four days after falling into the frozen pit, the mammoth's life had been reduced to its essentials: breath, stay warm, hope.

Slowly the mammoth's eyes became clouded − first with rage and fear, then with exhaustion, and finally with ice as the mounting snowflakes began congealing on the rapidly cooling hide. The warmth would be the first to go. The next would be hope, and finally breathing would slow to a stop. Gradually, as its muscles relaxed, the mammoth sank passively into the frozen muck and yielded to sleep. As the snow piled up against the lee side of its head, its eyes blurred to nothingness and its will gave way to the howling wind.

3

The Wilderness

The Vermont mountains stretch extended straight.
New Hampshire mountains curl up in a coil.
— Robert Frost

Vermont has historically been a remote and inaccessible wilderness; therein lies much of its mystique and charm. Stretching four-fifths of a mile tall by a mountain range wide and over a half-billion years old, it is a vast expanse of hardwood-spruce forests and brambly underbrush draped over the rugged, metamorphic Green Mountains like a great rumpled blanket. Like Alaska or the Upper Peninsula of Michigan, you have to consciously go there to get there. Otherwise, you simply end up somewhere else.

In a strictly geographic sense, Vermont doesn't exist at all. In a perfect world, politics would divide the land like the water does. Political boundaries would run along the spine of drainage divides, not down the middle of lakes and rivers. In a perfect Vermont world, the valleys would be left intact and the divide would tiptoe along the crest of the Green Mountains, separating the hypothetical states of Champlain to the west, and New Connecticut to the east. A vestige of this separation remains. It is Vermont law and tradition that the Governor and Lieutenant Governor be elected separately, regardless of party affiliation, reflecting an old law which required the Governor and the Lieutenant Governor to be from opposite sides of the state, east of the mountains and west.

This inaccessible remoteness that defines Vermont has also been her undoing. Throughout history, travel was been relatively easy from north to south, up and down the river valleys of the Connecticut and the Hudson/Champlain. Until recent modern times however, it was virtually impossible to travel east and west over the spine of the Green Mountains, especially in winter, mud season or bug season. (*When all three occur simultaneously, as they do for about four months a year, the uninitiated are advised to stay indoors.*)

The first people to explore Vermont came into it from the south, following the great wall of ice as it retreated northward. To these explorers, Vermont was a desolate wash of frozen mountains, wasting ice and sparse tundra drained by broad plains of muddy sediments. But it contained enormous potential resources. Herds of large game were abundant, and far to the north lay an icy sea rich in nutritious marine life. These explorers ventured north, made brief stays and then returned to the south with the seasons – each year extending their world ever-northward. Eventually they stayed. The realm of the powerful Algonquins extended from far beyond the western horizon to the shores of the great long, deep finger of the sea that drained even farther northward to the ocean. They traveled through the eastern mountains to follow game and to fish in the valley beyond. The more agrarian, and sedentary Abanakis were drawn to the broad plain to the north, where the mountain ranges melted away. The tribes to the south and east controlled the broad valley of the Connecticut River that ran all the way to the ocean and the rich fishing banks just off shore. All groups used the mountains for game and for transit. In fact, it appears that Vermont may have been used for millennia by multiple native groups for hunting, fishing and traveling without significant, long-term conflict.

As people of European descent expanded across North America in the 17th and 18th centuries, they divided and parceled the land as they went. First coastal Massachusetts was settled, then the fertile valleys of the Connecticut, Hudson, Delaware, Potomac and James. They cleared and settled the wilderness of the Susquehanna River, opening the Great Valley, and then preceded over the mountains to Pittsburgh and down the Ohio River to Cincinnati, St. Louis and all points west. The mountains of Vermont however remained largely unchallenged.

• • •

There are few relatively easy places in which an east-west traverse across the Green Mountains can be made.

The combined valleys of the White and Winooski Rivers offer the best option, forming a deep cut through the mountains that has been used for millennia. The glaciers first carved it out, straightened it and smoothed it and then floored it with broad river sediments. Migrating animals, exploring humans, dusty coach roads and eventually railroads and modern highways further tamed it. The problem here however, is that the west-bound traveler drops out of the mountains near the middle of Lake Champlain and must then divert at least fifty miles either north or south to circumvent it.

Farther to the north, the traveler can go completely around the northern tip of the Green Mountains for an easy cross of the Richelieu River at the north end of Lake Champlain. This can be treacherous in the winter and diverts the traveler from the rich resources of the Adirondacks, if that is their goal. If their goal however, is the St. Lawrence River and access to the ocean, this route is preferable.

Migrants traveling from coastal settlements to the south towards Lake Champlain followed either the Connecticut or Hudson River northward. The Hudson route brought the traveler to a low divide that crossed into the northward flowing Champlain Basin. Travelers heading up the Connecticut River left the river at what is now Bellows Falls, and worked their way up the Black River, following the headwaters into the Green Mountains. Here they crossed the eastern ridge and entered a low, rounded valley at the top. At the summit elevation of only 1415 ft., the trail crossed the divide at what is now known as Mt. Holly, swung wide of a marshy bog and then worked back down through a second ridge and down the Mill River towards Rutland in the Champlain Valley. The advantages of this route were that it was relatively direct, low in elevation, and arrived at the south end of the lake where it could be crossed easily. The traveler then proceeded on to the Adirondacks and the productive wilds of northern New York and Pennsylvania.

This was the route first discovered by the migrating herds of mammoth, caribou and deer and utilized by the native humans that followed them. Later this would be the path followed by the trappers, the wagons and the settlers, as Vermont opened up to western civilization. And then, in a burst of technology, crews of workers cleared the trees, blasted the rock, evened the grades and rounded the corners — allowing the railroads to pierce the Green Mountains and connect western Vermont with the rest of the world.

4

The Walk Along the Tracks

Retired ship captain George Thorp had spent a lifetime at sea. He was not a rich man but he had managed his money well, and when the land winds blew him to a small farming settlement in western Vermont, he made the voyage gladly. The year was 1799. He had come to the small village of Charlotte in the Champlain lowlands to settle the estate of his late cousin, John Thorp, who had emigrated from Ireland four years earlier and had set up a mercantile and lumber business along the main road between Burlington and Rutland. The choice lands along Lake Champlain were being settled rapidly and Thorp's business prospered.

In addition to settling the estate, George Thorp sweetened the deal by marrying his cousin's grieving widow and settling down on the fertile lowlands adjacent to Thompson's Point. Very quickly he adapted to the life of husband, farmer, entrepreneur and country gentleman, building a house and small store on a quiet lane about a mile east of the lake in the morning shadow of Mt. Philo.

• • •

In August of 1849, the last stretch of the Rutland-Burlington railroad was nearing completion a short distance west of the Thorp farm. Two rail companies, the Rutland-Burlington and the Vermont Central were in fierce competition to complete the first railroad through the Green Mountains, connecting Boston to Burlington and eventually to Montreal. The Vermont Central was following the mid-State route through the Winooski Valley while the Rutland-Burlington was following the old stage coach route, crossing over the southern pass at Mt. Holly.

Both crews were composed primarily of hard-working, hard-drinking Irishmen driven from their homeland by the potato famine that had decimated northern Europe. Spurred on by promises of whiskey and bonuses, in two short years they had pushed west from Bellows Falls, penetrated the core of the Green Mountains at Mt. Holly and then dropped down into the Champlain Valley at Rutland. The port city of Burlington, the final terminus, was now less than 20 miles away.

In 1849, the Thorp family business was run by Captain Thorp's son, John. The farm and store remained a prosperous enterprise. Work on the railroad proceeded adjacent to his farm and over the course of the summer, John Thorp developed a friendly relationship with the railroad workers and often wandered down from his house to chat with overseers and observe the on-going construction.

Just north of Thorp's home, the railroad encountered a particularly bothersome grade over a small rise leading towards Burlington. William Wright had been contracted to grade and fill a three mile stretch of track from Thorp's Crossing northward through what was then known as Barber's Swamp. It was a wet, mucky area, where the thick vegetation retained much water. The workmen were moving slowly through the heavy wet sand and sticky-blue clay that underlay much of the area. The clay was thick and wet, sticking to their shovels and boots and threatening in spots to suck them in like quicksand. Almost as quickly as they dug, the area beneath their feet would fill with water. Their pickaxes and shovels would often strike submerged roots and rocks which impeded their progress, requiring them to drive the pick into the mud with all their weight and then quickly hurl whatever they had struck into the growing pile behind them. In this manner, the process of filling the swamp with a long straight ribbon of sand and gravel proceeded slowly and laboriously.

The warm August afternoon was pleasant. Cicadas buzzed in the tall green grass as Thorp strolled along the worksite amidst the clanking of tools and the labored shouts of workers. July had been an unusually hot month, with many days into the 90's, rare for Vermont. The weather in August had been more seasonal, although a bit wetter than normal. But with no recent stretches of hot sticky weather, the hordes of mosquitoes that had made life so unbearable in the spring and early summer were now greatly diminished.

With the sharp eye of a nosey Vermonter, Thorp walked slowly, scanning the piles of sand and clay unearthed by the busy workmen. After traveling about a quarter mile from the road his attention was drawn to what appeared to be an odd bone or a shattered root protruding from the pile of drying muck. It was smooth and leathery and fleshy brown in color. As he brushed clay from it, it had what appeared to be unusual indentations and grooves. It seemed to be part of a skull, although the skull of *what* he couldn't imagine. Some of the workers noticed him examining the objects, and mentioned how they had struck upon the skeleton of an animal earlier in the day and were perplexed as to how a horse or cow could have become buried at such a depth. Thorp asked the workers to show him the spot where the bones had been found and after further examination, he could see that the remains of what appeared to be an entire skeleton were still encased in the mud extending roughly perpendicular to, and away from, the tracks — into the blue clay.

As a farmer, Thorp knew immediately that these bones were not those of a horse or a cow, or for that matter, of any other animal that he had ever encountered. Thorp recalled reading that the bones of a fossil elephant had been discovered the previous summer in Mt. Holly during construction of the same railroad. The bones had been sent to Harvard University for examination by renowned geologist Louis Agassiz, and then had been returned to naturalist Zadock Thompson at the University of Vermont in Burlington.

Professor Zadock Thompson had already developed a reputation as an astute authority on natural history in Vermont and had authored a number of books and almanacs on the subject. He was the local expert on everything from birds to weather to physical geography. Whenever an answer or identification was required, Thompson was the authority to be consulted. Thorp approached Wright with the bones and asked if work might be discontinued at that particular site until Thompson could be contacted and shown the remains. Reluctantly Wright agreed and moved his crews to a different portion of the cut while two men were dispatched by wagon to Burlington with the box of bones for Professor Thompson.

5

The Young Naturalist

The lure of inexpensive land in the rapidly expanding Allegany wilderness appealed to Barnabas Thompson of Massachusetts. The Thompsons were the direct linear descendants of the hardy European pioneers who had immigrated to the northern colonies of America in the generation immediately following the Pilgrims. They settled about 12 miles west of Plymouth Harbor in the "alternative settlement" of Halifax, an indication that the original Plymouth colony was already beginning to stretch its physical and social boundaries.

But after 150 years of the Thompson family working the land, young Barnabas's father was finding it increasingly difficult to farm the sandy soils of coastal Massachusetts. The fractious events of the American Revolution had changed the social order and now the best lands inland were taken, and what lands that remained along the coastal plain were rapidly escalating in price. So in 1791, (the year that Vermont earned Statehood), Barnabas Thompson, his young wife, and two of his brothers, moved northwestward to the wilds of Bridgeport, Vermont. They chose a pleasant upland valley in the foothills along the eastern flank of the Green Mountains, a few dozen miles north of the southern pass that had taken animals and natives back and forth through the mountains for thousands of years. The Thompsons cleared the land and established a homestead. Two years later his father Noah joined them, and three years after that, Barnabas Thompson and his wife celebrated the birth of their second child: Zadock. Then through the riotous cycles of Vermont's four seasons – Winter, Mud, Bug and Fall – the intelligent and ever-curious young Zadock Thompson watched Vermont grow.

• • •

Zadock Thompson spent his childhood on the family farm, roaming the hills and fields with his brothers and sisters. Farm life in rural 19th century Vermont was a tough prospect. The short growing season, thin rocky soils, and long bitter winters guaranteed a life of hard work. But Vermont farmers have always been a proud and resourceful lot and by local standards, Zadock's family was better off than many, with both food to eat and warmth to share.

In 1808, in the spring of his twelfth year, a horrible accident nearly took the life of young Thompson. Little has come down to us about the accident and the details are sketchy because Thompson was an intensely private person and spoke little of the event in later years. All that is known is that he suffered a "sugaring" accident in which his foot was gashed severely. The cut was life-threatening and he nearly died before the bleeding could be stopped. Along the frontier, medical attention was unreliable and Zadock suffered fevers and infections that left him bedridden and frail for a lengthy period. Disability and infirmity as the result of the accident plagued Zadock for the rest of his life.

While confined to his bed, Thompson indulged his great loves of reading and learning, devouring what few books he could find on the Vermont frontier. He was intensely curious, a keenly observant scholar and a meticulous record-keeper. These traits acquired in his youth served him well throughout his academic life.

It was during his youthful days in Bridgewater that Zadock met Phoebe Boyce. Old maps show that Phoebe's father, Jacob Boyce, lived on the farm next to Zadock's older brother. Zadock was only two years older than Phoebe and it is likely that they knew each other as children. With a limited number of playmates and with their shared interest in the natural world, it's likely they played together as well.

By 1813, at the age of seventeen, young Thompson had exhausted local resources and enrolled in the academy at Randolph, adopting a cycle of studying and teaching that lasted for four years. In 1817 he left Randolph and headed "west" to Lima, New York. However, he again became ill and was forced to return to Vermont. It was during this period of infirmity that Thompson calculated his first almanac. Though highly regarded as accurate, the almanac didn't sell.

Finally, in 1820, Zadock moved to Burlington and enrolled at the University of Vermont (UVM). Upon his arrival he found a pleasant town on the eastern shore of Lake
Champlain, growing up the hillside towards the young
campus that had been founded along a grassy green at
the top by one of the Green Mountain Boys in 1791.

Burlington in the 1820's was a growing town of about
2500 residents. Although it lay far inland, over 300
miles from the ocean, its proximity to Montreal and the
St. Lawrence River gave Thompson a sense of connect-
edness with the greater world outside of Vermont. With
close economic ties to Montreal and a direct stage route
to Boston, 19th century Burlington enjoyed prosperity
unusual for a town so far removed from the remainder
of post-colonial New England. For a rural bumpkin from
Bridgewater, Thompson found the cultural and academic
atmosphere of Burlington to be refreshing.

Having spent the previous four years teaching during the winter and attending the Academy in Randolph
during the summers, Zadock was proficient enough to be
placed into the sophomore class, and three years later he
graduated with honors. Within a year of his graduation he
married Phoebe Boyce and two years following that they
purchased a small house along the University Green.

Phoebe shared Zadock's interests in nature and history
and worked actively to help him with his projects. No pictures of Phoebe Boyce Thompson have survived, but like
Zadock she was probably a quiet and stoic woman. In my

mind's eye, I picture her as petite and pretty in a plain sort of way. Zadock and Phoebe had three children: a son who died as an infant, their first daughter Harriet who died in childhood, and finally a daughter Adeline Phoebe, born in 1829. Adeline was the only child to survive to adulthood. She shared her parents' interest in nature and had a talent for drawing. (Adeline Thompson was the first artist to make illustrations of the whale bones for her father.)

Thompson continued to observe, catalogue and document the natural history of Vermont. By 1824 he had published the *Vermont Gazetteer*, and in 1825 he was appointed Tutor of Mathematics and Science at the University of Vermont. Also in 1825 he published *Youth's Assistant in Practical Arithmetic,* which finally began to garner him a degree of financial success.

By 1826, the Thompsons were able to piece together sufficient funds from the wages and royalties that Zadock was earning to purchase a small house for $1000. Located at 75 S. Prospect St., it was a plain but sturdy home with two pleasant acres. Two years later they enlarged the house substantially in preparation for transforming it into Burlington's first boarding school for girls.

The enlarged house at 75 South Prospect eventually became known as the "Torrey House" and could be found on University and Burlington maps until 1940. In that year, the entire house was placed on a huge trailer and moved, with great fanfare, down the street to 466 So. Prospect in preparation for the construction of UVM's Waterman Hall. (By scaling off old maps, the original location of the house can reliably be placed where the back portion of the North wing of Waterman Hall now rests.)

(Author's Note: The Torrey House is owned by UVM and is still in use. In 1994, I contacted UVM and asked if I could inspect the inside of the building, being used at that time by the Office of Employee Assistance. They granted my request, and I remember approaching the building on a sunny winter's day with great reverence. I entered through the old front door, the door through which Zadock had passed thousands of times. I gazed out the windows, trying to imagine the cottage and the green. I climbed the tight, narrow staircase imagining Zadock and Phoebe walking up and down the very same steps as they tended to the young residents of the boarding house. I asked if I could crawl into the attic, secretly hoping that I might stumble upon the long-lost drawings of young Adeline Thompson scrawled on the walls or rafters. The attic contained original old 18" floor planks with square-headed nails... and a great view out the tiny attic windows, but sadly, no drawings.)

The boarding school on Prospect Street succeeded for a couple of years but eventually failed and by 1831 the Thompsons were forced to sell the house and half the property to Professor Joseph Torrey for $1200. They then moved their small family next door into a cottage on the remaining acre. It was in this small cottage that Thompson lived the remainder of his life, and in which Phoebe lived until 1876 when she sold it for $2400 and moved to Northfield to live with her granddaughter.

6

The Cottage on the Green

"Zadock…" Phoebe Thompson called to her husband from the back door of the cottage, "two gentlemen from the railroad wish to speak to you."

53 year-old Professor Zadock Thompson, self-described "science master for the common man," was working in the garden and didn't particularly care to be disturbed. He craned his bony neck in the direction of his wife and then rising slightly, was just able to peer over the trellised bean plants that threatened to completely overtake his garden.

Thompson lived in a small, cluttered cottage across from the College Green on Prospect Street in Burlington, with his wife and two daughters. Although tiny, it was by all accounts a pleasant and comfortable home, surrounded by large spacious gardens filled with interesting and well-tended plants. The gardens were well-populated by hummingbirds, chickadees and a variety of small animals, and the cottage itself was a clutter of boxes and shelves containing rocks, fossils, bones and a variety of curiosities collected from all over New England. It was here that

Thompson carried out his investigations on everything from the medicinal value of plants, to the interrelationships of different kinds of animals, to changing weather patterns, religiously keeping a series of daily meteorological measurements that he maintained until just before his death in 1856.

The two men who now approached him wore the clothes of workmen and walked with an easy confidence. They carried a small wooden crate, which appeared to contain a load of firewood sticking out in all directions.

"My what a beautiful day, Professor Thompson!" The man offered his hand.

"Sir, my name is Mr. Jackson, and this is Mr. Boardman. We are with the Rutland-Burlington Railroad. If we could bother you for a little of your time, we'd like to show you some bones that we find completely puzzling."

Zadock cleared a work table and the men set the box down, telling the story of how the bones had been found. As Zadock listened, he carefully removed the clay-covered bones one-by-one, inspecting them as he went. He noted rib fragments, an apparent sternum and portions of what appeared to be a skull. Of this he was fairly certain, but they seemed to be from an animal with which he was not familiar. There were no limb bones, and from the shape of the skull, it appeared to be either saurian (lizard) or cetacean (whale). There were no teeth to offer clues as to the animal's diet, although the holes for dentition were empty and free of clay. This indicated to Thompson that the teeth had fallen out during the excavation and might still be recovered at the site.

Thanking Mr. Jackson and Mr. Boardman, Zadock enthusiastically assured them that he would travel to the work site immediately after examining these bones to collect what specimens might remain. Thankful that they had finally left, Zadock pulled up a chair and gave the bones a more careful inspection.

Although Thompson didn't know it yet, the bones had been entombed in the sediments of the former Champlain Sea for more than a hundred centuries. The bones had become saturated with water, and slowly the strengthening calcium was leached away leaving behind leathery collagen. While buried beneath the ground, the bones were protected from the atmosphere and the effects of surface weather. The wet muds kept them hydrated and remarkably stable, but upon exposure to the air, they risked drying out, shrinking and deforming.

By the time the bone fragments arrived at Thompson's cottage they had already begun to dry out and crack. Thompson was aware of the effects of aerial exposure on long-buried animals, having collected and preserved the bones of the mammoth found the previous summer in Mt. Holly. So he immediately coated the bones liberally with animal glue to preserve them and prevent further desiccation. Unknown to Thompson, this act of preservation would prevent future scientists from obtaining an exact age of the whale because the animal glue impregnated the bones with modern organic matter, making further carbon[14] dating impossible. You could try to date the bones, but you'd only get the age of the horse that gave its life to make the glue.

He set to work immediately — cleaning the dried clay from the bone fragments and hardening them as he went. Slowly, the vague outline of a thin elongated skull began to emerge from the fragments. Having stabilized the first group of bones, Thompson embarked immediately on the 25 mile journey to the site and collected as many fragments of the skeleton as possible. Most of the vertebrae and ribs were still intact in the clay and were removed after much effort. The skull however, the most diagnostic part of the skeleton, had been the first to be exposed by the worker's shovels and had been badly shattered in the early stages of excavation. Much of the skull had long since been discarded with the dirt and only through great effort was Thompson able to recover additional skull fragments as well as a few conical yellowish brown teeth. Unfortunately, some of the workmen had already removed bones from the site, and those bones were never recovered.

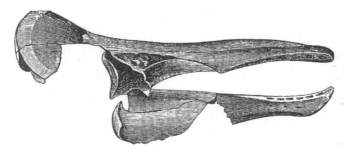

(Figure 2 – A woodcut of the skull that accompanied Zadock Thompson's first description of the whale in 1850. Note how much of the skull was originally missing.)

The bones that lay before Thompson spoke to him immediately. He knew from the rounded convex nature of the vertebrae that this animal moved by flexing its spine in an up and down manner, rather than side to side. The small, distinct chevron bones on the tail suggested the attachment of powerful muscles. The conical teeth implied an animal that fed by grabbing small prey and swallowing it whole without chewing or slashing, and the short powerful limbs suggested an animal that propelled itself horizontally by pushing and pulling rather than by moving up and down over the ground on limbs. The fragments of the skull, when put together even suggested the presence of a blowhole, a feature common to members of the whale family.

Thompson pondered these observations as he continued to work in his garden on the Green, taking his daily meteorological observations and giving his lectures on mathematics and natural history at the college. Although an astute observer of natural phenomena, Thompson was essentially self-taught. He had no one with which to confer and operated essentially alone as a scientific naturalist in mid-19th century Vermont. There existed no reference library on natural science in Burlington at the time and in fact, Thompson once remarked: "a respectable library for the use of a naturalist could not have been culled from all the public and private libraries and all the bookstores in Vermont." Despite these limitations, Thompson's natural instincts suggested to him that the animal he faced was in fact a member of the cetacean, or whale, family. So he consulted one of the few books available to him: Georges Cuvier's classic 1825 French text on comparative anatomy. From this book Thompson concluded that the bones that lay in his lab were most closely related to the small white whale that had been first described at the mouth of an arctic river in Russia in 1776, and which inhabited the far northern oceans of the world.

Curious.

But solving one mystery only introduced a host of other questions to be answered. Thompson stared at the bones scattered about on his work table, scratched his head and then walked into the cottage from the garden to ask his wife the question that would be asked many times in the years to come:

"Phoebe, how do you get a whale in Vermont?"

PART TWO

1849

7

The World in 1849

Late in 1848, word raced eastward at the speed of a rumor of the discovery of gold in the foothills of the Sierra Nevada Mountains of central California. Over the winter, dreams of fabulous wealth grew in the telling and the retelling and by the spring of 1849, the world was clamoring to make the treacherous journey to California. Fathers and husbands left families behind to seek the family fortune. Farmers left their fields untended and city slickers left secure but boring jobs for the adventure of seeking gold in the West.

In all, over 80,000 persons made their way west in 1849, and by 1852, the population of San Francisco had grown from a familiar 14,000 "non-natives" to a quarter-million hopeful Argonauts. Young people made their escape and many an adventurer invested their dreams and the entirety of their fortunes for the barest glimpse of gold. So many ships came into the San Francisco harbor full of treasure seekers that many were abandoned right there for want of a crew to sail them back out again. Nearly half of those ships were from New England.

In 1849, Zachary Taylor, "Old Rough and Ready," a distinguished veteran with tours of duty in the War of 1812, the Indian wars and the Mexican-American war, was inaugurated as the 12th President of the United States. By July of the following year he would be dead of undetermined causes. "Acute gastroenteritis" was listed as the official cause although the circumstances of his death are poorly understood and assassination conspiracy theories persist to this day. (Taylor's body was exhumed and tested for traces of poison in 1991, but no conclusive results were obtained.)

During his brief tenure in office, the national maelstrom that Taylor found himself embroiled in revolved around the issues of abolition and slavery — a debate that would eventually erupt in the Civil War a decade later. Although a former slave-owner himself, Taylor was adamant about upholding the law of the land, and when southern states threatened to hold a succession convention over the issue of slavery in the western territories recently gained in the war with Mexico, Taylor vowed to "lead the army myself" and hang anyone who resisted.

In 1849, Harriet Tubman escaped slavery in Maryland and made her way north to freedom along the Underground Railroad, only to return to the south over a dozen times, duplicating the perilous journey in order to help 300 former slaves also gain their freedom. "I never lost a passenger," she is reported to have said. In 1850, the State of Vermont, the first state to include abolition of slavery in its constitution, declared slavery to be a "crime against humanity," setting off a fervor of abolitionism and establishing Vermont as a preferred destination for runaway slaves.

In the lead-up to the Civil War, Vermont's abolitionist attitude is widely reported to have stirred the Georgia General Assembly to debate a resolution suggesting that the entire state of Vermont be chopped away from the rest of the country and "towed like a barge out to sea." Although this may accurately reflect the attitude of Georgia's legislators, who were generally regarded at the time to be a surly and disagreeable bunch, it has never been positively confirmed.

In 1849, lines for the "magnetic telegraph" were spreading across the country like giant webs, making communication with distant cities almost instantaneous. By 1847, Burlington was connected to New Haven and Boston, and the following year the line was extended to Montreal.

Also spreading was the railroad, replacing the overland stage and the canal systems and providing reliable and fast transit and transportation. In Vermont, two railroad companies were frantically competing to become the first to cross the rugged Green Mountains and link Burlington with the East Coast. Within a generation, railroads would span the entire continent, connecting New York to San Francisco along a continuous steel rail. In 1842, Vermont had neither railroads nor canals within its boundaries, but by 1850 there were ten railroads totaling 493 miles of track. Noted Zadock Thompson in 1852: "We little thought that the short period of ten years would witness the completion of a network of rail road over the whole country." By 1849, the fabled Erie Canal, which had opened up the Ohio Territory to a new wave of settlement just a generation before was already becoming outmoded and sat largely abandoned.

In the five years preceding 1849, four western states entered the Union and the Minnesota Territory was established. In the five years that followed, the state of California and seven territories were added. Western land was plentiful and inexpensive. With the invention of the steel plow by Vermonter John Deere, the fertile sod of the prairie could be turned over and converted immediately to crops – no trees to cut down or land to clear. For many New Englanders used to thin, poorly-draining soils full of stumps and rocks, the West presented the ultimate opportunity, and they left in droves. Growing to 300,000 residents by the early 1840's, Vermont failed to gain another 100,000 until well into the 20th century. During the 1850's, the wild years of the California gold rush and Nevada's silver boom, Vermont saw a net increase of only 978 persons! Some worried that New England might be totally abandoned – that the allure of cheap lands, the gold rush, and adventure might lure the youth away forever.

In 1849, a French physicist established the speed of light at 186,300 miles (300,000 km) per hour and U.S. patents were awarded for the safety pin, reinforced concrete, and the repeating rifle. Across the East and Midwest, thousands of farmers rushed to buy the new $100 McCormack reapers to replace the field workers who had left for the gold fields.

And also in 1849, just two years before Herman Melville published "Moby Dick," Professor Zadock Thompson discovered a great white whale of his own. Because he had been weak and sickly all his life, Thompson was unsuited to leave the security of the land that he knew so well and make the long hard journey by land or sea, to take his chances in the west. He was a Vermonter, free and proud and he was doing what he had always been meant to do. And so, in this swirling vortex of gold, national tension, expanding horizons and new technologies, Thompson repaired to his little cottage on the Green in Burlington, Vermont, to have a good, long look at a wooden box of bones that some railroad men had delivered to him.

8

The State of Science and Geology in 1849

"First there is a mountain,
then there is no mountain,
then there is."

— Donovan Leitch, 1960's folksinger

Zadock Thompson is sometimes portrayed as a back-woods naturalist — collecting, describing and toiling in northern isolation. While this may have been true during Thompson's early career, there is ample evidence to suggest that he became increasingly involved with the rapid advances that were taking place in the larger world of natural science.

He would have been aware of James Audubon's series of illustrations in *Birds of America*, published in 1838, and consulted it in his many bird identifications. He could also draw on Charles Lyell's *Principles of Geology*, published in two volumes (1830 and 1832) which broke new ground by suggesting that the Earth was both very old and that the surface of the Earth was dynamic and in constant motion, contradicting the previously held view that the Earth was young and static. Charles Darwin read the ship captain's copy of *Principles of Geology* during the four-year voyage of the Beagle and was greatly affected by it. Darwin's own five-volume report on the zoology of the voyage was completed in 1843 and served as a standard for expedition reporting procedures in the future.

Primary amongst those who influenced Thompson's thinking was Professor Louis Agassiz, the world-renowned paleontologist and comparative anatomist at Harvard University. Although trained in biology, Agassiz is probably best known for his revolutionary work on glaciers and their effects upon the landscape. Agassiz grew up in a French-speaking village in the foothills of the Swiss Alps amongst the seasoned mountaineers of Europe and regularly hiked the hills, mountains and glaciers. As an acutely observant hiker, he noted the effects of modern glaciers and compared them to landscapes where glaciers no longer existed. He claimed that moraines, erratic boulders, glacial polish and other features far from any present day glaciation were evidence of a large-scale Ice Age in the past. This set off a debate that raged in northern Europe and North America for twenty-five years.

Agassiz was a well-rounded naturalist – a scientist of the world with credentials in paleontology, systematics and earth science. His emergence as a preeminent authority and tireless promoter of science, made him somewhat of a celebrity in both Europe and New England where he quickly developed networks of regional naturalists who worked with him in a loose cooperative extension. These naturalists brought curiosities to Agassiz for consultation which in turn helped to further develop and promote a consistent base of knowledge. It was to Agassiz that the remains of a mammoth found in Mt. Holly, Vermont in 1848 were initially sent. It was also to Agassiz that Thompson took the remains of the Charlotte whale for consultation and verification the following year. The presence of Agassiz in Boston had a centralizing effect. It helped to root out rumor and misinformation and to create a basis for a standardized natural history. Within 10 years of his arrival in America, Agassiz, by then a full professor at Harvard University, opened the Museum of Comparative Anatomy in Boston.

In 1851, flush with the excitement of traveling to Harvard to meet and consult with Professor Agassiz, Zadock Thompson took the huge professional step of travelling to London to attend the London Exposition. There he was exposed to the great minds, ideas and personalities of the 19th century and this undoubtedly had a profound effect on him professionally. Within two years of his return, Thompson was named Professor of Natural History and Curator of the State Cabinet (Collection). That same year he published the *Appendix to Natural History of Vermont* containing his description of both the whale and the Mt. Holly mammoth. In 1852, Thompson attended a field trip to examine the enigmatic fossiliferous lignite deposits at Brandon, Vermont. Also participating in the trip were no lesser visionaries than James Hall and Charles Lyell. Thompson was now operating within a much more influential sphere of players.

Massachusetts's Henry David Thoreau, the philosopher/naturalist best known for his essay "On Walden Pond," was also a contemporary of Zadock Thompson. In 1842, the same year that Thompson published the first edition of "Natural History of Vermont," Thoreau published his own "The Natural History of Massachusetts." Both men were voracious readers and extremely curious about the work of their contemporaries. Since they worked in adjoining states at the same time, it can be assumed that they were familiar with each other and with each other's work. In fact, Thoreau was granted membership in the Boston Society of Natural History in 1850, the same year that Thompson appeared before that group to deliver his report on the discovery of the Charlotte whale. Thoreau was an avid collector of natural phenomenon but emphasized an important distinction between "master workmen" of science and the "mere accumulators of facts." Thoreau looked to men like Louis Agassiz to put order to the "facts" that he and others were collecting.

The mid-19th century was unquestionably the age of the "gentleman naturalists" — men of science with enormous curiosity who sought to make sense of the natural world by collecting and systematizing. Most, but not all, were men of independent wealth who toiled in isolation for the love of scientific discovery. In addition to the relatively isolated work of Thompson and Thoreau, others like Agassiz, Charles Darwin, James Dana, Benjamin Haldeman and James Audubon, were making important contributions to the rapidly growing body of natural history through systematic observation and collection.

• • •

Zadock Thompson was, above all, a keen observer of nature and chronicler of fact. There was little place in his writing for speculation and theory and therefore little has come down that would give us a sense of what he thought about what he was seeing and how he made sense of it. Finding an elephant and then a whale in two successive years in the wilds of Vermont — the two most important fossil finds in New England to that point — would be difficult for anyone to explain. Maybe that was Thompson's strength: he didn't attempt to explain what he saw — he simply recorded it precisely. He left little else, so in order to understand Zadock's thinking and the difficulty that he must have had in arriving at certain conclusions, one must look carefully at the state of geology and scientific thinking in the mid-19th century.

The science of geology is relatively young compared to the other sciences. Astronomy, biology, medicine, meteorology and chemistry have been around throughout human existence, but other than flint-knapping, gold-digging and various daring-do acts of alchemy, the study of the Earth's processes went relatively unexplored. In fact, for most of its history, geology remained intertwined with religion. The science of geology was only born out of frustration at organized religion's unwillingness and inability to process new information.

Intuitively, people saw the land change through erosion, earthquakes, storms and the simple passage of time. They found the bones of animals that no longer existed and noted the gradual development of new animal and plant types over time and through domestication. As early as the 4th century BC, Aristotle took note of the extremely slow rate of geologic change and speculated on the effects that might have on life. There seemed to be an element of time and gradual change that was unexplained. In western society, such questions were first settled in the Bible, and for well over a millennium they remained essentially unchallenged.

With the rediscovery of the New World in 1492, the exploration and examination of the Earth proceeded at an unprecedented rate. New maps revealed a world that was much more vast and complicated than the original Mediterranean-centered world. New mining techniques allowed the ground to be probed at deeper and deeper levels, providing even more insight into the internal structure of the Earth.

The Earth was seen to be made of layers but the "why" and the "how" of these layers remained a mystery. The layers were not continuous. In some instances they were consistent; in other cases they were highly variable. Layers might truncate against one another or pinch out and disappear. Marine beds with fossils were found in rock at the tops of mountain ranges and mountain tops were found in the sea. Even more vexing was the fact that the exact same sequence of rocks could disappear and then be found miles away – 100's or 1000's of miles away – but at different angles, sometimes overturned completely. Somehow it seemed that the layers of the Earth were interacting with each other but no mechanism could be found. Something was wrong with the equation. What was missing from the equation was *time*.

In the late 17th century, the storied James Ussher, archbishop of Armagh, Ireland, sat down and worked out the biblical math. By adding up the various "begats," he concluded that the Earth had been formed on Sunday, October 23, 4004 B.C. Shortly thereafter in 1701, an authorized version of the Bible accepted this as official church doctrine and the 6000 year-old age for the Earth became the gold standard by which all other estimates were judged. For nearly a century it was considered heresy to challenge it.

By the mid-18th century however, the challenge was on. Georges Louis de Buffon, a French zoologist, melted iron balls of varying sizes and then allowed them to cool. Buffon proposed that the age of the Earth could be determined by calculating the amount of time it would take the iron to cool from an original molten state. His work led him to conclude that the Earth was at least 75,000 years old, an astounding figure for that time. (Had Buffon not failed to take into account the heat constantly produced by the radioactive decay of elements in the Earth's interior, his figure would have been much higher.) Slowly, methodically, proposals for the age of the earth crept to a million years, then 40 million years, then a half-billion years, then many billions of years. It became apparent that the forces that have shaped the Earth have been operating for an unimaginably long time. Today the age of the Earth is estimated to be over 4.5 billion years old. Should new evidence arise, that figure may be altered in the future.

• • •

"We find no vestige of a beginning,
no prospect of an end"
— James Hutton, Scottish geologist

In the mid-19th century, the debate that drove scientific inquiry in geology was the schism between two schools of thought with the large and unwieldy names of *catastrophism* and *uniformitarianism*. There were many variations but the essential argument was this: *is the geologic change that we see on the Earth due to isolated, catastrophic events like earthquakes and floods, or is it due to slow, constant processes over time, like sediment tumbling along in a river?* Thrown into that was an additional wrinkle: *can all of the anomalous, unexplained surface effects be explained as the result of the biblical flood of Noah?*

It was not a new battle, to be sure. But with the lines firmly drawn, the essence of geology boiled down to three questions:

1. How old is the Earth?
2. To what degree has it changed over time?
3. What is the agent of this change?

James Hutton (1726-1797) was a brilliant thinker but a poor writer. In retrospect he is often considered to be the founder of modern geology, but in his day his writing was so awkward, cumbersome and difficult to understand that it had little effect until it could be "translated" by the writings of others.

Hutton is best known for a single extraordinary insight that he had while hiking with friends along the coast of Scotland. Upon reaching a promontory known locally as Siccar Point, he noted gray shales tilted almost vertically that were capped abruptly and perpendicularly by horizontal beds of red sandstone. This had the effect of forming the letter "t" and given the understanding of the day, made little intuitive sense. How could one layer of rock truncate and align fully 90° from another? How could baked, metamorphic shale lay against seemingly unheated sandstone with no effect?

Hutton understood that this could mean only one thing: that the formation of this outcrop implied many cycles and required a great deal of time. In his mind's eye he saw the shale being deposited as horizontal layers of mud in a marine environment, and then being metamorphosed and tilted almost vertically by subterranean forces. The key to his insight is what occurred next: he realized that the now-vertical beds of metamorphic shale had been eroded and then, on top of them, horizontal beds of sandstone had been deposited. The red nature of the sandstone suggested a terrestrial environment. The erosion of the shale indicated a hiatus, or a gap in the record. The rocks above and below the hiatus bore witness to both mountain building and erosion. The movie that played in Hutton's mind as he watched the silent outcrop contained the basis for modern uniformitarian geologic thought: The earth has been built by multiple, gradual, cyclic, reoccurring events over a very long period of time.

The influential French zoologist Baron Georges Cuvier (1769-1832) didn't quite agree. Cuvier was convinced that the physical and biologic history of the earth resulted from a series of planet-wide catastrophes that caused widespread destruction and change. Each catastrophe led to the alteration of the landscape and the elimination of animal life in the vicinity. Following the event, new life was either created or migrated to the area from elsewhere. Cuvier identified the most recent catastrophe as the biblical flood, making catastrophism particularly appealing to theologians.

Enter Sir Charles Lyell. In 1832, Lyell published the final volume of one of the most influential books in the history of geology. The title was simple: *Principles of Geology*. The subtitle was more ponderous: *An Attempt to Explain the*

Former Changes of the Earth's Surface by Reference to Causes now in Operation. Lyell stated simply what Hutton could not: small, incremental changes over enormously long periods of time can lead to major observable and measurable changes. "The present is the key to the past," he wrote, meaning that the processes operating today are identical to those that have operated throughout earth history.

• • •

We return to Zadock Thompson. In Vermont, and in fact all over much of northern Europe and North America, enormous quantities of sand, clay and gravel were piled up in beds. Some of these piles were neatly stratified while others were heaped in chaotic jumbles. Erratic boulders the size of houses were found perched in odd places often great distances from where they originated and often at high elevation. Frequently the bedrock was covered with curious linear scratches that pointed in the same general direction, but followed the lay of the landscape, especially in valleys and along mountains ranges. Those were the facts. They were easily observable. But how and why did they occur?

The biblical flood, the Great Deluge, was commonly used at the time to explain these observations without compromising the Bible. A huge, earth-wide flood could explain suspended beach lines high upon mountain sides, lowland clay deposits, and the jumbled remains of many animals deposited in enormous bone beds. Scrub and scour features that obviously resulted from catastrophic rushes of water could be found world-wide, and the presence of marine fossils at high elevations were explained as remnants of a great flood.

What a great flood could not explain was the presence of marine fossils locked *deep within folded and fractured bedrock* at high elevations, huge boulders suspended at higher elevations than they outcropped, and the great beds of chaotic, unstratified sediments. The biblical flood could also not explain the enormous range of geologic features across the planet. Floods tend to muddy differences and blur distinctions. They erode the highlands and fill up the holes. No flood, not even one of biblical proportions, was capable of throwing up mountains or baking and folding solid rock.

There must be other forces at work.

Thompson was a man of God and a man of science. This apparently caused him little contradiction. Again, he simply recorded what he saw. When he described the discovery site of the Mt. Holly mammoth, he recorded the depth of the organic muck, the ancient presence of beavers, the basal gravel deposit upon which the mammoth remains lay and the distance to undisturbed bedrock. When he described the whale site he noted the presence of organic matter in the unstratified blue-grey clay, the overlying stratified layers of sand and gravel, the vertical and horizontal orientation of the fossil and the elevation of the excavation.

Let's watch over Zadock's shoulder: Thompson was well-aware that Lake Champlain drained to the north and connected with the ocean via the Richelieu and St. Lawrence rivers. Either a rise in the land or a lowering of the sea could have stranded the whale in its current position. But which? The whale find was so important to New England geology because it represented the first time that a vertebrate marine fossil had been found so far inland. If, in fact, the sea level had dropped, then that should be observable world-wide. The evidence indicated quite the contrary: if anything, sea level had risen. With the discovery of the Charlotte Whale in 1849 it became obvious that glacial rebound and the effects of widespread glaciation, at least within the Champlain Valley, must be seriously considered. Agassiz was familiar with Vermont's glacial landscape having made multiple trips up the valley of the Winooski River. Because of Thompson's profound respect for his professional mentor, it seems unlikely that Thompson would accept the presence of stranded beach lines, erratics, unsorted deltas, glacial polish and upland marine clays in the Champlain Valley as anything but evidence of glaciation. Although Agassiz (and likely Thompson as well) went to his grave believing that the hand of God was still involved, it is Agassiz's work on glacial features in northern New England, Charlotte Whale included, that helped to drive the last nail in the coffin of the biblical flood as a serious scientific theory.

PART THREE

WHALES, FOSSILS, MUCK AND CLAY

9

The Singing White Whales

They may have been the original stuff of mermaid legends, these smallish white whales from the north that sang like canaries. Their incessant squeaking and bird-like chirping carried through the water and earned them the name "canaries of the sea" amongst early sailors. As they swam alongside the boats, the reflected light that rippled through the waves off their white skin may have looked to the lonely sailors like the pale, naked bodies of women with fins.

The White Whale (*Delphinapterus leucas*) also goes by the names of "white porpoise," "white squid hound" and "sea canary" although most commonly they are known as "beluga." Beluga whales are toothed whales recognized by their brilliant white to grey-white color, lack of a dorsal (back) fin, and the presence of a prominent forehead knob called a "melon." The melon, which causes them to bear an uncanny resemblance to a punch-drunk boxer who has just lost a fight, is actually a receptacle of thick oil. The melon oil helps focus incoming and outgoing sounds, allowing belugas to communicate with other whales and to use their voices as a sonar system to measure distance and location.

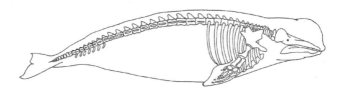

(Figure 3 – White "Beluga" Whale showing the relationship of the skeleton to the external anatomy.)

As whales go, belugas are fairly small, averaging 10 to 15 feet in length, with males generally larger than females. They differ from the larger baleen whales in that they have small, peg-like, cylindrical teeth that are nicely adapted for snagging small fish, squid and crustaceans which they then swallow whole without chewing. Their lips are lined with delicate muscles that permit them to forage along the ocean floor with extreme agility. These same muscles allow belugas to mimic a wide variety of human expressions and emotions – including smiling – a large reason why modern belugas are so popular at zoos and aquaria.

This is where our story becomes a little dicey. This is where we begin to confuse "were" and "are." When we speak of beluga whales do we speak of them in the past tense or in the present? To what extent can we use what we know about modern belugas to give us insight into those of the Champlain Sea? In fact, one of the biggest questions about the Champlain whales, maybe *the* biggest question is: What is the relationship of the Champlain Sea whales to modern belugas? They certainly exist in the St. Lawrence Estuary today, and because of the Charlotte whale, we know that they lived in the Champlain Valley eleven thousand years ago. Are they the same species? Could both populations mate and reproduce? There are minor differences but are these differences significant enough to separate them? These are questions that plagued Zadock Thompson and continue to intrigue us today.

There is an answer, and again it involves *time*.

In "human" time, eleven thousand years is an eternity. It predates every great recorded civilization and extends us back into the shadowy realm of prehistory. But in geologic time, in evolutionary time, eleven thousand years is barely a heartbeat. Geologic/evolutionary time is measured in millions of years… anything less than a million years is probably still happening. Even the evolution of whales themselves from land-dwelling animals (which is considered to be one of the most dramatically rapid steps in all of evolution) took at least ten million years. Eleven thousand years is scarcely enough time to catch evolution's attention, no less create a new species. There is little doubt (although in science there is always *some* doubt) that the whales of the Champlain Sea were genetically similar enough to modern belugas to be identified as the same species.

That being the case, we should then be able to use the traits and behaviors of modern belugas as reliable indicators of the traits and behaviors of ancient ones. Let's extend some of what we know about modern whales to the singing white whales of the Champlain Sea.

Belugas today are found world-wide in the cold circumpolar waters of the northern hemisphere. They follow the ice edge south during the winter and then summer in the brackish waters of estuaries and rivers. Because of this tolerance and even preference for freshened waters, belugas would have been very much at home along the ice edge and amongst the floating icebergs of the Champlain Sea. Physiological adaptations allowed them to stay submerged in icy waters up to 30 minutes at a time, coming up to breathe in small, protected, unfrozen areas of open water within pack ice.

The ice offered them protection from one of their greatest natural enemies but exposed them to another. Killer whales are most apt to attack belugas in open water where they can use speed and strength to out-maneuver the beluga's agility and cunning. Lacking a dorsal fin, belugas can skim beneath the ice with ease, taking advantage of small pockets of air. With neck vertebra that are unfused (unlike other whales) they have increased maneuverability, allowing them to move in and out of the jagged ice. In contrast, the large dorsal fin and general bulkiness of killer whales make them less effective as hunters in areas of dense ice.

Although the ice pack offered protection from below, being forced to breathe through small openings in the ice made them prey to their other natural enemy: polar bears. Blending in perfectly with their surroundings, polar bears wait silently near known air holes for belugas or small seals to surface. Once their prey is within reach, the huge bears haul the whales onto the ice and kill them.

No evidence of Ice Age polar bears has yet been found around the Champlain Sea, although given their numbers and lifestyles, fossil remains of large predators are statistically difficult to find. However, given the bear's potential payoff of a fat, nutrient-rich whale or seal, it would be hard to imagine that a beluga approaching an air hole from the quiet of the sea below wouldn't be instinctively weary of what might be waiting patiently above the ice.

10

The Sticky, Blue-Gray Clay of Charlotte

In sedimentology, the size of a particle is a reflection of the amount of energy in the environment at the time the particle is deposited. Raging mountain rivers contain large boulders that clunk against one another as the river pushes them downstream, while smaller cobbles, gravels, sands and silts are washed away by the current. As river gradients level and begin to slow, increasingly smaller pieces drop out and are deposited in gravel bars and point bars along the way. But the finest sediments – microscopic clays and tiny bits of organic matter, remain suspended until washed onto flood plains, into quiet backwaters or deep ponds or lakes where they gently settle, producing fine, mucky beds.

In the ocean the process is the same. The biggest rocks and boulders remain in the rivers — the river's power being insufficient to move them all the way to the sea. (Large rocks along the ocean shore, say the coast of Oregon or Maine for instance, are remnants of the erosion of bedrock right along the shoreline.) Along beaches and in shallow water where the wave energy is the greatest, the sands and fine gravels are constantly sorted and winnowed into layers of virtually indestructible quartz. But through all of this the fine silts and clays remain suspended. And again only in the quiet, deep waters are the miniscule, constantly agitated particles finally allowed to settle out.

The whale was found in a dense, sticky, blue-gray clay that is representative of the southern arm of the Champlain Sea. This is the clay that tormented the rail workers and was the clay reported by Zadock Thompson in the Appendix of his 1853 edition of *"Natural History of Vermont."* This clay was also confirmed at the depth of the original discovery by an exploratory pit near the site in 1993 (Chapter 16). Presence of the blue clay indicates quiet water, most likely deep water due to the lack of organic matter.

Thompson described the clay as being unstratified. However he also reported finding bits of organic plant material, interpreting the preservation to have been in a "quagmire." Not far above it he found stratified and cross-bedded sands and gravels containing sea shells similar to those found on the beaches of the North Atlantic today. This would be consistent with a pattern of shallowing and emergence as the land rebounded over time.

The 1993 exploratory pit confirmed the stratified sands and gravels over the clay but turned up little in the way of organic plant material. What the dig did discover were isolated, angular chunks of rock imbedded and suspended within the fine clay at the exact level that Thompson reported finding the whale.

Given the previous description of the conditions under which clay accumulates, how does one explain the presence of angular rocks and pebbles spread randomly through a thick deposit of fine, unstratified clay? Other than small boys throwing rocks from shore, (or more likely a rifle-armed outfielder for the New York Yankees) nothing immediately comes to mind. The shallowing of water or mass wasting from shore would leave tell-tale signs that can be easily identified.

There is one explanation.

Ice rafted debris (IRD) is material — sand, gravel and chunks of rock — that becomes incorporated into a glacier as it grinds over the land. When the glacier meets its terminus at the sea, large chunks of the glacial ice break off and float away as icebergs. As these icebergs melt, a slow but steady rain of rock material falls to the sea floor, landing upon whatever happens to be passing beneath them at the time.

What are the chances of an ice-rafted pebble landing at any given spot at any given time? Very small. What are the chances of finding them in a small excavation? Also small. But find them we did. Their presence helps confirm the timing of the whale's death during the late glacial stages of the Champlain Basin, and agrees with the tendency of beluga whales to live along the ice edge and amongst floating icebergs. It might also indicate that the depth of water at the time of the whale's death was at least deep enough to support floating icebergs.

What does this tell us? Well, not much, and a whole lot.

11

The Gelatinous
Muck of Mt. Holly

The exhausted Ice Age mammoth at Mt. Holly managed to survive through most of the night but by the time the sun came up all life had passed from the great beast. The few scavengers that wintered in the mountains attempted to exploit the meat but were only able to reach those bits that weren't frozen solid and remained exposed above the ice. Quickly the carcass became frozen and was buried in the ice and snow.

But with the coming of spring and the brief summer, the carcass thawed and was eagerly scavenged by a wealth of animals thankful for the rich meat. The bones were broken and scattered – some disappearing on land, others sinking into the murky water. Quickly the meat was consumed. The enormous skull and tusks sank slowly and slid with time toward the deepest part of the bog, and there the remains settled and came to rest.

The bog was not really a bog in the beginning. It started out as a depression filled with melt water – possibly a kettle hole resulting from a melting block of buried ice, or simply a hollow in the bedrock caused by erosion. Water flowed through it on its way down the mountains, but as the years, decades and centuries went by, the summers got longer and the land became greener. Gradually the pond began to fill with debris from a succession of plant communities: tundra lichens to low plants to study bushes to pioneer trees to mature forest.

Throughout most of its early history the pond maintained a flow of water, keeping it open and fresh. The pond remained that way for a thousand years or two, until beavers came along and cut down the trees, driving the sharpened trunks deep into the mud, damming the flow and creating a large, quiet pond. With water flow restricted, the pond began to fill with organic debris — slowly at first — but then more and more rapidly until the beavers could no longer maintain their homestead and moved on to find other small depressions to dam.

• • •

Meanwhile at the bottom of the bog, the skull, the tooth and the few scattered bones sat motionless in the oxygen-starved muck. Over succeeding millennia, water permeated every cavity, tissue and cell until it completely filled every space, virtually suspending the bones in fluid. With unlimited mobility, acids resulting from decay saturated the remains and slowly leached out calcium phosphates and other structural minerals, leaving behind little but a leathery, water-soaked sponge of slimy collagen. Only the enamel of the tooth was able to resist.

In the cold anoxic waters, dead plant material accumulated faster than it could rot. Through the same basic process it was reduced to rubbery cellulose that shook like jelly and rapidly and thoroughly dried out upon removal from the bog. (In his notes, Zadock Thompson reported that the saturated gelatinous muck lost fully 7/8 of its mass upon drying.) The bones of the mammoth were no different. Upon removal they too lost half their volume and rapidly cracked beyond repair.

● ● ●

Migrating animals continued to pass by the small bog, most stopping to drink and browse, some undoubtedly becoming entrapped in the frozen muck of winter. Early human explorers passed along its edge as they followed the animals through the mountains. Eventually a military road widened the trail, followed by a toll road and a stage coach route.

Then one day a small group of surveyors arrived at the bog on horseback. They took some measurements and drew some maps. They viewed the pass from every angle and discussed it from every vantage point. But regardless of how they plotted it, they kept coming back to the same conclusion: the new railroad had no choice but to cut directly through the middle of this muck.

12

The Escape From
The Bog At The Pass

By mid-summer of 1848, the railroad construction crew had finally reached the top of the southern mountain pass. It wasn't a particularly steep climb, but it was a psychological milestone. They had endured thick brambles, folded metamorphic mountains and mosquitoes the size of berries, but they had finally breached the rugged Green Mountains. From here it was westward and all downhill into the valley of Lake Champlain and then a hundred easy miles along the flat farmlands that ringed the lake north to Burlington, and eventually Montreal.

Ahead, just east of Mount Holly, in a depression that marked the trail summit at 1415 feet elevation, was a small boggy marsh. A low rim of rocks lined its western edge, marking the drainage divide between the Connecticut River and Lake Champlain. To the east, water collected into Branch Brook and flowed out through a river gap between Ludlow Mountain and Sawyer Rocks to join the Black River, flowing down the eastern slopes toward the Connecticut River. To the west, just beyond the rim of rocks, Mill River gathered for its run towards Rutland. The railroad was following the old Vermont Toll Road, the route that the stage coach between Boston and Burlington had followed. The stage had followed the migratory trail of the native Indians, who had followed the game, who had followed the historical path of least resistance.

Surveyors had already determined that the tracks would need to traverse the wetland before they could cross over the drainage divide and descend into Rutland. It would be a fairly easy matter of blasting through the low ridge of rock, draining the swamp, digging down to bedrock, and then back-filling with sand and heavy gravel before laying the track and moving on. They had done it through countless bogs and swamps already, and would cross many more before they finished. It was routine.

As the workman shoveled loads of muck from the track's path, it became obvious that this swamp had been a beaver pond at least once in its history. Large lodge poles of maple, beech, birch, spruce and hemlock were pulled out, still containing the chew marks so characteristic of beavers. As they dug through the gelatinous mire to un-consolidated glacial gravels and drift, and finally bedrock, one of the workmen in the middle of the morass called out. He had struck something unusual and a knot of work-ers slowly gathered around him as he removed and then cleaned what seemed to be a large tooth. It was roughly rectangular in shape, eight pounds in weight, about the size of a small loaf of bread with folded sheets of enamel, still gleaming brownish white. Amidst speculation as to what sort of animal it might be, other workers digging in the same area uncovered portions of bones and finally, two sections of what seemed to be a giant antler or tusk. There was no shortage of opinions: diluvian monsters, ancient dragons… surely victims of the great flood of Noah. Frankly, no one had a clue. The perplexed railroad engineers packed up the bones and sent them back down the line to Harvard University in Boston, where they landed in the lab of Professor Louis Agassiz.

Meanwhile, Zadock Thompson traveled to the discovery site from Burlington on the old Vermont Toll Road. He arrived at the scene traveling in the opposite direction that the mammoth had been following. Thompson drew a rough map, paced off distances and measured depths. He noted the presence of beaver marks and described the species of submerged trees. He observed that the gelatinous muck "quivered like jelly" when cut into sections and held in the hand, and that it became "light as a cork" when allowed to dry. As an indication of his respect for Louis Agassiz, he concluded with the following:

"I have prefixed to this account the specific name of the Mammoth, or the fossil Elephant of Europe, but have little doubt that ours is a distinct species, and I am happy in knowing that one of our best comparative anatomists is now investigating this very subject."

• • •

"*Sckloritigisch-glauk-utuk*," was the sucking sound that the fossils made as the Irish railroad workers pulled them from the muck at the bottom of the bog. "*Sckloritigisch-glauk-utuk*," was the sound that their boots made as they struggled to carry the bones back to the train. "*Scklori-tigisch-glauk-utuk*," was the sound of Zadock Thompson looking to extract just one more piece from the gelatinous quagmire. But it no longer smelled of death; it now smelled of life. The mammoth would finally make it over the pass and down the other side. Patience is a virtue. After being entombed in the dank, dark muck of Mt. Holly for what seemed like an eternity, the mammoth had finally managed to escape.

13

The Silent Vigil and the Unmarked Grave

On January 19, 1856, less than seven years after finding the whale, Zadock Thompson passed away in the small cottage on the University Green amongst the gardens and specimens where he had lived for so many years. He had been feeling poorly all winter and had finally become bed-ridden. He was lethargic and depressed because it was becoming more evident with each passing day that he would not be able to complete his series of books on the natural history of Vermont. When the end finally came, his wife Phoebe was at his bedside as he offered his final words: *"May God's will be done."*

The most endearing and poignant moment that I encountered while researching this story occurred as I was reviewing some of Thompson's materials in the State Historical Museum in Montpelier. Zadock Thompson kept a meticulous set of daily climate records – temperature, barometric pressure, precipitation, clouds, and comments – dating back to 1832. It was a strict part of his daily regimen. In his last days, when Zadock became too ill to continue to record his observations, Phoebe faithfully took over recording them for him. By comparing their hand-writing, it is apparent that Zadock recorded his final entry on January 6th, with Phoebe taking over from that time onward. On January 19th, the day that Zadock Thompson died, along with the usual information on temperature, humidity, etc., Phoebe dutifully recorded in the comments section:

"Mr. Thompson died today at 5 pm."

She then went on to record his weather data for many years before turning the job over to the fledgling U.S. Weather Service's Burlington office.

A year after his passing, Phoebe Thompson sold his natural history collection to the State of Vermont, thus passing the Charlotte whale into the State Cabinet, where it has remained to this day. Thompson's collection largely replaced the previous State Cabinet which was tragically destroyed in a great fire that burned the old wooden State House to the ground in January of 1857. Ironically, much of Thompson's original collection (which was stored in the basement office of the State Geologist in Montpelier) was destroyed in the Flood of 1927 — to this day Vermont's historic flood of record. Fortunately, the whale managed to avoid both catastrophes.

During his professional career, Thompson authored dozens of books and maps, and personally collected, cata-logued and described over 250 subspecies and varieties of plants and animals including 47 quadrupeds, 141 birds, 40 fish and 38 trees. He served variously as Professor of Natural History, Curator of the State Cabinet and Episcopal Reverend, and was a member of the first geologic survey to traverse Vermont. He is generally regarded as Vermont's first, foremost, and greatest natural historian. Zadock Thompson is buried in an unmarked grave[1] in Burlington, Vermont. It is hoped that this book will help spearhead an effort to obtain a proper headstone.

---

1 Thompson's tombstone (Lot #4-2-1, Elmwood Cemetery) has suffered over time and no longer exists, rendering the grave "unmarked". By contacting the cemetery office, I was able to obtain a plot map of the cemetery and the following verbal instructions on how to find Zadock Thompson's grave: *Go in the main entrance off Elmwood Street and walk in until you see the Pomeroy Monument (with curbing all around). Walk past; look for monuments with either "Blush" or "Robinson" bordering the walk. These define an area that has, in succession: "Reynolds", "Simpson", "Lathrop", "Bronson", "Thompson", "Safford", "Porter" and "Smith".*

14

The Burlap Skull
and the Plaster Smile

On a snowy January evening in 1857, workers who hadn't yet left for the day noted smoke issuing from the floor near a heating vent in the Vermont State House in Montpelier. Before help could be raised, Vermont's capitol building was completely engulfed in flames. Volunteers were successful in rescuing furniture and many of the items from the library, but the bulk of the natural history collection — scattered about the building in cabinets and alcoves — was lost.

Architects and contractors were hired to design and build a new State House that was to be taller and grander than the one that preceded it and work progressed swiftly. As Curator of the State Cabinet, Albert D. Hagar was charged with providing display specimens for the new building. But with the bulk of the State's display collection destroyed in the fire, he had to quickly acquire new material.

Zadock Thompson had passed away the year before and his widow, Phoebe, was contacted to see if she would be willing to sell Zadock's natural history collection to the State. With her husband gone and with only the scant income from the royalties on Thompson's books and almanacs, she gladly sold the entire collection to the State of Vermont for $1,000. Included within this collection of rocks, mounted animals, pressed plants and historic artifacts, were a couple of boxes containing the assorted ribs, vertebrae, teeth and shattered skull bones of the fossil whale uncovered during railroad construction in 1849.

Hagar realized immediately that the whale fossil could be a major attraction, but in its present state it was unrecognizable as a fossil, no less as a whale. So he set Charles Hancock, Jr. to the task of reassembling the bones into a display specimen. Hancock arranged the bones in order and developed a support system from which to suspend them. Missing vertebrae were carved from wood and the limb bones were positioned as best as could be determined. Hagar and Hitchcock were working without the oversight of a trained anatomist and this was reflected in the final product. The mounted skeleton was ramrod straight as if the whale was "standing" at attention. Many of the bones were mounted in the wrong location — most notably reversed vertebrae and the shoulder girdle which was mounted at the bottom of the rib cage (posterior) rather than the top (anterior.)

Fig. 340.

Fossil Whale *(Beluga Vermontana.)*   [F.-F. Currier Del.—J.Bruen Sc.]

(Figure 4 – A woodcut of the whale as it first appeared in Albert Hagar's 1861 "Geology of Vermont.")

The most pressing problem however, was the skull. Since it was the first part of the skeleton encountered by the worker's shovels, it was severely damaged and many pieces were missing. The cranium was largely intact but half of the upper jaw and the opposite half of the lower jaw were completely gone. Only nine of the thirty teeth had been recovered.

Albert Hagar was a fine scientist but he was also a showman. He knew that the specimen would need to have a recognizable skull if it was to become a popular attraction, so he set about to make one. Using wire, plaster and coarse burlap, Hagar and Hitchcock fashioned a skull for the specimen that contained all of the bone fragments in their correct relative positions. They then painted the entire mount brown and installed it in an alcove of the new State House.

In his 1861 *Report on the Geology of Vermont*, Hagar included the following note:

"It may be proper to remark that the bones of the head were so much broken by the workmen who encountered it that but an imperfect idea of its shape could be obtained from

the preserved fragments by one not familiar with comparative anatomy. The outline of the head, therefore, may not be true to nature, but the writer acting in the capacity of curator, concluded that an artificial head, embracing the bones that had been preserved, if attached to the skeleton, even if it were not a perfect model of the original, would be more attractive to visitors than the remaining portion of the skeleton would be without a head. Hence he fitted it up, not to elicit the criticism of the learned zoologist, but to render the skeleton more interesting to the casual observer."

This crippled wretch of a skeleton that has come down to us over the years — with its misplaced bones, burlap skull and plaster smile — has been very troubling to some. Dr. G. H. Perkins wanted to reconstruct it in 1908 but lamented that *"...it has been impossible to remount the specimen at present, if indeed it can be done at all without serious damage to the bones, the old mountings having become firmly fixed in place."*

In 1992 during a renovation of the museum, the whale was removed from its case and stored in a back classroom where lucky visitors were able to observe it up close. There were discussions concerning potential reconstruction, but in the end it was decided that it was much more important as a historical specimen than it was an anatomical one, and so it was returned it to its display case unchanged.[2]

---

2 See *"The Tiny Harmonica"*

15

The Professor
and Indiana Jones

(Montpelier, Vermont, 1906) Vermont State Geologist Dr. George Henry Perkins was not satisfied with the current state of affairs and had decided to undertake a more thorough and systematic study of the whale. The fossil whale specimen on display at the State House in Montpelier was still considered to be the type specimen for the species *Delphinapterus vermontanus,* but there was growing debate over the claim that it constituted a separate species distinct from the modern beluga whale (*Delphinapterus leucas*). To compound the problem, the "Montpelier specimen," as it was then known, had never been properly described in scientific literature. Although Zadock Thompson's 1850 account was a superb description for the era in which he worked, it no longer stood up to the increasing rigors of modern science.

(Since Thompson's time, the specimen had been variously referred to in the literature as *Beluga vermontanus* [1853, 1861], *Delphinapterus vermontanus* [1890, E. D.

Cope], and then *Delphinapterus leucas* [1896, J. Dana.] The confusion arose from the incompleteness of the fossil specimen and the natural variation within white (beluga) whales themselves.)

Perkin's original intent was to do a complete literature search on the Montpelier specimen – pulling together anything that had ever been written about it and compiling it into one place. He also wanted to take a complete set of photographs to replace various old ink drawings and woodcuts that had been used for 50 years.

Shortly after beginning the project and possibly as the result of it, Perkins received a call from Dr. F. W. True of the U.S. National Museum in Washington D.C. True was also interested in the whale and pledged the assistance and resources of his organization, even offering his own collection of articles related to the whale and arranging to have the photographs taken.

Perkins initially intended to study only the Montpelier specimen. He consulted all previous accounts and made a detailed series of measurements. However the incompleteness of the skeleton, along with the haphazard way in which the skeleton had been reassembled (most especially the skull) forced Perkins to look for other similar whales with which he could make comparisons. He soon found there to be a treasure trove of other whales found in Pleistocene sediments throughout northwestern New England and southern Canada. His research led him to the Provincial Museum in Halifax, the Geological Museum of Ottawa, the Redpath Museum at McGill University in Montreal and the American Museum of Natural History in New York City. When he contacted the American Museum, he was referred to an eager young whale expert named Roy Chapman Andrews

• • •

Roy Chapman Andrews is widely considered to be the original role model for the notorious movie character *Indiana Jones*, played by actor Harrison Ford in the series of George Lucas films beginning with *Raiders of the Lost Ark*. His career at the American Museum of Natural History would eventually span six decades. He would go on to become one of the most exciting personalities in American science – leading a perilous and swashbuckling expedition in the 1920's across fragmented, pre-Communist China to the Gobi Desert to return with a fabulous collection of heretofore unknown dinosaur fossils. Included in his treasures were the world's first fossil dinosaur eggs. (Casts of these exact eggs are in the UVM collection.) His discoveries would shed light on dinosaur physiology, predator/prey relationships, and the relationship between dinosaurs and birds.

In 1906 Chapman was just beginning his museum career as a graduate fresh out of Beloit College in Wisconsin. On a whim, he ventured to New York City with what little money he could scrape up to seek a job at the museum. He told the interviewer that he'd "sweep floors if necessary," and when the interviewer asked Chapman if a college graduate would be happy sweeping floors, Chapman replied: "Oh, not *anyone's* floors, just the *museum's* floors." He was hired on the spot and there is no record of him ever performing janitorial work.

One of Chapman's first assignments was to collect and study a whale carcass that had washed up on the New Jersey shore. He took to the project with the enthusiasm and thoroughness that marked his professional career. Within a couple of years he had become the museum's leading authority on cetaceans. And so it came to be that when Prof. George Perkins contacted the American Museum for information on fossil whales, it was with Roy Chapman Andrews that he was put in touch.

After a few rounds of correspondence, Perkins packed up his notes, his photographs and some of the sturdier and more interesting bones, and traveled to New York to meet with Andrews.

"In order to decide so far as possible..." Perkins wrote, *"several...questions that had arisen in course of my study of the Montpelier skeleton, I took photographs of the entire skeleton and larger ones of the different parts to the American Museum of Natural History, New York. Here there are numerous cetacean skeletons, mounted and disarticulated. By the courtesy of Mr. Roy C. Andrews, I was not only able to use this material freely and most helpfully but, what has been of much further assistance, Mr. Andrews freely gave me all aid in his power, and to this and to his experience as special student of the cetacea I am greatly indebted..."*

Together, Perkins and Chapman examined every whale specimen in the museum's collection — fossil and modern. They compared how bones articulated with one another, pondered the variations in dental configuration and discussed the evolutionary relationships of different species. Andrews produced diagnostic examples of critically related parts such as ear bones and was able to demonstrate how the missing portions of the Montpelier specimen functioned. Perkins credits Andrews with pointing out some of the finer points of whale anatomy that he might not have noticed on his own.

Following his consultation with Andrews, Perkins returned to Vermont to write the definitive scientific account of the whale and published it as part of his *Report of the State Geologist on the Mineral Industries and Geology of Certain Areas of Vermont, 1907-08.* Perkin's report contained accurate descriptions, historical references, photographs and measurements of the fossil and placed the "Montpelier specimen" firmly within the scientific literature. Although it didn't resolve the naming problem directly, it finally allowed others to sort it out.

PART FOUR

THE CHARLOTTE WHALE

16

The Gunter Chain and the Fourteen-Foot Hole

Paleontology — the study of fossils — is a lot like a crime scene investigation. By the time the investigators finally arrive, the crime has already been committed, the perpetrator has left the scene and all that remains are the sparse leavings of the act. In paleontology there is seldom a trail of blood, lust or money. Over the course of thousands, or millions, of years the trail can grow very, very cold.

In the case of the Charlotte whale there was a dead body, but very little else. There was no murder weapon, no spent casings. It wasn't even apparent whether the victim was found at the murder scene or whether the murder had happened elsewhere and the body moved. For that matter, it was only known in the most general of terms where the body was originally found. New insight required new evidence and new evidence required a different approach. But where to start?

In 1992 a small group of staff and volunteers at the University of Vermont's Perkins Museum decided to attempt to locate the original whale site as described by Zadock Thompson. The group included Jeff Howe (Perkins Museum curator), Robert Trithart (museum volunteer and Charlotte resident), Dr. Stephen Wright (UVM geology professor), Mary Ann Schlegel (UVM geology grad student), Stephen Bechtel (UVM geology grad student), Douglas Griffen (Charlotte resident) and Mary Lighthall (Charlotte Historical Society).

We knew that the actual whale site itself had been destroyed during the construction of the railroad, and that 10' to 20' on both sides of the track had been disturbed by associated berms, trenches and access roads. However there could still be much to be gained by exploring the immediate vicinity.

Our original goals were simple:

1. Pinpoint the original discovery site as precisely as possible.
2. Get permission to dig a hole down to the depth of the whale discovery.

Why? Curiosity mostly. What if the Charlotte whale was just one of a group of whales that had been preserved in the same vicinity? What if there were associated young? What if this was some sort of bone-bed and there were the preserved remains of other Ice Age creatures? What if we could find organic materials or microfossils that would allow us to more accurately date the site? The "what ifs" were enticing.

In his account (published in the Appendix to the 1853 edition of his *Natural History of Vermont*) Zadock

Thompson describes the discovery location in relation to two east-west roads that cross the north-south railroad tracks on both sides of the site. The "south road" is clearly Thompson Point Rd. (TPR), still in use and prominently shown on both modern and 19th century maps. The "north road" (NR) however, which once crossed over the tracks on a sixteen-foot high bridge, had fallen into disuse over the years and its trace had long-since been plowed under by local farmers. Thompson gave his measurements in "rods", the working measurement of the railroad crews in the mid-19th century. A modern rod converts to 16.5 feet. According to Thompson, the distance between the two roads was "about" 80 rods (1320'), and the site was located 55 rods (907.5') north of TPR and "perhaps" 25 rods (412.5') south of NR.

Using a 200' retractable rule, we marked off the tracks starting from the center of TPR. Using Thompson's account we established the mathematical locations for the discovery site and the NR but, given the local topography, nothing about either site made intuitive sense. Up until this point, Zadock's measurements and descriptions had always been accurate and complete… he couldn't be this far off. Something wasn't right. We left our markers in place and returned to the museum to make a few phone calls and re-check our thinking.

We contacted Mary Lighthall of the Charlotte Historical Society who was very interested in our project and she was able to provide us with clarifying information on

Thompson's account. She verified that the south road was TPR and that a faint trace of NR could still be found in the form of a rut road that led from the rear of the James Lawrence house, the only 1800's house along that section of Greenbush Rd. She also indicated that even though there may be a distance problem with Thompson's 80 rods, she felt that the 55/25 proportion would probably prove to be correct.

So we located the rut road. From the railroad bed it's not readily apparent where a road might cross, but from the farm fields there was only one obvious route. We followed the trace down to where it dead-ended at the tracks. At the same location, buried beneath an ocean of poison ivy, we found a pile of rough field stone (potential foundation of the bridge) and a geodetic marker (M-18, 1935). Measuring backwards we obtained a new distance of 2567 feet between TPR and NR. Further, when we scaled that distance to the 55/25 ratio, we obtained a potential whale discovery site at 1771 feet north of TPR. The topography of this new potential site made much more sense. But the problem was that the established distances where almost *exactly twice* that of those given by Zadock. He could never be that far off.

When something is radically wrong – *something* is radically wrong. There had to be an explanation.

We returned to Mary Lighthall. She suggested that we try measuring the tracks with a Gunter Chain, the instrument used as the standard in the 1840's by the railroad engineers. Invented in 1581 to serve as a surveyor's tool, it was a steel chain composed of a series of linked brass segments arranged in a repeating pattern of exacting length. Lighthall added that the Charlotte Historical Society had a Gunter Chain in their collection (#75/001/26) that they would be willing to loan to us. (Further research indicates that this may actually have been a Ramsden's Chain, or Engineer's Chain, an American version.)

(Figure 5 – A Gunter chain used for surveying and measuring distance along the railroad tracks in 1849. From the collection of the Charlotte Historical Society.)

Before beginning, we stretched out the chain and measured it. To our amazement it turned out to be 33 feet in length — exactly two rods! Could it be that Zadock Thompson, using the railroad engineer's method of measurement — a method possibly not familiar to him — reported his distances in chain lengths, thinking he was reporting in rods? This would certainly explain the discrepancy in distances, and if so, this would put Zadock right on the mark. Measuring with the chain and using the 55/25 ratio, we determined that our new potential discovery site was 53.5 lengths (1765.5') north of TPR and 23.5 (775.5') lengths south of NR – a total of 77 lengths. For measurements along the track, Thompson likely accepted the word of rail surveyors... who were on the scene and who were at that time by far the best equipped to measure distances. Maybe Thompson measured it alone using their equipment, unaware of the proper conversion factor. Or maybe he watched silently as they measured, noting the number of chain lengths. In either case, it appears that there was a technological miscommunication at some point in the process... but in the end, we seemed to have stumbled upon our answer.

Given the uncertainties of different types of measurement, whether one measures from road edge or center, the conversion factor and that Thompson was measuring over a muddy construction site, we felt that we were well within the degree of accuracy that we required and that we were easily within less than 100' of where the Charlotte whale was discovered in 1849.

We had found our site. Now it was time to dig a hole.

• • •

On a sunny and pleasant October morning in 1993, a small group of people clustered along the edge of an alfalfa field bordering the railroad tracks in Charlotte, Vermont, 1765' north of Thompson Point Rd. Present that day were members of the UVM Geology Dept., the Perkins Museum, Charlotte Historical Society, UVM Anthropology, UVM Public Relations, the Lake Champlain Maritime Museum, Vermont Information Systems and a small but spirited group of Charlotte residents. In addition, there were two videographers from UVM media services and a photographer from the *Burlington Free Press*.

Through the efforts of a local resident, the volunteer services of a local excavation company had been secured. The excavation company provided a backhoe and a highly skilled operator (the owner – who said he wouldn't miss this for anything). The landowner had given us his blessing and by 10:30am, after a two-hour delay in order to comply with Dig-Safe regulations, we were ready to dig a hole.

Within 40 minutes the backhoe operator produced a beautiful, clean, rectangular hole, about 8' x 8' at the top and 11' deep. An aluminum extension ladder was the first thing lowered down into the hole, followed by an orderly progression of geologists, anthropologists, marine historians, stratigraphers, statisticians, videographers, reporters and local residents who had stopped by to see what the fuss was all about. Dr. Stephen Wright provided a detailed layer-by-layer analysis of the sediments and Dr. Peter Thomas expertly troweled off the upper layers and pointed out more recent relationships such as plow zones and root casts. Both descriptions were recorded and lie somewhere within the UVM video archives.

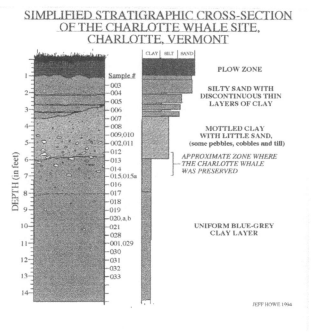

SIMPLIFIED STRATIGRAPHIC CROSS-SECTION
OF THE CHARLOTTE WHALE SITE,
CHARLOTTE, VERMONT

(Figure 6 – A stratigraphic cross-section of the exploratory pit.)

A few observations from the day included:

1. No vertebrate remains or direct evidence of whale activity was found.

2. Zadock Thompson was accurate in his overall description of the stratigraphy. His 4' of unstratified sand, over 2.5' of stratified sands and clays, over a dense "quagmire" of mucky, blue clay is essentially what we found... minus the "quagmire".

3. A number of curious 2 – 5 cm rounded black nodules of either organic material or weathered shale were found by Stephen Bechtel. Their exact significance is unknown. It was suggested at the site that they be compared to manganese nodules that have been found at the bottom of Lake Champlain.

4. Interclasts of harder, dryer clay were found within the pastier blue clays.

5. Pebbles and cobbles (to 8") and till materials were found in the stratified sands and clay at depths between 4'6" and 6'6".

6. The nature of the clay, at least at levels below approximately 8' – 9' was dense and pure with little evidence of sand or silt.

We analyzed the pit as completely as possible and then asked the backhoe operator to go down another 3' to allow us to take a few samples at the bottom. The last few feet became very wet and mucky and fearing that the side walls might collapse, we climbed out of the pit and had the operator fill it back in

In the end, the exploratory pit did little to further our knowledge of the Charlotte whale. We found nothing new; we made no stupendous discoveries. The participants soon scattered to new jobs and opportunities and the samples were never tested, the results never written up and I've been left with this story rolling around in my head for the last 20 years. The event was essentially just a group of like-minded people, enjoying a brisk autumn day and hoping to stumble onto something exciting. And even though we found little but a few rafted pebbles, we speht a convivial day in the low autumn sun getting good and muddy and talking whale theory from sun up to sun down. Fossils or no fossils, there is still something very holy and special about descending into a freshly dug pit and placing your hand upon the cold, spongy dampness of ancient Ice Age clay.

17

The Charlotte Whale –
What We Know and
What We Don't Know

It is the whale that this story is about, but it is about the whale that we know the least. The life that the whale lived and the fate to which it finally succumbed are both obscured by over 11,000 lost years. Over those years the land and the climate have changed and a dozen scenarios have played out on the Charlotte landscape – the rebound and emergence of the land, the freshening of the water, the tundra yielding to vast pine-spruce forests which in turn yielded to hardwoods, the first humans following migrating animals into the valleys, and finally cars, railroads, dairy cows, tourists, traveling skiers and modern civilization.

In addition, despite the conscientious, and in some ways heroic efforts of Zadock Thompson to preserve the fossil and the site information professionally and completely, the actual process was haphazard and rushed – performed in a backwoods environment lacking proper facilities or equipment. The bones were hacked out with shovels and pick axes, packed in wooden boxes and carried by horse cart over dusty, bumpy roads to Thompson's cottage in Burlington. There Thompson slathered them with an "animal glue" to prevent further desiccation, but also unwittingly rendered them insensitive to any further carbon[14] dating. The result is that the whale has come down to us with little actual information. What we are left with is precious little fact, interesting anecdotal evidence, a healthy amount of speculation based on fact, and more than a few pure flights of fancy.

So which is which? What are we to believe? Is it actually possible to make sense of all this? Well, yes it is. We begin by stripping away the trappings of legend, filtering through the misinformation, and going back to the original sources to determine exactly what we do and do not know.

For instance, it has been widely reported that the whale was a female. There is, in fact, no real evidence to support this. This conclusion, speculation really, originated from those of us who were working on the reinterpretation of the whale in the early 1990's. We reasoned that since the whale appeared to be found in shallow water (a false assumption), and because females and young frequent the shallows while the males stick to deeper water, that this whale "could" be female. On some levels this also tied in conveniently with the name "Charlotte" as we told the story to school groups and museum visitors. But in reality, there were no young found in association with the Charlotte specimen, nor is there anything about the skeleton (hip structure, etc.) that would allow us to determine sex. Therefore the sex of the animal remains open to speculation.

Similarly, mention is made from time to time that the whale was "beached." This was most likely inspired by frequent popular news stories about beached whales. But if that were truly the case the whale bones would be preserved in courser, stratified beach deposits. Most likely however, if the whale had been beached it would have been attacked by scavengers and waves, scattered about and not preserved at all. There is no evidence that the Charlotte whale was ever beached.

Some are also arguing that the Charlotte whale is a recent anomaly, a misguided whale that took a wrong turn and ended up stranded in modern Lake Champlain. The sediment in which the whale was preserved shows that the whale predated Lake Champlain and the presence of similar whale fossils around the basin prove that "Charlotte" was not alone.

A frequent and legitimate question that comes up about the Charlotte whale is one that played a prominent role in the original State Fossil hearings: *Is the whale fossil old enough to be called a fossil?* The answer is: *yes*, if only by the thinnest of geologic hairs. By definition a fossil is the remains or trace of life that existed before the end of the Pleistocene period, more commonly known as the "Ice Age". This date, as currently (2009) recognized by the International Union of Geologic Sciences, has been set at 11,700 years b.p. ("before present). Everything after that date is considered to be "modern" or "recent." As previously mentioned, absolute age dating of the Charlotte whale is not possible due to contamination. However, relative dating and anecdotal evidence reliably places the whale at *about* 11,500 years old. I feel comfortable placing "about" in the $+/-200$ years range necessary to bring the whale within compliance. So by the age of an old tortoise (or a young redwood), the whale qualifies.

A question that remains unanswered is: *how deep was the water and what was the depositional environment like at the time the whale carcass settled?* The site where the whale was found (as reported by Z. Thompson, using the original railroad survey) was 60 feet above the level of Lake Champlain. Workers dug down 10 feet to reach it. Lake Champlain itself currently sits at about 150 above sea level. By that reckoning the whale site itself has risen at least 200 feet relative to sea level since the whale's burial. Modern geologic maps put the whale site at an elevation of around 190 feet; the railroad dug down 10 feet or so. As a ballpark figure, it's safe to say that the site has risen (due to rebound) around 200 feet in the last 11,500 years. During that time, sea level has also risen. It's unclear how much erosion has taken place. In short, the depth of the water and the distance to shore are not known, although they could surely be calculated using rates of rebound and correlated beach lines and sediments.

Zadock Thompson suggested that the whale was buried in a salt-marsh or plant-filled "quagmire" based on plant remains that he reported in association with the whale. This would imply a shallow, near-shore environment with lots of organic material. The exploratory pit dug in 1993 found very little in the way of organic plant material although it did turn up root casts that penetrated the clay from above.

The delicately fine clays in which the whale was buried can only form in quiet waters. Not necessarily deep waters, but quiet waters. The exploratory pit confirmed that this clay is overlain by alternating sands and clays, consistent with shallowing and emergence. There is nothing in the sediment that suggests that the whale was in a near-shore environment at the time of burial and preservation.

What we DO and DO NOT know about the Charlotte Whale

What we do know:
- The whale is a small, toothed whale of the species *Delphinapterus leucas.*
- It was preserved in a thick layer of unstratified sticky blue clay containing ice-rafted pebbles.
- The whale was found in sediment similar to others associated with the Champlain Sea.
- The whale appears to have been an adult based on skull sutures and tooth wear.

- The skeleton is incomplete however the skeleton was found fully articulated, with the bones all in their original positions relative to each other.
- There has never been any evidence of predation (teeth marks, etc.) found on the specimen.

What we do not know:
- the exact age or sex of the animal
- how long it has been buried
- the cause of death

What we can surmise based on what we know:
- Based on the current terrain, the whale was buried in a down-slope area on the west side of a north-south running underwater shoal. Barber Hill, the highest point on this ridge, was possibly a small island.
- Based on the presence of rafted pebbles, the water was at least deep enough to accommodate floating icebergs
- Based on the current terrain and present and past sea levels, the whale was buried in water as deep as 200 ft.

PART FIVE

SO, HOW *DO* YOU GET A WHALE IN VERMONT?

18

How DO You Get A Whale In Vermont?

et's set our imaginations free once again like we did
on Greenbush Road at the very beginning of this
book. Pretend that the summer trees and fields of western
Vermont are the waters of a blue-green arm of the ocean,
and the flocks of birds and herds of dairy cattle are distant
schools of fish. Transport yourself back eleven-thousand
years, to a time when Vermont was very different. Squint
your eyes, puff out your cheeks, wiggle your tail and imagine that you are a beluga whale named "Charlotte" swim-
ming in the Champlain Sea.

Got it?

Good.

The water is frigid, at times only a few degrees above
freezing, but your thick layer of blubbery insulation keeps
you warm and comfortable. The shimmer of the surface
above you ripples with sunlight, while at times the depth
below you fades into blackness. The water around you is
a blue-green diorama made slightly hazy by fine, blonde,

glacial rock-flour that pours into the sea by the ton from surrounding rivers and streams. The slight turbidity creates searchlight cones of light that ply the depths but always trace directly back to the sun.

You let out a series of chirps and clicks as you swim along, receiving them back as they reflect off objects in the environment. The water is abuzz with these beluga songs – coming and going between the other members of your pod as the group continues to explore and communicate. You are easily able to filter out the extraneous noise and take in only what is important to you. You sense the ice edge, the depth of the water and the configuration of the bottom. You are aware of a nearby school of fish and the positions of the other whales. There is no confusion or alarm… to you it is quiet and peaceful.

Given the wear on your teeth and the sutures in your skull, you are an adult. Because you are an adult your hairless hide is white, allowing you to blend in with your icy surroundings. You use your peg-like teeth (about as thick as a human's little finger) to chomp into the edge of a small school of fish that you have managed to overtake. You catch about a dozen of them and swallow them down whole as they struggle to get free. Three manage to slip away but you take another chomp and snag another dozen. This time only one escapes.

Despite your name, you might be a male… or you could just as easily be a female. Presumably *you* know and so do your friends, but to the world beyond your species it's awfully difficult to tell. Your sex is very important in establishing your role and rank amongst the other whales.

Hopefully your life is rich and meaningful in a beluga sort of way — you eat well, lead a good life, and have mated and passed on your genes. You'll need to use your imagination here because, in reality, we know very little about your life. As for your death there is only one thing of which we can be sure: at some point you passed away. The details will likely never be known but the end result is very certain.

You may have been attacked by a predator in open water. A large killer whale might have attacked the pod and you were severely wounded but not killed. At the last moment the predator may have elected to slay another victim and you were able to swim off only to die later from your wounds. You may have survived the initial attack but were left severely crippled, unable to care for yourself and compete for food

Maybe you were foolish in trying to run too far beneath the shifting, refreezing ice. The cruel wind that blew above the surface sucked any remaining warmth from the air and all of the reliable, open air holes froze over unexpectedly and you drowned without making it to the surface. Maybe you miscalculated the cold fresh water falling from the ice pack and became trapped as it refroze. Maybe you managed to find an open air hole but also found a large bear waiting patiently for you when you surfaced. The predator mauled you with its huge paw but you were able to escape, although mortally wounded.

Maybe you just died of old age, or disease, or from a broken beluga heart. Whatever the cause, at some point you passed away – the spark left your eyes, the life left your body and your carcass drifted to the bottom of the sea.

You may have tumbled, you may have slid, or you may have dropped gently from above. You may have died in open water and sank, or you may have died in the shallows and your carcass bloated with gas and floated to deeper water before rupturing and sending you to the bottom. How you ended up where you did is not known, but eventually you came to rest on the west side of a gentle underwater ridge, with your head pointing southwest, about 18" below your tail. It is likely that the gentle underwater slope positioned you this way, with the added weight of your head settling into the muck accounting for the angle.

The water was quiet and sufficiently distant from in-flowing rivers. It was deep enough for an occasional iceberg to float by but potentially shallow enough to allow sparse vegetation to grow. Most importantly however, regardless of the circumstances of your death and demise, you arrived at your final resting place intact. There has never been any reported evidence of teeth marks or other feeding traces. This is important because it indicates that you weren't savaged by predators or scattered by scavengers. Your intact carcass settles to the bottom and turns from white to moldy grey, slowly decomposing as a gentle rain of glacial leavings buries you in the mud.

But even as you are being slowly buried you are rising up.

Way before your time, way before the Champlain Sea even existed, huge glaciers pushed down from the north. They combined with smaller alpine glaciers that flowed down from the mountains to form a massif of ice over two miles thick. The enormous weight of this ice crushed the land beneath it, compressed the rock and pushed it deeper into the Earth.

In addition to being pressed downwards, the rock itself was compacted. Water and air were squeezed from all remaining spaces and even the tiniest cracks and crevices were forced closed to accommodate the weight. Thus liberated, microscopic bubbles of water and air worked their way upward and outward through the rock and ice seeking the surface. Dormant faults and slip surfaces were reactivated permitting the rock to grind against itself, compacting even further — sliding together like freshly shuffled cards. And when every remaining volatile had been squeezed from the rock and every conceivable space was crushed shut, the ice pushed the land down even further.

With no spaces left to close, the surface layers were pressed into neighboring layers below. Uncomfortable density differences were set up, potential energy was stored, and rocks were forced down into depths at which they were not comfortable. Like cattle pressed together in an overcrowded holding pen, there was pushing and shoving and complaining... but nowhere to go. Crushed, compacted and forced to unnatural depths, the bedrock waited patiently as the mountain of ice above it continuously reworked and reshaped the surface.

The bedrock didn't need to wait long. The overlying ice waxed and waned throughout its stay in the valley but after a couple million years – barely a three-day blizzard in geologic time – the northern engine that supplied the ice began to sputter and the ice began to retreat. It didn't actually flow backwards; it simply wasted away without supply lines of reinforcements.

As the weight was slowly lifted from the shoulders of the land, the bedrock relaxed and began to expand, but the ice melted much more quickly than the bedrock was able to respond. The two miles of ice had pushed the surface of the land down so far that it had been depressed below the level of the sea. When the ice finally retreated north of the St. Lawrence River, the ocean rushed in, seeking its own level – forming the Champlain Sea. Following the ice edge, your beluga ancestors entered the sea and found it much to their liking.

• • •

It takes little time, probably a season or less, for your carcass to completely rot away leaving nothing but a skeleton. Water begins to permeate your bones and a gentle rain of sediment slowly covers your skeletal remains. Even as you are being buried deeper in the mud you are rising up. You, the mud, and in fact the bedrock itself are all rising... imperceptibly. Slowly, in geologic time the land is rebounding from its confinement beneath the ice. Like a sponge that has been squeezed and then released it is rising up to resume its old form. Water is penetrating small cracks, slip surfaces are releasing their tension and isostatic forces are reasserting themselves.

As the land continues to rise, the ocean slides down its side, exposing the bottom and rolling the sandy beach down over former deep water muds. The water above you becomes shallower and shallower as the beach approaches. Sediment particles become more coarse and the beds show evidence of wind and water movement. Eventually your gravesite emerges from the water, but there is still an accumulation of clay, mud and sand above your head. As the land above you rises beyond the beach, deposition ceases and erosion begins. Soil begins to form; grasses grow and help to retain the soil. Soon they are joined by trees and bushes. And for thousands of seasons, this is how things remain.

Your grave goes from below sea level to above and when the entire basin tops sea level the water begins to drain northward into the St. Lawrence River and back into the Atlantic Ocean. Over time the salt water of the Champlain Sea drains away and is replaced by fresh water from the mountains. In response, the marine animals migrate back to the sea and fresh water populations take over. As the land continues to rise, you move further inland and away from the lake.

The question then becomes, technically, not "How do you get a whale in Vermont?" but rather, "How do you bring Vermont to the ocean?"

• • •

As you rest, encased in the mud, big changes are taking place on the surface. In 1791, the former fledgling independent republic of New Connecticut straddles the crest of the Green Mountains, extending from Lake Champlain in the west, to the Connecticut River in the east. Ill-defined and carved from the northern wilderness following the French and Indian War a generation earlier, its fringes are easily accessible by water. Its interior however remains a virtually unbroken wilderness, a mountainous land of thin, rocky, clay-rich soils — remote and untouched — waiting for settlement. New York claims it from the west; New Hampshire claims it from the east. The United States Congress shows no interest in making it a state until Great Britain attempts to capture it from the north. Congress then moves swiftly.

With a constitution already in place, last minute boundary disputes with New York and New Hampshire are settled and the Independent Republic of Vermont is transformed into the State of Vermont, the 14th state of the new American union. The first article of the new constitution guarantees "that all persons are born free and independent", establishing Vermont as the nation's first abolitionist state. In so doing, Vermont sets itself upon a course to which it will hold throughout its storied history: independence, self-sufficiency and tolerance.

Congratulations. You are now a Vermonter.

The land becomes settled, the trees are cut down and the soil is plowed and cultivated. Because the thick layer of clay in which you lay blocks the drainage of water, a murky swamp known as "Barber's Swamp" forms above you.

In the mid-1840's, railroads are spreading across the country like rapidly growing crystals of frost. Two competing rail companies are rushing to see who can cross the Green Mountains first – connecting Burlington with the East Coast. One group, the Rutland-Burlington Rail Road, has managed to cross over the southern pass through Mt. Holly and is now pressing northward along the shore of Lake Champlain. The previous summer they had unearthed the remains of an ancient elephant, and now, in 1849, they are about to tackle Barber's Swamp.

Get your things together, you are about to be discovered...

THAT'S how you get a whale in Vermont.

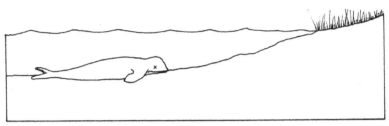

Figure 7 – The whale dies and settles to the bottom of the Champlain Sea.

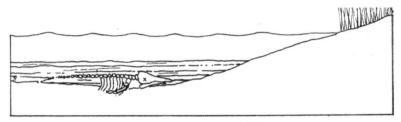

Figure 8 – The carcass decomposes and is slowly covered by fine sediment.

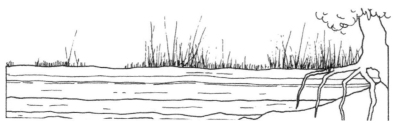

Figure 9 – Glacial rebound slowly raises the burial site above sea level and a succession of plant communities take over the dry land above.

Figure 10 – Construction for the railroad in 1849 exposes the skeleton, severely damaging the skull but preserving the remaining bones in the clay.

PART SIX

AFTERMATH

19

The Bill and The Governor

I was sitting in my basement office at the old Perkins Museum at the University of Vermont one snowy winter day, talking to museum volunteer Robert Trithart, when the phone rang. I can never seem to remember where I put my keys, but for some reason I remember that incident very clearly. It was a teacher from Charlotte Central School asking me for suggestions on ways to get her students involved in a meaningful way with the Charlotte whale. The three of us bounced ideas around and I remember saying, largely in jest, that the Charlotte whale should *really* be the official State Fossil. The conversation eventually concluded, and I went back to my meeting with Trithart.

A few weeks later, I traveled to Charlotte Central School to do an assembly presentation on the whale for the students. Again, I suggested to them that the Charlotte whale would make a great State Fossil. In due time, I received word that the students of Charlotte Central had, in fact, contacted Mary Lighthall of the Charlotte Historical Society and petitioned a special committee of the Vermont

State Legislature. Hazel Prindle, the Charlotte Representative had introduced, and was championing, a bill to have the Charlotte whale designated as the Official State Fossil of Vermont. In my capacity as Curator of the Perkins Museum I was asked to attend a series of hearings in Montpelier to testify as an "expert" witness.

Arriving at the miniature, golden-domed State House in Montpelier a few minutes early, I paced the checkerboard, black and white Vermont marble floor in the main hallway, pondering what I might be asked and what I would say. Eventually, I was ushered into an ornate meeting room and shown to my place at a long, fabulously polished, wooden table.

On one side of the table sat a trio of Vermont's blustery-best legislators. They were elderly, overweight men, hair meticulously combed, dressed in expensive suites and smelling thickly of aftershave. On the opposite side sat five or six elementary school students, arms fidgeting on the table top, legs dangling from tall wood and leather chairs. They stared at the legislators. The legislators stared back at them.

It was a stand-off.

To be fair, there has always been a little controversy in Vermont over a couple of paleontological sticking points concerning the whale. Namely:

1. Is the Charlotte whale really old enough (~ 11,500 years) to be declared a "fossil"? and,

2. What about the Mt. Holly mammoth, or the world's oldest reefs at Isle Le Motte, or the Brandon lignite,

or various Cambrian trilobites? Shouldn't they be considered as well?

Fair questions. The legislators got right to the point. *"I hear that there are whales, just like this one, that are alive today up in the St. Lawrence River. What makes this one so special?"* The little girl to whom the question was being addressed, looked to her teacher, looked to her friend and then replied: *"Those whales are new whales. Our whale was dead a long time. Our whale deserves it."*

The members of the committee nodded to each other and exchanged a series of winks. The largest, scariest legislator of them all, the one to which the others deferred, cleared his throat and peered in mock gruffness at a young boy sitting directly across from him. *"Young man, what should I say to the students up in Grand Isle who tell me their trilobite should be the official fossil instead of yours?"* Feet dangling 10 inches off the ground, the young boy was forehead to chin with the old man. *"Everybody knows,"* he said without the slightest hesitation, *"that a BIG fossil is better than a little one."*

That appears to have sealed the deal. I don't believe they asked me anything. The Bill passed, and on June 7, 1993, I was invited to Charlotte Central to share the stage with Governor Howard Dean as he signed the bill proclaiming the Charlotte Whale to be Vermont's Official State Fossil.

We sat on metal folding chairs, alone on the gymnasium stage: the Governor, the Bill, and I. As I sat there, looking out on the faces of the school children, their teachers and the assembled dignitaries and members of the media, I reflected upon the long and interwoven series of events and personalities that had brought us to this point: Vermont's premier 19th century naturalist, an ice age mammoth, Professor Louis Agassiz, Francois Cuvier, the first railroad through the Vermont wilderness, George Perkins, Henry David Thoreau, the son of a ship captain, a Statehouse fire, a museum renovation and a solitary "sea canary" slathered in horse glue.

It all made perfect sense.

The Governor said a few words and then stepped down to a special table that had been set up especially for the occasion. He took out his pen and signed Vermont Act#66 (1993) to the delight of the students and their teachers.

20

The Charlotte Whale Web Site: An Early Web Pioneer

This chapter is about, of all things, an old and historic *web site*. Not just any old web site, but one of the *very first* educational sites on the World Wide Web. This takes place in the early 1990's. At that time I was the Curator of the Perkins Museum of Geology at the University of Vermont, and was overseeing a major renovation of the museum and all of its exhibits. In a back corner of the museum - in a dusty old wood and glass display case the size and shape of an oversized coffin — rested the bones of a the Charlotte whale. The story of this whale was poorly told and I was researching every source of information available for the new exhibit.

There was at that time a visionary computer-guy at the University by the name of Wesley Wright. He was unorthodox... an out-of-the-box sort of fellow. but he knew his stuff and he was way ahead of the curve when it came to computer applications. At that time, serious computers still took up entire rooms, and home computers were thought to have few applications beyond storing recipes and Christmas card lists. Wright however, had a clear picture of the future potential of computers and specifically, he had a vision for what was at that time only little known: the World Wide Web.

Because the University was interested in promoting the new museum when it was completed, and because Wright was familiar with my work on the whale, he came to me one day and suggested that we construct a "web site."

"What's a web site?" I asked.

"It's information on our computer," he replied, "that can be accessed anywhere in the world by other computers on the World Wide Web."

"What's the World Wide Web?"

And so it went. Although I had recently purchased my first computer (a little *Mac Classic* the size of a toaster oven which later became a door stop) I knew next to nothing about them and was completely unfamiliar with the emerging web phenomenon that was just beginning to take hold. I was, however, familiar with the concept of HyperCard, and although I had never seen an actual web page before, when he explained the idea of the site itself, I immediately saw the potential. I sat down and wrote the story and constructed an outline of nested pages that could be cross-linked to each other. I did some drawings, assembled some photographs and gave the whole mess to Wright who quickly transformed it into something that was, and still is, quite beautiful.

But that's just background. Here's the best part of the story, the part that you computer geeks and nerds will really like. The site was completed and made its debut late in 1993. (It can still be found at <u>www.uvm.edu/whale</u>.) It was an immediate hit and people started asking how they could find it on their computers.

"First," I would tell them, "you have to get on the World Wide Web." THAT was the hard part as there wasn't much access in that day. "Once you get on the Web, click on the icon that says *'What's New on the Web Today'.*" Yes, that's right, there used to be a single icon on the desktop for anything new on the web that day! And if you clicked it, it listed three or four new sites – mostly obscure government or university programs.

I would simply tell them to go to a specific day (I don't recall which) and look for the University of Vermont. It remained that way for about six months until the web started to fill up so much that a specific address was needed.

Go there. The site is still intact and is still extremely functional. Wesley Wright has elected to leave it as it was, so it has changed little over the years and remains a relict, a souvenir, a fossil just like the whale that it describes. The site continues to receive awards and I still get emails from kids in Australia, Indiana or France looking for more information on the Charlotte Whale.

But think of that! "What's New on the Web Today." There was actually a time when you could hold the new sites on the web each day in the palm of your hand…

just three or four. Today there are probably millions every hour.

21

The Tiny Harmonica

There is a rumor that circulates amongst the school children of Vermont. It tells of a tiny, one-inch, four-holed harmonica that hangs suspended by a thin string inside the skull of the Charlotte whale. Legend has it that it was placed there by a former, departing museum curator in appreciation and acknowledgement for all that Charlotte had been through, and for all that "she" has come to symbolize.

"Always keep a tune in your head, Charlotte," the curator is said to have whispered as he left the museum for the very last time.

It is also said that the harmonica (if it really *does* exist) is hung high within the skull so as only to be visible to the smallest of school children, standing wide-eyed in the front row, looking up at the specimen from below. Adults who attempt to see it are inevitably brought to their knees.

There may be a grain of substance or truth to the matter, or there may not. It's really hard to say.

Good science would dictate further observation.

Author Jeff L. Howe with "Charlotte" during a museum renovation in 1993.

Author's Notes

This story frequently interchanges modern names such as "Green Mountains," "St. Lawrence River" or "Mt. Holly" with features in the ancient Ice Age landscape. This is done to help orient the reader. It uses the term "Ice Age" interchangeably with the geologic epoch known as the Pleistocene, which lasted from 2.6 million until 11.7 thousand years ago.

The spelling of Zadock's wife's name appears alternately in the literature as "Phebe" and "Phoebe." Although "Phebe" appears most frequently, the author has chosen to use the spelling "Phoebe" because it is the one most familiar to modern readers.

This is not a rigorous scientific document, nor is it a piece of fiction. It should be viewed as a cultural/scientific history, told by a storyteller. The author has taken existing primary accounts, viewed them in the light of modern scientific understanding and then set them against the backdrop of scientific understanding in the mid-19th century. If anything, it only proves that there is much more research that is necessary if we are ever to know the complete story of the singing, smiling whale found in Charlotte.

APPENDIX

I - A History of the Specimen

The Charlotte whale has made three trips out of Vermont since its discovery: a brief trip to Boston to visit with Louis Agassiz at Harvard in 1850, a journey to Springfield, Massachusetts for a meeting of the American Association for the Advancement of Science in 1860, and a trip to the New York Museum of Natural History with George Perkins in 1906. Over the years it has escaped fire and flood and managed to survive being accidently tipped over in the back of a truck. The following is an account of its movements.

(Note: In Vermont the term "State Cabinet" refers to the official State collection of natural history objects.)

1849

The partial skeleton of a small whale is discovered in Charlotte, Vermont during construction of the Rutland-Burlington railroad. The bones are collected and brought to Professor Zadock Thompson at the University of Vermont. Thompson returns to the site on at least two additional occasions to collect any remaining pieces. After consulting Georges Cuvier's *Ossemen Fossiles*, Thompson declares the skeleton to be that of a White (Beluga) Whale.

The first illustrations of the bones are made by Thompson's daughter, Adeline.

1850

Selected bones (including the periotic?) travel with Thompson to Harvard University where he consults with comparative anatomist Dr. Louis Agassiz about their identity. Agassiz confirms Thompson's identification.

1856

All specimens in the State Cabinet are stored in room #14 of the State House in Montpelier by Albert D. Hagar (acting State Geologist, 1856-57). The whale was apparently not part of the collection at this time.

Zadock Thompson dies on January 19.

1857

A major fire sweeps through the Vermont State House in January and destroys all but 50 specimens in the State Cabinet. (The whale was not part of the collection at this time.)

Phoebe Thompson is approached by the State of Vermont and agrees to sell Zadock Thompson's geological collections to the State Cabinet for $1000. These specimens are intended to replace those lost in the fire. The unmounted whale bones are part of this collection.

1857-1860

The bones are restored and mounted for display in the State Museum by Edward Hitchcock, Jr., who then exhibits the skeleton at the American Association for the Advancement of Science at its Springfield (MA) meeting.

Albert D. Hagar makes a makeshift skull of plaster and canvas "not to elicit the criticism of the learned zoologist, but to render (it) more interesting to the casual observer."

1858

The collections are placed on exhibit in the new State House.

1861

A wood cut illustration of the specimen appears in Volume II of Albert D. Hagar's 1861 *Report on the Geology of the State of Vermont.*

1880

A lithograph of the skull appears in the 3rd Edition of James D. Dana's *Manual of Geology.*

1899-90

The whale is reported in George H. Perkin's *Report of State Geologist on Mineral Resources of Vermont,* 1899-90, to be "mounted in the long case just under the gallery", presumably in the New State House

1906

Professor George H. Perkins travels to New York with selected bones to consult with Roy Chapman Andrews at the Museum of Natural History.

1908

George H. Perkins thoroughly describes the specimen in his 1908-09 Report of the State Geologist. This report utilizes photographs of the specimen made for the U.S. National Museum at the request of Dr. F. W. True.

1909-10

State Geologist George H. Perkins issues *History and Condition of the State Cabinet.* The whale is mentioned in passing.

1918

The State Cabinet is moved with the Vermont Historical Society to the new library and museum in a building authorized in 1915.

1922

Vermont's historical flood of record inundates Montpelier, flooding downtown buildings to the tops of the second floor. Biological specimens, labels and records stored with the State Cabinet in a basement storeroom of the State Geologist's office are destroyed. The whale is displayed elsewhere and escapes damage.

1944

By this time the State Cabinet is displayed only in alcoves and halls at the entrance to the building.

1957

The Vermont Historical Society (VHS) applies for space in a new building but is told that it will have smaller museum exhibit space. VHS offers to take the geologic and fossil specimens but says that it has no room for the larger cabinets and specimens. The whale would be included in this latter group.

1962

The whale specimen is moved from the basement of the State Library to Perkins Hall at the University of Vermont in Burlington by Dr. Allen Hunt and State Geologist Dr. Charles Doll. The specimen tips over while being transported in the back of a small truck and sustains minor damage to the plastered skull. The damage is easily repaired.

1992

A web site dedicated to the whale is designed and installed on the World Wide Web by Wesley Wright and Jeff Howe of the University of Vermont. It becomes one of the first sites on the Web

1993

The whale is reinstalled as a central exhibit near the main entrance of the Perkins Museum of Geology in Perkins Hall (UVM) as part of a major museum renovation. It is suggested that the skeleton be reconstructed to eliminate errors from the 1860 reconstruction including the old plaster and canvas skull, but it is decided that it is an important part of the history of the specimen and it remains untouched.

The whale is declared Vermont's Official State Fossil by the Vermont State Legislature and the bill is signed into law at Charlotte Central School in June by Governor Howard Dean.

2005

The University of Vermont Geology Department and the Perkins Museum of Geology move to Delehanty Hall on the old Trinity College campus in Burlington. The whale exhibit is moved at this time.

II - The Periotic Bone

One of the more curious and enigmatic items involving the Charlotte whale is the periotic bone. In Dr. George Perkin's 1907-08 *"Report of The State Geologist of Vermont"*, he mentions, for the first time, the presence of this small, bulbous, snail-like inner-ear bone that is a key characteristic of cetaceans, especially beluga whales, because of its important function in echo location.

The periotic bone of the Charlotte whale is curious for three reasons:

1.) Even the most casual observer will note, when viewing all of the Charlotte material together, that the state of preservation of the periotic is unique. Whereas the other bones have a dusty brown color and texture, the periotic has a shiny, resilient, almost opalescent quality. This may be due to differences in composition, to being protected within the braincase, or to other preservational or environmental factors. However, the difference is obvious and cannot be ignored.

2.) Experts note size differences between the Charlotte periotic and what would be expected in comparison with other known *D. leucas* specimens, although there is disagreement as to the interpretation. Roy Chapman Andrews mentioned the following:

"I have compared the bone with the ear bones of several specimens of *Delphinapterus leucas*. The resemblance except in point of size is very close indeed. The bullate portion of the periotic in your specimen is somewhat smaller in proportion to the total length of the bone than in *D. leucas*. The internal auditory meatus is also slightly different in shape. However, I believe that these characters are open to a slight individual variation. The difference in size seems to be an important one as it probably indicates that your specimen, if adult, is a smaller animal than *D. leucas*.

Andrew continues: "A comparison with the periotic of a very young individual of *D. leucas* shows this bone in the latter individual to be considerably larger than in your specimen. The bone itself agrees so closely with other specimens of *Delphinapterus* in general characteristics that there can be no doubt of its identity with that genus."

However, Dr. True of the National Museum notes: "The periotic of *D. vermontanus* appears to indicate that the species is distinct from *D. leucas*.

3.) The most curious aspect of the periotic however, is that Zadock Thompson never mentions the bone at all. "It is rather strange," notes Perkins, "that Thompson in his detailed account of the finding and identifying of these bones should not have mentioned the ear bone." And indeed, if one scours Thompson's accounts, there is no reference to this unusual and unique bone. This suggests at least the following possibilities:

a.) That the periotic bone was included in a series of miscellaneous bones that Thompson could not identify and left with Agassiz for further study. On page 262 of his 1850 description (American Journal of Science, etc.) Thompson states:

"There are several of the recovered bones, whose places are not yet ascertained. Some of these may be appendages to the hyoid bone and others may belong to a rudimentary pelvis. Professor Agassiz who has manifested, as already stated, a deep interest in these fossils, has kindly consented to give them that further careful investigation, and illustration, which their importance demands, and for which he is most ably qualified; I have, therefore, placed them in his hands for this purpose."

Perkins goes on to say (pg. 96):

"It may be noticed that Thompson says that the scapula and ulna of the right side were the only bones of the anterior limbs that were recovered. Other bones must have been recovered later, for in the specimen as mounted, all the bones of the left side are present." This leads credence to the idea that bone material was returned to the collection after Thompson's written report, and possibly after the transfer of the fossil to the State Cabinet following Thompson's death in 1856.

b.) The periotic was found at the original site but belonged to a different, smaller individual. It is always been a possibility that the Charlotte whale was one of a number of individuals in the same general vicinity and that some bone pieces were scattered and intermixed. Although this is highly unlikely, it must be considered as a possibility. The 1992 dig hoped to shed some light on this but found nothing to either confirm or contradict the idea. Perkins speculated: "… as only this one individual specimen has been found in the state it must have belonged to it." This is likely the case, but cannot be assumed.

c.) The periotic belongs to another specimen and was inadvertently included with the Charlotte specimen in some subsequent comparative study. This is admittedly speculative, but the possibility cannot be ruled out. From Zadock Thompson and Louis Agassiz on down, the whale has been in many hands.

There is no solid evidence, anecdotal or otherwise, to support the last two options, leaving the first as the most reasonable: that the periotic was left with Agassiz for further study and returned to Thompson at a latter date, possibly without comment.

Intuitively, at least to this author, there is something about the Charlotte periotic that doesn't quite fit. It is naggingly enigmatic. Unfortunately, this small piece of the puzzle must necessarily remain hidden, at least for now, as there appears to be no surviving correspondence between Agassiz and Thompson in the collections of Agassiz's letters at Harvard, or Thompson's at the University of Vermont.

Bibliography

References Pertaining to the Charlotte Whale

Bailey, Horace W., 1913, Thompson: Interesting facts regarding..., Comments on Thompson in obituary of his sister Eliza, Burlington Free Press, June 10, 1913.

Basset, T., 1977, Zadock Thompson (newspaper series running 2/27; 3/6,13,20,27;4/3,10,17,24/77) Burlington Free Press, Burlington, VT.

Bristol, Theresa Hall, "Notes on Some Early Vermont – New York Settlers," New York Genealogical and Biographical Record 44 (1913): 285-289

Bonnichsen, R., Jacobson, G.L.Jr., Davis, R.B., Borns, H.W.Jr., 1985, The environmental setting for human colonization of northern New England and adjacent Canada in Late Pleistocene time, Geological Society of America Special Paper 197, pp. 151-159.

Chapman, D.H., 1937, Late-Glacial and Postglacial History Of The Champlain Valley, American Journal of Science, vol. 23, no. 200, August, 1937, pp. 89-124.

Cutting, H.A., 1875, Report of the Geologist and Curator State Cabinet for 1874 and 1875, Vermont Historical Society, Montpelier.

Dann, K., 1984, The Oldest Vermonter, Vermonteer, September 8, 1984, (newspaper feature).

Dodge, Bertha S., 1977, Tales of Vermont Ways and People, Stackpole Books, Harrisburg, Pa. ISBN 0-8117-1722-4

Erickson, Jon, 1996, Glacial Geology: How Ice Shapes the Land, Facts On File, Inc., An Infobase Holding Company, New York, ISBN 0-8160-3355-2

Evans, P.G.H., 1987, The Natural History of Whales and Dolphins, Published by Facts On File, Inc., N.Y.

Fairbridge, R.W., 1977, Discussion Paper: Late Quaternary environments in Northeastern Coastal North America, Ann. N.Y. Acad. Sci., 288: 90-92

Fisher, Dorothy Canfield, 1953, Vermont Tradition: A Biography of An Outlook on Life; Little, Brown and Co., Boston

Follette, Clara E., 1962, History of the state cabinet, Vermont Historical Society reference report to Comm. of Dept. of State Admin., 12/28/62, Vermont Historical Soc., Montpelier.

Gaskin, D.E., 1982, The Ecology of Whales and Dolphins. Heineman Educational Books Ltd., London, 459pp.

Gingerich, Phillip D., 1994, The Whales of the Tethys, Natural History, April, 1994, pp. 86-88

Graffagnino, J. Kevin, 1979, Zadock Thompson and The Story of Vermont, Vermont History, Proc. of Vt. Hist. Soc., vol 47, no. 4, Fall 1979, pp. 237-257.

Graffagnino, J. Kevin, Samuel B. Hand, and Gene Sessions, eds., 1999, Vermont Voices, 1609 through the 1990's. A documentary history of the Green Mountain State, Montpelier: Vermont Historical Society, 1999

Harrington, C.R., 1977, Marine mammals in the Champlain Sea and the Great Lakes., Ann. New York Acad. Sci., 288:508-537.

Harrington, C.R., 1981, Whales and seals of the Champlain Sea. Trail and Landscape, 15:32-47.

Hitchcock, E., et al., 1861, Geology of Vermont, Vol. I, pp. 162-165, Vol. II pp. 938-939.

Imbrie, John and Imbrie, Katherine Palmer, Ice Ages: Solving the Mystery, 1979, Harvard University Press, 224 pgs., ISBN 0-674-44075-7

Jackson, C.T., 1854, "On a recent mine of gold, silver, lead and copper recently opened at Bridgewater, Vermont": Boston Society of Natural History proceedings, vol. 5, p 62.

Levenson, Thomas, Ice Time: Climate, Science and Life on Earth, 1989, Harper and Row, 242 pgs., ISBN 0-06-016063-2

McGee, R., 1974, Beluga hunters: an archaeological reconstruction of the history and culture of the Mackenzie Delta Kittegaryumiut. Newfoundland Soc. Econ. Stud., Mem. Univ. Newfoundland, St. John's, 13:1-125.

Mchedlidze, G.A., 1976, General Features of the Paleobiological Evolution of Cetacea (translated from Russian), Published for the Smithsonian Institution Libraries and the National Science Foundation, Washington, D.C., by Amerind Publishing Co. Pvt. Ltd., New Delhi, 1984

Ogden, J.G., II, 1977, The Late Quaternary Paleoenvironmental record of Northeastern North America, Ann. N.Y. Acad. Sci., 288: 16-34

Perkins, G.H., 1908, Fossil Cetacea of the Pleistocene of the United States and Canada (with special reference to *Delphinapterus vermontanus*, Thompson), Report of the State Geologist of Vermont, 1907-1908, pp. 76-112.

Perkins, G.H., 1909-10, History and Condition of the State Cabinet, Report of the State Geologist of Vermont, 1909-10, pp. 1-78.

Philbrick, Nathaniel, 2006, Mayflower: A Story of Courage, Community, and War, Penguin Group, New York. ISBN 0-670-03760-5

Pippard, L., 1985, Status of the St. Lawrence River population of Beluga, *Delphinapterus leucas*, Canadian Field-Nat., 99:438-450.

Raymo, Chet, 2006, Walking Zero: Discovering Cosmic Space and Time Along the Prime Meridian, Walker and Co., New York. ISBN 0-8027-1494-3

Reeves, R.R., and E. Mitchell, 1984, Catch history and initial population of white whales (*Delphinapterus leucas*) in the river and gulf of St. Lawrence, eastern Canada. Nat. Canadian (Rev. Ecol. Syst.), 111:63-124.

Sirkin, Les, 1977, Late Pleistocene vegetation and environments in the Middle Atlantic Region, Ann. N.Y. Acad. Sci.. 288: 206-217.

Smith, T.G., D. J. St. Aubin, and J. R. Geraci [ed.]. 1990. Advances in research on the beluga whale, *Delphinapterus leucas*. Can. Bull. Fish. Aquat. Sci. 224: 206p.

Stewart, B.E., and Stewart, R.E.A., *Delphinapterus leucas*, Mammalian Species, no. 336, pp. 1-8, 3 figs. (Published 12 May 1989 by The American Society of Mammologists)

Stilwell, Lewis D., Migration From Vermont. Montpelier, Vermont: Vermont Historical Society. 1948

Thompson, Z., 1850, An account of some fossil bones found in Vermont, in making excavations for the Rutland and Burlington Railroad, American Journal of Science, vol. 9, no.26, March 1850, pp. 256-263. (Also hand-written copy by Thompson)

Thompson, Z., 1853, (Reference to both the Mt. Holly mammoth and the Charlotte whale), Thompson's Vermont, Appendix, pp. 15-20, figs. 1-13.

Thompson, Z., (no date), Autobiographical sketch. (from Special Collections, Bailey-Howe Library, University of Vermont, Burlington, Vt.)

Turner, Frederick Jackson, 1920, The Frontier in American History, 4th printing, 1997, University of Arizona Press. ISBN#0-8165-0946-8

(The Fossil Remains Of Vermont, Hours At Home: A Popular Magazine of Religious and Useful Literature, September, 1866, Vol.III, #5.)

Also By Jeff L. Howe:

What The Next Moment Might Bring
Tales from the Road to High Adventure

A collection of short stories and essays from over sixty years out upon the road to high adventure including: *When the Baby Exploded, The Best Ten Cents* and *A Stripper Bar in Baker, Montana.*

Available in soft cover and eBook and available at Amazon.com and a growing number of book stores where you live.

See **jeff-howe.net** for details.

Milton Keynes UK
Ingram Content Group UK Ltd.
UKHW021331301024
2473UKWH00040B/377

A ROCKY ROAD
MEMOIRS

ABRAHAM LEVY
WITH SIMON ROCKER

HALBAN
LONDON

First published in Great Britain by
Halban Publishers Ltd
22 Golden Square
London W1F 9JW
2017
www.halbanpublishers.com

A CIP catalogue record for this book is available
from the British Library.

ISBN 978-1-905559-81-7

Illustration No. 33 Photo Copyright © Suzie Maeder/Lebrecht
Music & Arts

Every attempt has been made to acknowledge all illustrations.
Please approach the publisher if any illustration has not been
acknowledged.

Typeset by Spectra Titles, Cambridgeshire
Printed in Great Britain by
CPI Group (UK) Ltd, Croydon CR0 4YY

For Estelle
You took on a role you did not seek
and you did it with grace,
elegance and sincerity

Contents

Preface

THERE WAS AN irony about the invitation to speak at an interfaith conference at Alcala University, one of the oldest seats of learning in Spain. At one time, no Jew, let alone a rabbi, would have been allowed to set foot inside its doors. It was founded a few years after one of the most traumatic episodes in Jewish history, the expulsion of the Jews of Spain in 1492. Its founder, Cardinal Ximenes de Cisneros, had become confessor to Queen Isabella the very same year that she and her husband King Ferdinand signed the expulsion decree. Now I was being welcomed by leading churchmen and the King of Spain himself.

When I finished my talk, to an audience robed in gowns of blue or red, King Juan Carlos said with a hint of surprise, "You speak very good Spanish." However, I could not explain how I knew the language. The Jews of Madrid, anxious to avoid any diplomatic embarrassment, had made sure to warn me, "Whatever you do, don't mention that you are from Gibraltar." The quarrel between Spain and Britain over my birthplace was not uppermost in my mind. I had come in the interests of reconciliation, following a visit two years earlier to take part in Sepharad 92, the programme to commemorate the 500th anniversary of the expulsion. The year of remembrance was meant to herald a new era in relations between Spain and the Jews and I was happy to grasp the hand of friendship extended to me. My connection with Spain goes back a long way. Among the estimated 200,000 Jews who left in that involuntary exodus five centuries ago were my ancestors.

Many Jews had seen Spain as their new promised land, only for the *conviviencia*, the co-existence they had once enjoyed with Christians and Muslims, to come to a bitter end. Those who did not choose exile remained at a price, by abandoning their faith and converting to Christianity. The policy of forced baptism had begun a century earlier but the "new Christians", as they were called, aroused suspicions of paying only lip-service to their new religion. Those accused of religious insincerity could fall prey to the heresy-hunters of the Inquisition. Despite the dangers, some of the converts continued secretly to practise Jewish customs. Long after the end of the Inquisition, people from Spain and Portugal have told me of hidden traditions still observed by their families. Some even light Shabbat candles and put them behind a metal grill to escape notice.

In the preparations for Sepharad 92, I wrote to the Vatican, urging that it make a statement acknowledging the horrors of the Inquisition. When the Spanish Church issued a declaration which spoke of the need for *teshuvah*, repentance, as well as for a common effort to "overcome the tragedies of history", I welcomed it as a positive step. I said, at the time of the commemoration, that it was our first duty to remember those who suffered but I also believed the occasion should be something else, an opportunity to recall the unique Jewish culture that flowered in medieval Spain and, for Sephardim in particular, to recapture its spirit.

In my address at Alcala, I highlighted how attached the Jews had felt to Spain. Moses Maimonides, the greatest scion of Spanish Jewry, who was born in Cordoba, fled after the invasion of the fanatical Almohads from North Africa in the 12th century. Nevertheless, as we know from the signature on his manuscripts, he remained proud to call himself "*Ha-Sephardi*", *El Espagnol*, the Spaniard. Yehudah Halevi, dreaming of a return to Zion nearly a thousand years before Herzl, could still write of the "good things" of Spain. Despite the shock of their ejection, the Jews retained nostalgia for their former home. You could take the Jews out of Spain but you could not take Spain out of the Jews.

A myth grew up among some Sephardim that they were descended from the ancient aristocracy of Israel, which they derived from a custom of letter-writers to append to their signature the Hebrew letters *samech tet*. The abbreviation was erroneously taken to stand for the words *Sephardi Tahor*, "pure Sephardi". A more plausible explanation is that the letters stand for *Sopho Tov*, "May his latter end be good", an exclamation of hope in days of persecution. Nevertheless, there was a certain cachet to being Sephardi, such that the word came to cover all non-Ashkenazi communities.

Some of the descendants of the exiles after 1492 kept the keys to houses where their families lived before the expulsion in the hope of returning one day. My own synagogue in London, the Spanish and Portuguese Jews' Congregation, still preserves Spanish within its liturgy. On the morning of the fast of Tishah b'Av, which commemorates the destruction of the Temples in Jerusalem, the *haftarah* from Jeremiah is read in Spanish. It was around the time of this mournful day in 1492 that the edict to expel the Jews of Spain came into force. On the night of Pesach, some families recite the Haggadah in Spanish as well as Hebrew. A few years ago, I reprinted an edition of a Haggadah from the early 19th century "*en Hebraico y Espanol*". It carries a dedication to Aaron Cardozo, head of the Jewish community of Gibraltar, who supplied provisions to the British Navy. Admiral Nelson's last words to him before the Battle of Trafalgar were, "If I survive, Cardozo, you shall no longer remain in this dark corner of the world."

Remarkably, even though Spain had driven Jews from its shores, it had not severed all connection with them. In 1556, King Charles V, the grandson of Ferdinand and Isabella, authors of the expulsion decree, knighted an ancestor of my mother, Jacob Cansino. He was able to practise Judaism openly as he was living in Morocco and he served as the Spanish envoy there. His coat of arms bears a gazelle, an animal known for its loyalty, and a pot. The pot is a symbol of abundance, although my grandfather used to say that it represented the *adafina*, the Shabbat hotpot, the Sephardi equivalent of *cholent*.

Since I grew up with the heritage of Spain and Portugal, naturally I take pride in it but its achievements are indisputable. Judaism would have looked very different without the contribution of Maimonides or Nachmanides, Yehudah Halevi or Ibn Ezra. The codification of Jewish law took shape, producing practical guides for Jewish living able to be followed by those without the skill to navigate the vast and dense text of the Talmud. Jewish philosophy reached new heights, setting out to clarify Jewish belief in a way commensurate with the most advanced ideas of the day. Not only were our prayer books enriched by the religious poems which came from Spain but poets such as Solomon ibn Gabirol also wrote verse on love and other worldly topics. They were the fathers of secular Hebrew poetry. While relatively few Jews indulged in mysticism, the Zohar, the central book of the Kabbalah, emerged there in the late 13th century. The Kabbalah sought to explain the hidden workings of the Divine and the spiritual forces that govern creation.

The Jews of Spain were, as I emphasised during Sepharad 92,

"masters of synthesis". They combined a devotion to Judaism with an interest in the world around them. Men like Ibn Ezra and Maimonides were versed in many branches of secular as well as religious knowledge. They evolved a type of religion which went hand-in-hand with active participation in the life of their country. They were able to attain influential positions in court. When Shmuel HaNagid, vizier to Habbus, the Berber ruler of Granada in the 11th century, rode into battle, he took with him his *shochet* to provide kosher meat. He was a poet, scholar and military commander who served both his God and his king without compromising either. Only a few days after the Jews began gathering their belongings and seeking refuge elsewhere, Christopher Columbus set sail for the new world in 1492 with astronomical tables which had been drawn up by a rabbi.

In a world now only too aware of religious fanaticism, the attractions of a faith that is rational, sophisticated and outward-looking ought to be apparent but the distinctive Sephardi ethos has fallen out of favour in recent times. The revival of Orthodox Judaism in the decades since the Second World War has been driven largely by a narrower vision. In a pamphlet I wrote more than forty years ago, *The Sephardim – A Problem of Survival?*, I observed that there had been a move to the religious right "with a punctilious preoccupation with all the minutiae and strictures of rabbinic Judaism". Many students attend yeshivot where they are immersed for years in Jewish studies. If they study science or medicine or other subjects, they tend to keep the two worlds – of religious and secular knowledge – apart, rather than strive, as did Maimonides and his contemporaries, to bring them together. The Artscroll publications which have become popular in many English-speaking synagogues typify this trend; while they have undoubtedly made Jewish texts accessible to a broader readership, they draw purely on rabbinic sources and exclude outside scholarship.

In that same pamphlet, I argued that the classic Sephardi experience had resulted not only in a certain worldliness which enabled positive integration in the wider society but also leniency and tolerance in the application of Jewish law. It was a legacy which I felt strongly then could help to heal the rifts between religious and non-religious in Israel. If anything, the divisions have only deepened and the animus felt by many Israelis towards the rabbinic establishment has alienated them from Judaism. Yet I have not lost hope that the pendulum will swing and the broadminded Sephardi tradition reassert itself.

There is something else I found in the experience of Spanish Jewry which always stuck with me. Horrified by the expulsion order, leading figures from the Jewish community went to the Alhambra Palace (a site originally developed by the son of Shmuel HaNagid) to try to change the minds of the King and Queen. "After all we have done for Spain, how could you do this to us?" they asked. The most prominent of these courtly appellants were Don Isaac Abarbanel and Don Abraham Seneor. Abarbanel was a philosopher and rabbinic scholar who wrote commentaries on the Bible. He played an important role as a financier, replenishing the royal coffers. Seneor helped to broker the marriage of Ferdinand and Isabella, which united the regions of Castile and Aragon and so laid the foundations of modern Spain. He became chief justice of the Jews of Castile but was not renowned for his Jewish learning. Despite their service to the kingdom and all their eloquence, their pleas fell on deaf ears.

When it came to the crunch, Seneor, a secular but not a spiritual leader, opted to remain in Spain and converted to Christianity. Abarbanel, the knowledgeable Jew, however, packed his bags and headed for a new life in Italy. The contrast was striking and appeared a lesson from history, one that I took to heart as I set out to become a rabbi: our survival depends on education.

I

The Levys of Gibraltar

CARMEL COLLEGE HAD opened in 1948 as an attempt to marry the best of English public school tradition with a solid foundation in Judaism within a Jewish milieu. The rabbinic exemplars of synthesis from the Golden Age of Spain might have approved of such an educational experiment. Its founder and principal, Kopul Rosen, was the model of a modern rabbi. Elegantly turned out, imposing, he was a magnificent preacher. The inimitable *Jewish Chronicle* columnist, Chaim Bermant, once said that when Kopul Rosen spoke, even the heads of the foxes on the women's fur coats would look up and take notice.

Shortly before the establishment of Carmel at Greenham Common in Berkshire, Rabbi Rosen had suffered a setback because he had expected to be appointed Chief Rabbi but instead was overlooked in favour of the much less charismatic Israel Brodie. He had also been the senior rabbi of the Federation of Synagogues but had not been happy in that role. Carmel was an opportunity to put his vision into practice. "One day there would be so many Carmeli rowers in the Oxford and Cambridge boat race that it would have to be postponed from Saturday to another day because they couldn't break Shabbat," he told us.

By the time I had reached barmitzvah and spent a year under Kopul Rosen's sway at Carmel, my heart was set on the rabbinate. My mother had always wanted to have a rabbi as a son, although whether the weight of her expectation fell on me in particular rather than my two brothers I can't say. When Rabbi Rosen asked my class what we wanted to do with our lives, alone of the boys, I said I wanted to be a rabbi. He seemed more disappointed that I was the only one who did rather than gratified that at least one of us aimed to follow in his footsteps, for the pulpit was hardly the preferred profession most well-to-do parents had in mind for their children. In those days – and this may seem surprising now – we wore our kippot only for praying, eating or Jewish studies and were not otherwise allowed to cover our heads unless granted special permission. Having declared my rabbinical ambition, I asked Rabbi Rosen, "Now may I keep my kippah on?"

We could count several rabbis in our family tree, on my father's side. The first we know of, nine generations before me, was Rabbi Yeshua Levy, born around 1640, who dispensed Torah in Tetuan, the Moroccan port some fifty miles south of Gibraltar. Rabbi Yeshua was one of the *megorashim*, as the exiles from Spain were known. We can be sure of our descent because the *ketubot*, the marriage contracts, that passed down the family record that these conformed to the "established conditions of the holy communities exiled from Castile". The *megorashim* regarded themselves as more educated and cultured than the *toshavim*, the Jews who had put down roots in Morocco hundreds of years before. Evidently, Rabbi Yeshua, or his grandson of the same name, made his mark because there used to be a road in the old Jewish quarter of Tetuan called after him. The second Rabbi Yeshua may have been the first of the family to spend time in Gibraltar, which by then would have been under British control.

2

According to the Treaty of Utrecht between Britain and Spain in 1713, no "Jew or Moor" was supposed to reside in Gibraltar but the pragmatic British, happy to take advantage of the trading links maintained by the Jews of Morocco, paid scant regard to its provisions.

Once under British sovereignty, the Jews of Gibraltar looked further afield for spiritual support. The head of the Spanish and Portuguese Community in London, Haham David Nieto, who had a reputation as a philosopher, sent his son Isaac to minister to the Jews of the Rock. At the same time, more kabbalistically inclined rabbis from Morocco continued to settle there. So Gibraltar became a bridge between Jewish East and West, absorbing influences from both in a way that was perhaps unique. By the end of the 18th century, the 600-plus Jews in Gibraltar represented more than a quarter of its civilian population.

My great-great-great-grandfather, Don Moses de Isaac Levy, a merchant with a flourishing maritime business who traded in timber, coffee and sugar among other commodities, was one of the leaders of its Jewish community in the early 19th century. In 1807, when he sailed to Lisbon to open a branch of his enterprise there, the Inquisition was still in force and Jews were forbidden to set foot in Portugal. Although advised to conceal his religion, he refused to do so and disembarked only when a special permit was arranged for him by Admiral John Jervis, the conqueror of Napoleon's fleet at the Battle of Cape St Vincent ten years before. The Portuguese ban on Jews was not formally lifted until 1822.

Don Moses was a well-connected man whose circle of contacts included Giovanni Maria Mastai-Ferretti, later to be chosen as Pope Pius IX; he and his fellow Gibraltarian, Judah Benoliel, were bankers to the cardinal. However, the earlier favours Pio Nono, as he was known, had been shown by Jews had seemingly passed from his mind at the most notorious incident of his papacy. In 1858, police snatched a six-year-old Jewish boy,

Edgardo Mortara, from his home in Bologna and took him to Rome on the grounds that he had been secretly baptised by a maid and was therefore a Christian. Pius IX ignored an international campaign to return the boy and even refused to meet the most famous Jewish figure in Europe at the time, the Victorian philanthropist Sir Moses Montefiore. The boy, whose story is being made into a film by Stephen Spielberg – *The Kidnapping of Edgardo Mortara* – was never returned and grew up to be a priest.

Don Moses was thought to have spent his final years in Israel, according to the monograph on his life published by my nephew, Isaac S. Levy of London. We know that his youngest son, Joshua, and most of Joshua's family died in the Galilee in the Safed earthquake of 1837. Don Moses's prosperity enabled his pious eldest son, Rabbi Isaac, to devote himself mostly to the pursuit of the Torah rather than matters of commerce and to sponsor the scholarship of other rabbis. Rabbi Isaac Levy himself wrote two halachic tracts, one of which *A Morsel of Bread,* about dietary rules, was translated from Hebrew into English by my brother-in-law Alan Corré. The rabbi was particularly stringent about the danger of insect infestation in fruit and vegetables and abstained from cauliflower, for example, because he considered it too difficult to clean.

Rabbi Isaac was also generally worried about over-eating, even on Shabbat, when it is a mitzvah to consume three meals, remarking that over-indulgence only created "food for worms". His abstemiousness clearly bore the influence of Kabbalah. Although I found some of the ideas of the mystical tradition attractive, I cannot claim to have inherited his asceticism. What I do share is the name of one of his sons, Abraham E. Levy (though I was not actually named after him, Abraham came from my mother's side), who ran the Lisbon end of the family business for a while and was consul-general for the Bey of Tunis in Gibraltar. In 2004, I was privileged to speak at the centenary of the synagogue in Lisbon – the first built in the city post-Inquisition – which great-great uncle Abraham had helped to found.

On one occasion, Abraham E. Levy hosted Sir Moses Montefiore, who was returning from Morocco on one of his many mercy missions to intercede on behalf of co-religionists in trouble abroad. The governor of Gibraltar laid on a banquet and the visiting knight was serenaded by a military band. In gratitude, Sir Moses was reported to have given my ancestor the silver statue of a woman, her nose partly removed in order not to transgress the commandment against graven images. Alas, the heirloom has disappeared; it was later presented to the Jewish centre in Lisbon but believed to have been taken in a burglary.

I was born in July 1939, a few weeks before the outbreak of the Second World War, the middle of five children, flanked either side by a brother and sister, Solomon and Nita who were older, and Loli and James. However, my earliest memories belong elsewhere than to Gibraltar, because when I was a year old, we were evacuated. Hitler, it was feared, was poised to take Gibraltar with the blessing of General Franco. While the young men remained to defend the garrison, the women and children were dispersed to various parts. Some went to England, some to Jamaica, while we were lucky enough to be sent to Madeira. To go there, my parents had to prove that we had sufficient means to keep us for a year. Little did anyone expect that we would remain there for five. When our funds ran out, we had to be supported by the British government.

On our island haven, the war passed us by. We shared a house with my paternal aunts and, while we had little and life was spartan, the cost of living was so cheap that we could still keep a maid. Although there had been Jews in Madeira in the 15th century, no indigenous Jewish presence remained. The house of the president of our community, David Benaim – who was later to become Israel's first consul in Gibraltar – doubled as a makeshift synagogue. He was a poultry *shochet*, religiously qualified to act as a slaughterer, and so able to ply his congregation with kosher chicken.

For amusement, I had a single comic which I learned by heart, about a lollipop which wandered out in the rain and as a result became very thin. I used to be asked to stand up and recite it as a party piece. Towards the end of our stay, we were moved to the Savoy Hotel, where the boys would cut rubber from under the carpet stairs to use as erasers for homework. My father Isaac told us much later that what had kept him sane through this period were the speeches of Winston Churchill he heard on the radio. After the war, when I was in synagogue with my father in Gibraltar, we would have to stay behind after the end of service as others left. "Avram," he said, "I have now got to pray for the life and health of Winston Churchill."

The 300-year-old Jewish community of Gibraltar was one of the few in Europe which survived the war intact. While some of the evacuees chose not to come home, those on Madeira returned to resume their lives, although it was more than a case of simply picking up where they had left off. Everything was in a state of disarray. Our homes had been taken over by the army and some of the ancestral silver was missing. My father, now in his mid-forties, was a notary public, a legal official whose certificate of practice is to this day signed by the Archbishop of Canterbury, but not a position that came with a salary enabling him to support a family.

Most of the wealth bequeathed by Don Moses and his successors had long gone, although my father's sisters liked to maintain an air of stylishness that reminded them of former glories. Their house had once been much bigger and, before being divided, had contained a stable for horse and carriage. They would proudly show me the room which in days gone by used to be reserved for visiting rabbinic emissaries from Palestine.

Whenever I visited them and was tempted by some of the fish they were frying, I was not allowed to sample it in the kitchen; I would be directed to the dining room, where a maid would bring a piece on a tray.

My father possessed a number of properties which had been in the family for 200 years but were in a poor state of repair. Although he could not mend their leaking roofs, he was resourceful and built on top of them, which made him in effect one of Gibraltar's first developers. He later erected a block of flats which we named Carmel House after the school. The small flat in Governor's Lane in which we lived belonged to my mother's family and, when it was acquired in the 1730s, was the first piece of Jewish real estate in Gibraltar. My mother's grandfather later gave it to charity and the rent we paid went towards the upkeep of the Jewish poor. Sephardim have long had the tradition of assigning some of their properties for the use of charity and the Gibraltar community have owned several houses for generations which subsidise good causes. When one of the trustees once offered a lease on such a property which my father thought too cheap, he threatened legal action to protect the amount of charitable income.

Despite the meagre size of our flat, there was still room enough for two maids, who lived in a little room upstairs. Spain was poor and people were hungry. They would readily come to work for board and lodging and three pounds a month. Occasionally, we would have a Spanish maid who had never met a Jew before. My mother recalled telling one of them, "You know we are Jewish?" The maid looked around, shocked and surprised. My mother asked her why. She replied, "Because we were always told that Jews had tails. I am looking at you and you haven't got one." Some of our maids remained with us for years. Our nanny Isabel, who is still alive, evidently retains fond memories because she still carries photographs of us as children with her.

Every week we would cross the frontier with Spain to buy food in the town of La Linea and twice a year my mother took us there to have suits made for us for Pesach and Succot. Since English cloth was superior, we brought the material to the tailor and my mother always made sure we had matching caps made as well but then travel became more difficult following the Queen's post-coronation visit to Gibraltar in 1954 when the Spanish closed the border; to get to Spain subsequently, you had to take a boat via Tangiers.

We enjoyed an easy childhood, never more so than in summer, when every day we would go to the beach and have tea in the tent put up for us. Each family had its own tent, side by side on the sand, like a little encampment of Israelites. After work, my father came to swim and buy fresh fish off the boats in the evening, which my mother cooked at home two hours later. One of the local delicacies was *pez espada*, swordfish, whose kosher status has long been a matter of rabbinic debate; I no longer eat it, though some still do.

My mother Rachel, who was nine years' my father's junior – they married when he was thirty-six – was an elegant woman from a privileged family, the Hassans. In the 1920s she would regularly stay at the home of her cousin Isaac Cansino in Manchester, where another guest was Haham Moses Gaster, the retired head of the Spanish and Portuguese Community in Britain; since he had become blind, she would read to him. She was a woman of great piety but little Jewish education, for girls at the time were not even taught to read Hebrew. She knew all her prayers off by heart in Spanish and every night would go near the mezuzah to recite them. I still have copies of some of the prayers which I transliterated from Hebrew into Spanish so she could follow parts of the service. On Shabbat she would attend the synagogue frequented by her family, while we would go to the Abudarham, the Georgian synagogue the Levys helped to establish in 1820. On festivals she would come to ours.

Her pièce de résistance was Shabbat, the pinnacle of her week. She would begin preparations for Friday night dinner on the Thursday evening, when out would come the best linen and the antique silver. On Friday the maid would be dispatched with the *adafina* to bake in the Jewish communal oven. The lamps which shone over our Shabbat dinner table were not wax candles but oil, lit with wicks my mother made herself.

Traditionally, one is supposed to make 100 *berachot*, blessings, a day but because the Amidah prayer for Shabbat has fewer *berachot* than its weekday equivalent, it is more difficult to fulfil the quota. So before reciting Kiddush on Friday night and Shabbat morning, my father, following Gibraltar custom, would add some extra blessings over food to make up the number: olives, considered a fruit as they grew on a tree, beetroot or artichoke as vegetables, and thirdly, some fried fish which always came with garlic sauce. My father offered a fourth blessing, making the *berachah* for a pleasant fragrance over a lemon.

We had another family custom during Kiddush. Just as my father would commence the blessing over wine, my mother would tip a little water into the silver goblet. It harked back to ancient days when the wines of the Land of Israel were said to be so full-bodied and strong that one diluted them with water.

On Saturday morning, when we returned from synagogue, the hot *adafina* would be waiting, fetched by the maid in her black dress and white collar. She did not always come back from the communal oven with the right pot. More than once, my mother exclaimed as we sat down to Shabbat lunch, "I don't remember putting those beans in the *adafina*."

By the standards of observance of most of the western diaspora, Gibraltar was a relatively religious community, if not a particularly learned one. No Jew who owned a shop in the high street would dare to open it on Shabbat. There was a story that when the future King Edward VII visited Gibraltar, he wanted to see an antique shop owned by our cousins, the Benoliels, on a Saturday. Mr Benoliel would not violate Shabbat even for a prospective monarch but waited until the next day when he took some of his prize pieces to the Prince of Wales's boat, moored in the harbour. In one respect, however, the community had grown more lax as a consequence of the Second World War. Since the young women had been evacuated, the young men who remained had little opportunity of meeting a Jewish girl. A number of Jewish men instead found romance with Spanish girls and after the war wanted to marry them. So they went to Morocco, where conversions were easier to obtain, and returned with their Jewish bride.

Not everyone in Gibraltar welcomed the conversions but then there have been few areas in Jewish life which have been so contentious over the past century. While some rabbinic authorities such as the London Beth Din today pride themselves on the stringency of requirements for converts as a test of sincerity, there are sources for a less arduous entry to Judaism. Morocco, at the time, leaned heavily towards leniency. And perhaps there is a lesson in that for some of the grandchildren of those girls who converted after the War ended up in prestigious Israeli yeshivot.

A few years ago I returned to Gibraltar to spend Kippur – Sephardim do not say Yom Kippur for the Day of Atonement – in the family synagogue for the first time in more than fifty years. I could not fail to be struck by the spiritual intensity of the prayers. As sunset fell during the closing Neilah service, I could see tears among some of the congregation before a band of six shofarot brought the fast to a resounding end. The historian Cecil Roth, one of my tutors when I was studying for my degree, told me that he had never experienced such a moving service as Neilah at the Abudarham Synagogue in Gibraltar. Where I grew up, everyone worshipped together, regardless of their level of practice or belief. We were spared the denominational divisions that elsewhere fractured contemporary Jewry. Whatever else it did, my upbringing impressed on me the need to strive, wherever I could, for Jewish unity.

At the end of their long day in synagogue on Kippur, the worshippers are exhorted to go home and "eat your bread with joy and drink your wine with a merry heart" in the confidence that their prayers have been accepted. The Judaism we experienced was never a burden nor driven by anxiety or fear. It was part of our natural habitat. We never questioned whether to keep Shabbat or not. It was not characterised by the kind of over-fastidiousness that would, for instance, worry precisely what amount of matzah it was necessary to eat at the Seder. We had our family tradition that you ate a mouthful of matzah and were content to put our trust in that. As the American scholar, Rabbi Professor Haym Soloveitchik, observed in a famous essay, "Rupture and Reconstruction" published in the journal *Tradition*: "On Pesach evening one is obliged to a minimal amount of matzah – a quantity equal to the size of an olive. Jews have been practising the Seder for thousands of years, and no one paid very much attention to what that *shiur* [required minimum] was. One knew it automatically, for one had seen it eaten at one's parents table on innumerable Passover eves; one simply did as one's parents had done." It was only in the last years with the growing influence of the yeshivot post-War that people became more preoccupied with the question of whether contemporary olives were as big as in the days of the ancient Sages.

Local custom flavoured our festival celebrations. At my aunts' Seder, the *charoset*, the symbol of mortar the enslaved Israelites had to use in their labours, came sprinkled with a little brick-dust. When the time comes to break the middle matzah at my own Sedarim, I will take the piece for the *afikoman*, tie it round my neck in a serviette and set off in an exodus around the table, with the Seder plate, chanting the verse from the Haggadah, *Bivhilu*

Yatzanu Mimitzrayim, "In haste, we left Egypt". On Purim, when we were children, my siblings and I would wear costumes my mother had specially made for us each year. At Pesach, my parents would order extra matzah for non-Jewish friends who looked forward to the seasonal flat bread and at Purim send them pastries; they would return the compliment at Christmas, going to the kosher baker to buy a cake for us. Many years later, when Purim once coincided with Good Friday, the Jews refrained from wearing fancy dress in the streets out of respect for the sombre Christian holiday. It was symptomatic of the religious tolerance that existed between neighbouring communities. Gibraltar never had need of a local chapter of the Council of Christians and Jews.

If ritual was important, what was paramount were honesty and integrity. In the early 1930s, the Levy brothers' business, which was run by my father's cousins and must have been one of the biggest firms in Gibraltar dealing in olive oil and sardines, went bankrupt. They were honourably discharged with around eighty per cent of their debts paid off. Nevertheless, although my father was not involved in the business, he devoted a year of his spare time to earn extra money, which he gave to his cousins to cover the twenty per cent they still owed.

A story I heard many years later from Jules Braunschvig, the head of the Alliance Israélite Universelle, also illustrates the emphasis my family put on right conduct. I had an uncle by marriage in Tangiers, David Edery, who was a successful dealer in Moroccan leather; he had no children, so he considered us his own. Not long after the war, Jules Braunschvig, went to Tangiers to launch an appeal for the Alliance and visited the wealthiest Jews ahead of the meeting to see what they would pledge. My uncle said he would give him 1,000 or whatever – I don't know in which currency. When the night of the appeal came, they went round the tables asking what each would give. The richest Jew of Tangiers said, "700"; next they called on my uncle, who also said

"700". When the meeting was over, my uncle went up to Jules Braunschvig and told him, "I will give you the 1,000, but I didn't want to embarrass this man who was richer than me."

When we returned to Gibraltar from Madeira, I was sent to "the nuns" for my education, a local convent school but after a year I moved to the Jewish school reopened by my father and David Benaim. While Spanish was our mother tongue at home, we were educated in English, which explains why to this day I can count only in English, not Spanish. Our proximity to Spain meant that we spoke modern Spanish, rather than the old Castilian which the Ladino-speaking Jews of Turkey and other communities preserved after the exile of 1492. Our Jewish curriculum gave us a thorough grounding in synagogue skills; we learned our prayers by heart and every week we read a portion from the Sefer Torah. The Torah became familiar from an early age rather something opened for barmitzvah.

In the Hebrew school, on the wall of the room that had once served as the Gibraltar Yeshivah – which had been financed by my family – there hung an old document with a list of signatures. We regarded it as particularly holy although we didn't understand it. Only many years later did I find out what it was. Someone sent me a publication in Hebrew which had a photograph of the same document with a transcription. It represented the attempt by a small group of Sephardi mystics in Jerusalem in 1754, headed by Rabbi Shalom Mizrachi Sharabi, to set up a spiritual commune. The signatories, many of whom bore the family names of members of the Spanish and Portuguese Community, pledged to "love one another and to consider each other as if each person was but a limb of the other". We might not have been able to scale such peaks of piety but it did express the kind of personal ethic which my family tried to instil.

By the age of eight or nine, I was going to synagogue for *shacharit*, the morning service, during the week before school and became known as "the religious boy". One of my most distinctive memories is being given by a relative some of the old, beautifully bound prayer books which had been in her family for centuries; they sowed the seeds of a fascination that later made me an avid collector of Judaica. When I was eleven, as there was no Jewish secondary school then, I went to the Christian Brothers. Such was their reputation for strict discipline that whenever I subsequently mentioned my schooling to Christian acquaintances, they volunteered their sympathy but I was only with the Brothers for a year.

Although I attended Jewish classes after school, my father did not believe this was enough and he resolved to send me, like my brother Momy (Solomon), abroad, to Carmel College, the newly founded Anglo-Jewish boarding school. His property ventures had proved successful enough to afford private education. Still, it was a tremendous sacrifice. On top of school fees, the flights to England cost £60 – the equivalent of £1,800 now – and took a whole day, with changes at Madrid and Bordeaux. "I am going to educate you all well," my father told us, "and if there is money in the pot afterwards, consider it a bonus." My father himself had been the beneficiary of an education abroad. A prosperous uncle had decided to invest in his academic promise and financed him to go to a Jewish boarding school in Frankfurt, before the First World War.

I had never been to England when I arrived for my first term, travelling with my brother Momy and Robert Seruya, who now has the best shops for cigars and perfumes in Gibraltar. We reached Greenham at night and when I awoke, I was captivated by the beauty of the parkland and the lake stretching out around me. I had never seen such scenery before. Here was a slice of Jerusalem in England's green and pleasant land. It was a small school; I was the 160th boy to enter (girls coming only in the 1960s). Whereas the Cousinhood, the established families that had dominated pre-War British Jewry, preferred Polack's, the Jewish house at Clifton College, those who went to Carmel were the sons of more recent immigrants made good. My peers included Ivor, a nephew of the businessman and philanthropist Sir Isaac Wolfson, Joe Dwek, who became a prominent figure in the Manchester community, and Philip Refson, whose grandfather Solomon Sheckman founded the Essoldo cinema chain (named after himself, his wife Esther and daughter Dorothy). Another was Emmanuel Grodzinski, from the kosher baking family, which made him an inevitable rival in our eyes with Michael Ostwind, whose parents had a large cake shop in the East End of London.

England was still in the grip of post-War austerity. For the weekly expedition we were allowed to make into town in Newbury, we used ration coupons to buy chocolate in Woolworths. One boy used to receive packages of sliced chicken from his mother every Friday, which in those days was something of a luxury. We did not go hungry, although our diet depended on plentiful servings of bread and gravy. I am certainly not a finicky eater.

The conditions were spartan but I did not pine for home comforts. Inside the mansion at Greenham, I slept in a dormitory with three to five other boys, having been spared the larger dormitories. Later, when a couple of years after my arrival, Carmel relocated to Wallingford, Oxfordshire, I shared a study bedroom with Joe Dwek. It was housed in a nissen hut and, although we had bunk beds and had to use an outside toilet, we felt privileged since we were only two to a room. The slipper and cane regularly administered to many of my peers as part of the public school experience I managed to escape myself. Overall, I benefited from boarding. It toughened me up and for that I am grateful. My wife Estelle believes it made me more independent, if more emotionally self-contained.

If Rabbi Rosen had hoped to turn out a rabbi or two to grace the sanctuaries of Anglo-Jewry, the Carmelis at that time were by and large not ready material. In truth, only a few of us were religious; the joy I had the first time I put on tefillin in school was not universally shared. Some of the Israelis who were sent from their new state to receive a European education were completely secular, like Benny, later Major, Shalit. He was to become the centre of a who-is-a-Jew controversy, which went all the way to the Israeli Supreme Court in 1970 when he and his Scottish, non-Jewish wife successfully demanded the right to register their children as Jewish by nationality, rather than religion. (That brought an immediate change in the law to restrict registration to a religious definition, to the child of a Jewish mother or a recognised convert).

At the end of my first year, I celebrated my barmitzvah back home. In a letter to my father, Kopul Rosen said that he had planned to attend but had been prevented by work, adding the generous assessment that my "deep attachment to all things Jewish indicates that the Jewish community may one day expect to have in Abraham an outstanding Jew". My rite of passage provided a salutary lesson in the cost of ignoring my father's advice. From the money I was given for my barmitzvah, I wanted to buy a bicycle, so my father took me along to a friend to buy one. In Gibraltar it was the norm to give ten per cent off the price to a friend. This time, however, the vendor was not playing ball and refused any discount. "Avram," my father said, "my advice is that you do not buy this bicycle," but I was adamant that I was going to have it. Within a couple of days, a great-uncle of mine who had missed the party came to see me and said that he wanted to give me a bicycle. I lost out even more. I had not only paid more for a bicycle than I should have. My great-uncle instead gave me an electric shaver, which I couldn't use until some years later anyway.

My father used to enjoy the Ashkenazi tunes Momy and I picked up at school, which reminded him of the ones he used to sing himself during his schooldays in Frankfurt. Whenever we returned to Carmel from Gibraltar, our aunts would stage a little ceremony for us, throwing sugar on the stairs and asking us to walk over it, so that we should have a sweet departure. Our parents maintained contact by writing sometimes twice a week, my father in English, my mother in Spanish. If I misspelt a word in one of my letters, my father would always take the trouble to correct it in his reply, counselling me on one occasion, "A future scholar has to be careful with his style, grammar and spelling."

Academically, Carmel served us well. I learned Greek for a time, until my teacher, Murray Roston, left to become lecturer in, and eventually professor of, English at Israel's new Bar-Ilan University. The formal Jewish education, however, was patchy. A teacher from Israel inducted us in the rigours of Hebrew grammar but our religious tuition generally fell short of what Carmel's founder must have hoped for. We remained, of course, in awe of Rabbi Rosen, who was an inspiring teacher – when he turned up to the classroom. His erratic brilliance did not stretch to a firm grasp of the timetable and I would be regularly designated to knock on his study door to remind him that he was supposed to be teaching us, though I did not always succeed in locating him.

The collective celebration of Shabbat provided some of the most enjoyable times at school: there was plenty of singing on Friday night and on summer afternoons we would have a *shiur* in the grounds, when Rabbi Rosen might give us a verse from the Prophets to learn in Hebrew, such as *Higid Lecha* from Micah ("It has been told you, O man... what the Lord requires of you – to act justly, love mercy and walk humbly with your God"). The Holocaust was barely spoken about, though a tattooed number on the arm of one of the young women who worked in the kitchen reminded us of what had befallen so many of our co-religionists only a few years earlier.

Apart from Rabbi Rosen, another important influence was

Abraham Carmel, who taught me English and Latin. Originally called Kenneth Cox, he had been a Catholic priest who was in the process of converting to Judaism when he came to Carmel in order to live in a Jewish atmosphere. In his book about his journey to Judaism, *So Strange My Path*, he painted a lyrical picture of Friday nights there. "As the Sabbath descended upon the school, the presence of God seemed very close... There shone on every face a sweet enchantment." He took considerable interest in my spiritual welfare and rabbinic aspirations. He was concerned that my good intentions should not be derailed by the less religious boys. There were no drugs then, though some of the more adventurous pupils would go into town to meet girls. A rather lonely figure, Abraham Carmel spent three weeks in Gibraltar staying with my parents shortly before his circumcision and often returned there for holidays. Unfortunately, he fell out with Rabbi Rosen and was asked to leave the school. He became a teacher at Flatbush Yeshivah in New York and was so well loved that they instituted a memorial day in his name. In his obituary in the *Jewish Chronicle* in 1982, I wrote that English Jews had not really appreciated him, whereas the Americans recognised "what a treasure they had in their midst".

Rabbi Rosen sold the school's first site at Greenham Common to the Americans for an airbase, later the site of the women's anti-nuclear peace camp. I was chosen to take part in the official opening of the new home in Wallingford in 1953, when I declaimed a passage from Amos which I had learned by heart. Carmel remained there until its closure in 1997.

It was decided that I should not stay at Carmel for my A-levels, but instead do them at Jews' College in London, the seminary founded a century earlier to train men for the Anglo-Jewish ministry. Dr Isidore Epstein, the principal of Jews' College, already had his eye on me as a potential recruit. Because it was too expensive to fly back to Gibraltar, for half-terms I used to go to my cousins, the Benoliels, who had remained in London after the War. Dr Epstein's son Jack taught physics at Carmel and he would invite me round to his parents' home for tea. Since the Benoliels lived in Maida Vale, I began going along to the Spanish and Portuguese Synagogue in Lauderdale Road, the start of an association that has lasted more than sixty years. The top hats of the worshippers were not a novel spectacle since we wore them in Gibraltar too but everything inside this cathedral synagogue was on a much grander scale.

I can remember only one thing about my interview for Jews' College when I faced a panel of three interrogators; Dr Epstein, editor of the first edition of the Talmud in English; the Reverend Dr Abraham Cohen, a respected scholar who had edited the Soncino Chumash, the five Books of the Torah, and Bible; and Sir Alan Mocatta, chairman of the college and a leading light in the Spanish and Portuguese Community. At one point, Sir Alan fixed his gaze on me and asked, "Do you play cricket?" My contributions to Carmel had been more to the synagogue, where I regularly read from the Torah, than on the sports field and I was more interested in service of the Lord than Lord's. "I do play, but I'm not much good at it," I confessed, prompting Dr Cohen to add, "He does it for *melachah* [work] rather than pleasure."

Fortunately, I was never asked to go in to bat for Jews' College. While we prepared for our secular exams, we also pursued our religious studies there, focusing mainly on Chumash, Rashi and the Talmud under the guidance of teachers of such calibre as Eli Cashdan, best known for his translations of the Singer's Siddur. Once we had our school qualifications under our belt, we went on to a three-year Semitics degree at the University of London, to which the college was affiliated, followed by a two-year ministerial diploma course. At the end of that we would earn the title "Reverend". The BA was a tough examination, demanding that we wrestle with subjects such as comparative grammar and North Semitic epigraphy. At the same time we continued our study of Jewish texts as well as undergoing practical training. We had a non-Jewish tutor for homiletics, who used to come and discuss our sermons with us. The first time I preached for real was at the old Willesden Synagogue when I was nineteen or twenty.

At the time, our apprenticeship for the pulpit would have seemed pretty conventional. Now, when most of the Orthodox rabbinate is trained exclusively in yeshivot, the idea of including a programme of academic Jewish studies would be considered radical, even dangerously so. For our BAs, we had to learn about the "higher criticism" of the Bible which had begun to be influential in the 19th century. The Torah, it contended, was not divinely transmitted to Moses in the wilderness but the edited work of several authors over centuries. Exposure to such ideas might have been seen as a test of faith but it was assumed that we would take no more account of them than was necessary to pass our exams and would no more embrace them than we would walk into a restaurant and order a plate of non-kosher beef. When one of our lecturers, Rabbi H.J. (Hirsch) Zimmels, who later became principal, brought up higher criticism, he would make sure to insist, "But please, you mustn't believe this, the Torah is *min hashamayim* ("from heaven")". We were not given any classes in systematic theology but were aware of the writing of Orthodox scholars like Rabbi David Tzvi Hoffman, who defended the Torah as a unified whole against the claims of the higher critics. Today future Orthodox rabbis are largely shielded from such debates and if they do academic study of the Bible, it is more about philosophy and literary analysis.

While traditional belief in the divinity of the Torah remained a given, we nevertheless received a good introduction to *Wissenschaft des Judentums*, the historical approach to Judaism pioneered by such figures as Leopold Zunz in Germany in the previous century. If you take a historical approach, you tend to think differently and it helped me better to understand the kind of problems that congregants would later raise and to avoid saying things in the pulpit which would sound absurd. The retreat from such an approach was brought home to me many years later by one of my rabbinical students. He had written a piece on the Haggadah to try to explain how the Jews, before they left Egypt, knew about the laws of *chametz*, leaven, which must not be eaten on Passover. For me, that was a non-question. "Tell me," I asked him, "do you believe that Abraham kept the whole Torah? Did he put on tefillin?" The student looked shocked. I believe that Abraham observed the laws of morality and the commandments that God revealed to him but it was never necessary for me to believe that Abraham put on tefillin before the specific commandment given to his descendants or that Jacob sat learning in a yeshivah just like students today. Nor to take midrashic legend as literal truth rather than parable with a profound message.

We were lucky enough to be taught history by the doyen of Anglo-Jewish historians, Cecil Roth. Underwhelmed by the state of our knowledge, he would tell us, "The extent of your ignorance is only paralleled by the shortness of your memory." I got on well with him and he loved Gibraltar. My uncle, Sir Joshua Hassan, became friendly with him. My uncle had a collection of ten beautiful *ketubot* in parchment and he told me, "I promised Cecil Roth a gift. Take them to him. You can keep one for yourself but give him all the rest." So I took them to him and, fool that I was, showed him all ten, including the one I had reserved for myself, which was the most interesting. "I tell you what," he said, "you give me that one and keep the other nine." I held out though and refused to give it to him.

I was lucky, too, to attend Jews' College in what now seems its golden age. The institution has ridden a few crises in its time but its rabbinical school was then flourishing and produced some of the leading rabbis of Anglo-Jewry and the Commonwealth in that generation. Among my contemporaries were Cyril Harris, future rabbi of St John's Wood Synagogue and Chief Rabbi of South Africa, who managed that community's transition from apartheid to the new era of Nelson Mandela, and Raymond Apple, first at Hampstead Synagogue and then Australia's pre-eminent rabbi at the Great Synagogue, Sydney. Jeffrey Cohen led the United Synagogue's largest community, Stanmore, for many years, Eddie Jackson went on to Hampstead Garden Suburb and Philip Ginsbury South London. Irving Jacobs later became principal of the college himself, while Stefan Reif excelled in academia as a Cambridge professor and head of its research unit into the Cairo *Genizah*.

When I entered the college, it was housed on the single floor of a building in Woburn Place, Bloomsbury but shortly after, it moved to magnificent new premises in Montagu Place with accommodation for more than a dozen students. We were spoiled; our rooms had their own sinks and were cleaned daily, and our meals were cooked. Our smart West End location gave us a sense of privilege, while conveniently I remained within comfortable walking distance of Lauderdale Road if I needed to go there for Shabbat. At Montagu Place, our numbers were swelled on Shabbat by some of the members of the embryonic Marble Arch congregation who would come to use our synagogue before they had their own. On Saturday nights, the college student society would arrange a *melaveh malkah,* for boys and girls – all perfectly respectable of course, though no doubt mixed events would be frowned on today in certain circles. A number of women students were taking teaching diplomas there, one of whom was Paula Unsdorfer, mother of Zehava, wife of Daniel Taub, the Israeli Ambassador to the UK from 2011 to 2016. Rabbi Faivish Vogel, one of the people who made Lubavitch the force it has become in Britain today, had just arrived as a young man to represent it and he would sometimes lead the entertainment at our soirées.

My move to Jews' College led to deeper ties with Lauderdale Road. In late 1956, when I was still seventeen, the congregation appointed me a student hazan, supporting my studies with a scholarship of £75 a year. I believe Sir Alan Mocatta had a soft spot for me, since even though I might not have been English, I was British, whereas both the spiritual leader of the community, the Haham, Dr Solomon Gaon and its long-serving hazan, the Reverend Eliezer Abinun, had been recruited from Sarajevo. Proudly I began to dress like the natives for Shabbat, sporting my stiff collar, black jacket and striped trousers.

As it was a forty-minute walk to Lauderdale Road from the Benoliels, who had moved from Maida Vale to West Hampstead, I went to live with some other cousins who were closer to the synagogue, the Sequerras, before eventually taking up residence in the college's new West End home. I taught in the Sunday classes and took services, leading the High Holy Day overflow minyan. In 1958, the Haham wrote to me to say that he had received "gratifying reports" of my conduct of the High Holy Day services. The following year, I was promoted to student rabbi with an honorarium of £250 a year, my letter of appointment expressing the wish that after obtaining a ministerial diploma and an MA, I would go on to do a postgraduate year at Oxford or Cambridge. To the lay leaders of the time, an Oxbridge degree was considered a far more valuable asset than a spell in even the most prominent yeshivah.

My father, while supportive of my choice of vocation, was keen to look after my interests and would not leave me to the mercies of the Mahamad (the executive of the congregation) until he had negotiated the details of my appointment in person. He recalled having come to London in 1956 before I accepted the scholarship to study at Jews' College, when he had "made it distinctly clear to the Gentlemen of the Mahamad that in accepting the assistance they were giving me, Abraham's future would not be tied and that he would be a free agent." I doubt whether the Mahamad were used to being spoken to in such forthright terms.

After a while I was seconded to assist the Reverend Nissim Levy, the elderly hazan of another community, Holland Park, which had been founded by immigrants from Greece and Turkey. Some had travelled to show their Oriental carpets at the Franco-British Exhibition of 1908. Although nominally independent, Holland Park was attached to the Spanish and Portuguese congregation and had to incorporate some of our customs, whether it liked it or not; the hazan of the Spanish and Portuguese, the Reverend David Bueno de Mesquita, had helped to secure a legacy from the prominent Indian banker Sir Sassoon David, which enabled Holland Park to open its synagogue in 1928, while Bevis Marks Synagogue owned the freehold.

I found it easy to settle there particularly because I was able to speak Ladino, the Judeo-Spanish dialect, with its members. The Turkinos, as they were known, were good people but not the most religious community. Mostly small traders who had shops and stalls, they felt they had to work on Shabbat to make ends meet. Some of the early settlers had been quite impoverished, receiving clothes and other help from the Spanish and Portuguese. Despite their lack of money, the new immigrants were always generous with what they had and if a hungry visitor turned up at the door, they would be welcomed, "Don't worry, *mas agua para la holla* – more water for the soup pot!"

Latterly, after many families left the area, the congregation has been kept going by wealthy benefactors but has remained loyal to its roots: when I once suggested that they move lock, stock and barrel out of west London to join the growing Jewish population in Hertfordshire, they gave short shrift to this sacrilegious idea.

My time at Holland Park is memorable chiefly for the fact that it was there that I met my wife, Estelle Nahum. Her paternal grandfather, who dealt in *tapetes*, carpets, had come to England from Izmir in Turkey for the big exhibition. After he settled in London, one of the things he used to do was repair carpets for the English aristocracy. He married his Salonikan wife in Bevis Marks in 1909 and was one of the first members of Holland Park. Their son married Estelle's Ashkenazi mother in Holland Park.

Estelle, who lived in Acton, used to attend a Sephardi youth group I started called Ven Aqui ("Come Here") and she also came to Lauderdale Road as a student teacher. One summer we helped to run a seaside vacation for a group of deprived children in Bracklesham Bay sponsored by the Children's Country Holiday Fund. I asked Estelle out immediately I finished my BA when I was twenty-one and she was seventeen and studying for her A-levels – she always claimed to have been baby-snatched. For our first date, I took her to a J.B. Priestley play in the West End, *A Majority of One,* which starred Robert Morley.

Estelle's father Leon spoke Ladino and years later, when we were on holiday together in Spain he would use it to order a beer or coffee in a café. The waiters must have thought we had stepped out of Cervantes. The language had been fossilised for centuries, though it had acquired words from other places where the exiled Spanish Jews had settled, such as the greeting *Ke haber*, "How are you", from Turkish. The Ladino romanzas which Estelle remembers him singing would bring tears to his eyes. We still have a tape of Ladino favourites, such as *Avraham Avinu*, "Our Father Abraham," and the lullaby *Dorme, Dorme*, which we play in the car.

Estelle and I became engaged in 1962 and were married the following year. My father, on a trip to London before the wedding, told me he approved of my choice. "You know one of the things I most like about her is that she is dignified and very quiet," he said. He did not appreciate small talk; he was quite Victorian like that. For wedding presents, Cecil Roth gave us two of his books, one on the Duke of Naxos inscribed to me and the other, on Dona Gracia, to Estelle, which recounted the lives of two of the most extraordinary figures in Sephardi history. Crypto-Jews who fled the Inquisition, Joseph Nasi and his aunt Dona Gracia rose to prominence in the Ottoman Empire and eventually received a portion of land from the Sultan in the ancient city of Tiberias to found a Jewish settlement in Israel. On the day of our marriage, Cecil Roth offered his congratulations with typical wryness, "I hope this will be the unhappiest day of your lives."

2

Top Hats and Talletot

IN THE OPENING chapter of Israel Zangwill's humorous novel about Jewish life in the East End of London at the end of the 18th century, *The King of Schnorrers*, Grobstock, the wealthy Ashkenazi financier runs into the eponymous "king", Manasseh da Costa, a Sephardi beggar. Far from displaying the expected attitude of subservience, da Costa acts as if it is he who is doing the philanthropist a favour by being gracious enough to accept his charity. In a defiant outburst, he harangues Grobstock: "You are the immigrants of yesterday – refugees from the ghettoes of Russia and Poland and Germany. But we... have been established here for generations; in the Peninsula our ancestors graced the courts of kings, and controlled the purse-strings of princes; in Holland we held the empery of trade. Ours have been the poets and scholars in Israel. You cannot expect that we should recognise your rabble... We made the name of Jew honourable..." Behind Zangwill's comic exaggeration lies more than a grain of truth. The Sephardim of London have always been proud of their pedigree as the forebears of modern Anglo-Jewish community, dating back to 1656 and the resettlement of the Jews in England in the days of Oliver Cromwell.

The Spanish and Portuguese Jews' Congregation I entered in the late 1950s cherished their historic traditions like prize antiques. While other mainstream Anglo-Jewish bodies now used English in their articles of governance, the Spanish and Portuguese still retained various terms in Hebrew or Portuguese in homage to their past. Whereas other organisations were run by an executive and collected subscriptions from members, we had the Gentlemen of the Mahamad and asked *Yehidim* to pay *finta*. The community's elaborate constitution appeared set in stone, which might have given it a certain mystique but also had its downside, as I reflected when I gave a sermon to mark my twenty-fifth anniversary as a minister in 1987. Appealing for genuine partnership between lay and spiritual leaders, I wondered whether "the bulk of the *Yehidim* know that the congregation is still being governed by rules written some 300 years ago when the rabbis were thought of as functionaries and not as leaders; when the rabbis are still excluded from the deliberations of the congregation, and when the decisions taken are, as a rule, not communicated to them."

The conventions which the community upheld so diligently, nevertheless, did have the virtue of ensuring dignity and elegance in worship. On Shabbat morning at Lauderdale Road, you could hear a pin drop. When I first began going to the synagogue, I was intrigued by the custom of bowing, which spoke of a certain refinement. To this day, when you are called to the Torah, in acknowledgment of the mitzvah you do not shake hands, you bow; when the man after you has finished his blessing, you bow to each other, you bow to the Ark and bow to the wardens as you return to your seat. The aesthetics of ritual were important to the Spanish and Portuguese, who saw it as part and parcel of *hiddur mitzvah*, the principle of not simply performing a mitzvah but doing so as beautifully as you can. They tended their sanctuaries with loving care. While the Sephardim strove to keep up appearances, the East Europeans were less bothered about bricks and mortar.

The congregation's attachment to formality was apparent in the clerical regalia ministers had to wear. The gowns and winged bibs which portraits in our hall show were sported by Hahamim down the ages were obligatory for services. Those who represented the congregation were expected to look the part. I remember once, when I had been at Lauderdale Road for a few years, bringing a youth who had been newly appointed as a student minister to the Mahamad. The Parnas Presidente (its chairman) cast his eye up and down the new recruit, then turned to me. "He's got to appear in synagogue on Shabbat, Abraham," he said. "Please take him and buy him a decent suit and good pair of shoes so he looks correct."

When I officiated at a wedding then, it was de rigeur for a rabbi to wear tails but, over the past twenty or thirty years, there has been a determined rebellion within British synagogues against old-fashioned dress; top hats have vanished from the wardens' boxes in the United Synagogue and rabbis have discarded canonicals as too anglicised. The Reverend Isaac Livingstone of Golders Green United must have been the last to be comfortable in a dog collar. In spite of modern fashion, I remain an unapologetic wearer of bib and gown on formal occasions, which for me still embody the congregation's best traditions of decorum. When he was chief rabbi, Jonathan Sacks might still be spotted at special events in gown and ceremonial hat. He'd sometimes ask me when we went off to a function together, "Does my hat look all right?"

Among our laymen there was none more sartorially correct than Raphael de Sola, who would rarely be seen in the street without his top hat. A stockbroker, he was a descendant of the editor of the de Sola prayer books used in our congregations. He was a keen horseman and kept a yacht in Cowes. He also had a boat called *Purim* which took part in the evacuation from Dunkirk. Before the Second World War, his sister Esther had won the affections of one of England's most eligible bachelors, Sir John Ellerman, owner of the country's most famous shipping line, which would not have been a problem if he had been Jewish. Sir John was determined to marry the girl and asked the synagogue what he could do. There was a lot of anti-Semitism around and the Reverend David Bueno de Mesquita felt it would create even more if a member of an eminent Christian family were to convert. Although they did not have a Jewish marriage, Esther maintained a kosher home and attended synagogue on festivals.

On Kal Nidre, Raphael along with many of the other more prominent members of our congregation would come to the service in white tie and tails, though he insisted on retaining his white tie for the whole of the following day's services, too. (Tails gave way to dinner jackets in the 1990s and now it is lounge suits.) Once a year, Raphael would turn up to synagogue without his topper, on the fast of Tishah b'Av, instead appearing in a green Eden hat. It so happened that he was buried on Tishah b'Av so, as a mark of respect, I asked all the rabbis not to wear top hats to the funeral. He left his collection of top hats – of which there must have been more than a dozen – to the synagogue. I picked them up from his house myself; each was slightly different and its shape sketched on the outside of the box in which it was stored. They are still worn in synagogue to this day, bearing his initials.

It didn't take me long to acclimatise to Lauderdale Road and I never felt like the proverbial provincial in the big city. Being at boarding school had made it easier for me to adapt to new surroundings, while I had come to regard Lauderdale as my second spiritual home when staying with my cousins during half-terms at school. The liturgy was broadly familiar with what I knew from Gibraltar. Poems, such as the poignant appeal to God, *El Nora Alilah*, chanted at the twilight of Kippur, or *Et Shaare Ratzon*, dramatising the conversation Abraham had with Isaac before almost sacrificing his son, which is sung before the blowing of the shofar on Rosh Hashanah, were part of my own religious inheritance.

Nevertheless, there were details of the service at Lauderdale Road which I still had to learn to master as a student hazan. When I arrived, Sir Alan Mocatta would see me at his house personally in order to teach me how to recite the *Zemirot*, the opening prayers. Sir Alan was a man of distinction who had reached the higher ranks of the judiciary at a time when prejudice made it not so easy for Jews to do so. It was he who set the tone of the congregation. A rabbi then would not be allowed to begin proceedings until the *shamash*, the beadle, went up to the Parnas Presidente and the Parnas would say, "Will you tell the rabbi to commence the service?" The service began at 8.30 am and if Sir Alan, who attended every Shabbat, did the introductory *Zemirot* himself, he would come at the start. The *Zemirot* were to take fifty-seven minutes precisely, before the choir, in their little hats and gowns, burst into *Shir Hayam,* the Song of the Sea. If Sir Alan was not taking the prayers, he would walk into the synagogue at 9.27 prompt. He was a stickler for strict timing. If a hazan deviated from it or departed in any way from established custom, one glance at Sir Alan's raised eyebrows would inform him of the error of his ways.

While such meticulousness must seem impossibly rigid today, it did set high standards for ministers to follow in leading the service. I was already reading the *parashah*, the weekly Torah portion, at Lauderdale Road and had had a good deal of experience at it from school but still I approached the *tebah*, the reading platform, with trepidation. When I was at Jews' College, Chief Rabbi Brodie told me the following story. "You know a fellow called Pereira Mendoza? He arrived at the college on a Monday morning looking downcast. So I said, 'Pereira Mendoza, why do you look so sad?' He said, 'Because I forgot a *revia* in last week's *parashah*.'" *Revia* is one of the notes for the cantillation of the Torah. Nothing less than perfection was acceptable for the old school. Today, they might forget a dozen *reviot* and no one would say a word.

In a packed memorial service for Sir Alan at Bevis Marks in 1990, I recalled that I had once told him that if I had not been a rabbi, I should have liked to have been a lawyer. He had responded, "If I had not been a lawyer, I would wish to have been a rabbi." No one could question his respect for Judaism yet it is true that the Judaism with which he and much of the leadership of the Sephardi community of his generation had grown up had become primarily a matter of ethics. In their dealings with people, they were upright, upholding the commandments *bein adam l'chavero*, between man and his fellow, but the long struggle for acceptance into English society had led to a relegation of ritual outside the synagogue walls.

Before the Second World War, religion still played an important part in English life so the more gentrified Jews were keen to show that they had fashionable places of worship to go to, such as the New West End in Bayswater or Lauderdale Road. They might have shunned bacon and shellfish but they were not so particular about other practices. Sir Alan would keep only one day Yom Tov, even for Rosh Hashanah when most would keep two, but he would not travel to synagogue by car. He insisted that his home should be within walking distance of both Lauderdale and Lord's. While they maintained high moral principles, the lack of ritual observance among many of the leading families of Anglo-Jewry made Judaism barely indistinguishable from Christianity, leaving it harder to persuade their children why they should still marry within the faith.

Against the allure of assimilation, we looked for ways to inspire our youth. The recently established state of Israel offered one new avenue. In 1962, I was invited by Dr Gaon to lead a group of young people who included Estelle on a trip to Israel on behalf of the World Zionist Organisation. "It is my earnest hope that the party will return better Jews and keener Zionists," Denzil Sebag-Montefiore, one of the leaders of the congregation wrote to me. And since the pleasures of the experience would be "marred by a certain amount of work", the Mahamad proposed to help with my expenses – though not extravagantly so; they offered £20 off the £70 flight. You could never accuse the lay leadership of being over-generous to their ministers. Their attitude was rather like the aristocrats of *Downton Abbey* towards their servants, expecting them to be content with a roof over their heads and food on the table but little else.

The Haham himself was an unapologetic Zionist who did everything he could to encourage support for Israel, which took some courage for among parts of the community there remained a residual anti-Zionism. In this, he was following the example of his predecessor, Haham Moses Gaster, an early patron of the Jewish national movement who introduced Theodor Herzl to England. Dr Gaster's lay leaders had not approved of his activities and insisted that any endorsement he gave to Herzl's political enterprise was as an individual, not in his capacity as Haham. Like much of the Anglo-Jewish hierarchy around the time of the Balfour Declaration, they feared that the plan for a Jewish homeland would cast doubt on their loyalty to Britain. Chief Rabbi Adler refused even to meet Herzl. The Reverend David Bueno de Mesquita, who considered himself an Englishman through and through, might have prayed for Zion but deprecated Zionism. Even after the creation of the state of Israel, it took some years for the Spanish and Portuguese Jews' Congregation to include a blessing for it; indeed, when the phrase "state of Israel" first replaced the previous formula, "our brothers who live in the Holy Land", I recall that one or or two people walked out of the synagogue.

Our guide in Israel was a young man from a Spanish and Portuguese family in Manchester, Dan Leon, who had made aliyah a few years earlier. Infused with the dream of building a new Jewish society, he was an ardent kibbutznik and a persuasive advocate for its collectivist ideals. He made a deep impression on us as he pointed out the achievements of the young state. In one case at least, the tour fulfilled Denzil Sebag-Montefiore's hopes to make its participants "better Zionists" – perhaps even more than he wanted – for one person decided immediately afterwards to go on aliyah.

What lodged in my mind more than the ancient sites that we visited – the Old City of Jerusalem lay beyond our reach, behind barbed wire – was an egalitarian spirit that permeated beyond the kibbutz. A Hebrew University professor was earning the same as a bus driver. Very often the drivers who took us around were great scholars themselves who, as they waited for us to finish our sightseeing, would have their heads buried in a textbook.

None the less, as we were to discover, a belief in social equality did not apply everywhere. When we were taken to the Knesset, we were greeted by a delegation of half-a-dozen or so Sephardi MKs. However, when I later boasted to someone about our VIP reception, he was unimpressed and dismissed the Sephardi politicians as nobodies who were just there to make up the numbers and reel in the Sephardi vote. His attitude demonstrated the disdain felt by much of the Ashkenazi elite towards the Sephardi population.

When we met Eli Eliashar, the president of the Sephardi community in Jerusalem, he told me something revealing too. He had tried to get into the Knesset in the early 1950s on a Sephardi ticket but Ben-Gurion viewed him as an adversary, because Israel's

Prime Minister realised that if the Sephardim became more politically organised, they would gain more seats. Eliashar, like Israel's fifth president Yitzhak Navon, hailed from one of the older Spanish-speaking families who had lived in the country generations before most of the Ashkenazi immigrants and would have been entitled to consider themselves a kind of Zionist aristocracy. He was a direct descendant of the Rishon le Zion, the spiritual head of the Sephardi community, who had befriended Sir Moses Montefiore in the 19th century. When Sir Moses offered to give money to yeshivot to teach their students Arabic, there was an outcry from the religious leadership, which objected to introducing any subject into their institutions other than Talmud. Rabbi Jacob Eliashar, however, sprung to the defence of Sir Moses who, he said, "values the glory of the Torah and Jerusalem above all wealth". After all, the Rishon le Zion observed, did not even Maimonides himself write some of his works in Arabic? Here was a classic instance of the flexible Sephardi tradition that was able to make accommodation with the outside world.

As soon as I had obtained my ministerial diploma from Jews' College in 1962, I moved on to the rabbinic ordination course. My father, ever-protective of my interests, was keen to ensure my duties at Lauderdale Road did not hinder my studies. When the Mahamad wanted to appoint me a hazan of the congregation, my father did not think it good enough. "I certainly will not tolerate any humiliation on you being compelled to accept a post below your status," he wrote to me. So I was accorded the title of youth minister as well, the term "minister" carrying a little more weight than it does now. "I owe my present position in life from almost nothing to my stubbornness in opposing injustice," my father impressed on me.

Our rabbinic studies were supervised by Rabbi Kopul Kahana, who had been a pupil of the one of the leaders of Orthodoxy in Poland, Rabbi Israel Meir Kagan, known as the

Chafetz Chaim after his most famous work. Possessed of a prodigious knowledge of Jewish sources, Rabbi Kahana had arrived in Britain just before the War barely speaking a word of English and went on to gain a degree from Cambridge. He penned learned articles on jurisprudence in general as well as a book comparing English, Roman and Jewish law. He was very short-sighted and used to hold the book close to his face when he read, but his memory was extraordinary. "Open any volume of the Talmud you want and put your finger anywhere on the page," he would challenge me. From the position of my finger he would declare the very words it was pointing to. He was a lonely man who had lost his family in the Holocaust and his second wife died prematurely. He came to our house quite often and when our son Julian was a baby, he would feed him from the bottle. Julian came to know him as "Rabbi Banana".

We would study at the college three days a week, Monday to Wednesday, from 10 o'clock to 3 before returning to our congregational duties. Remind your members to please be kind enough not to die on one of those days, Rabbi Kahana would tell us: he was unquestionably one of the greatest Jewish scholars in the community's history. Taken as a whole the college was blessed with a generally accomplished faculty. Apart from his talmudic labours, Dr Epstein was a prolific author, whose books included *Judaism: A Historical Presentation* for Penguin and *The Faith of Judaism* – a staple of the ministerial diploma course and a work thought worthy enough to be translated into Hebrew in Israel. We benefited too from Dr Naftali Weider, who had married a cousin of mine, as it happened, who taught us Talmud, Bible commentaries and liturgy. He used to set us passages of Shakespeare to translate into classical Hebrew and, glaring at our efforts, would comment, "This is below criticism." He had no doubt of his abilities: "If I am doing some research," he told us, "and I think my interpretation right and the Messiah comes and says 'Weider, you are wrong,' I will say '*Melech Hamashiach*, it is you who is wrong.'"

When the *Jewish Chronicle* reported an attack on the course at Jews' College made at a public meeting, a number of my fellow students and I sprung to its defence in a letter printed the following week. The ministry had become the community's "favourite Aunt Sally", we protested, and there was only so much formal training could do. What counted in a successful spiritual leader, we contended, was also "outlook, approach, personality and example". My contemporaries at the college remained a constant source of support. If anyone was in trouble, Raymond Apple was always there to help. Irving Jacobs was scholarly, meticulous and unswerving in his commitment to the truth. Eddie Jackson was a great pastor with a wonderful human touch. Philip Ginsbury was learned, humble and always sensitive to other people's feelings.

Jeffrey Cohen, who had come from Gateshead, showed how to manage the change from yeshivah learning to the intellectual challenges of *Wissenschaft*, the scientific study of Judaism. There was never a dull moment with Cyril Harris, whose energy was irrepressible. When we sat half-asleep at breakfast, he would stride in and rouse us with a rhetorical call to arms, "Evil shall confute itself and truth shall prevail."

When we were on the diploma course, we had been lectured by one of the rising stars of the Anglo-Jewish rabbinate, Louis Jacobs. A product of the yeshivah system in Manchester and Gateshead, Rabbi Jacobs had started as an assistant to the doyen of German Orthodoxy in Golders Green, Rabbi Eli Munk, before coming to the most liberally-minded United Synagogue, the New West End. We had little idea of the storm that was about to break around him. His studies in Semitics at the University of London had convinced him of the validity of biblical criticism. The Torah could not have been transmitted in its entirety direct to Moses in the wilderness, he concluded, but was compiled over time with a human hand in its editing. In 1957, he published a small book, *We Have Reason To Believe*, which sought to reconcile commitment to traditional Judaism with academic scholarship as he saw it. The book caused no scandal when it first came out. The fuse it lit was slow-burning.

Rabbi Jacobs was charismatic and well-liked. I did not agree with his theology but I can't recall that any of us objected to having him as a tutor. I can acknowledge that there are difficult passages in the Torah but whereas he would say that they could not possibly have been written by God, my own view is that while I might be surprised that God said something and it defies my comprehension, I am not prepared to state that God did not say it. There are parts of the Bible I do not understand but I have faith to leave them in abeyance. I have always borne in mind the saying of the Spanish philosopher, Miguel de Unamuno, *"Una fez que no duda es una fez muerta."* "A faith that does not doubt is a dead faith."

Chief Rabbi Brodie either thought the book was not troubling enough when it came out or had not read it but later events spurred him into action. When Rabbi Jacobs was appointed moral tutor to the college, Dr Epstein – rightly – felt threatened. The principal of the college was due to retire and its chairman, Sir Alan Mocatta, had promised Rabbi Jacobs the succession. Not only that, but clearly Sir Alan and others envisaged the post as a stepping-stone for Rabbi Jacobs to become Chief Rabbi after Brodie. I can imagine Dr Epstein brandishing the book in front of the Chief Rabbi and crying – in his rather high-pitched voice – "Look, look!" Whatever happened, Rabbi Brodie blocked Rabbi Jacobs from becoming principal: two years later in 1964 when Rabbi Jacobs, his college career thwarted, wished to return to the New West End, the Chief Rabbi prevented him from resuming his old pulpit.

In my view, it was foolish for the United Synagogue to stop Rabbi Jacobs from going back to the New West End and I believe some in the London Beth Din thought so too. The community might have been less fragmented if he had been allowed to remain at New West End. The United Synagogue, however, was a changing organisation. It had once been led by members of the Cousinhood, who governed more out of a sense of *noblesse oblige* than Orthodox conviction. However, Sir Isaac Wolfson, who had become its president, was more of a staunch traditionalist. Exiled from the US, Rabbi Jacobs and his supporters from the New West End set off to start a congregation of their own and on their first Shabbat they found safe haven in Lauderdale Road. Dr Gaon was abroad, in America, and the Parnas Presidente, Nathan Saatchi, father of the famous advertising brothers, granted them permission to use the Montefiore Hall. But after only a week, the refugees were sent packing; Rabbi Solomon Sassoon, who was a founder of the Eastern Jewish congregations and thought the religious outlook of the Spanish and Portuguese too relaxed, went berserk and the Mahamad were forced to withdraw their hospitality. As a junior minister, I could only keep out of the fray and, though my phone rang constantly with reporters chasing comment, publicly I held my tongue. In retrospect, the episode proved a turning point for British Jewry; the balance of power within mainstream Orthodox had shifted to the right.

For all the drama of the Jacobs Affair, as it became known, our congregants were far less preoccupied with arguments over theology and what they most wanted from a rabbi was to be a good pastor. One of my favourite quotations, which reminded me to keep my feet on the ground, was from George Bernard Shaw's play, *Saint Joan*, "The thick air of your country [Britain] does not breed theologians." However well prepared we were by Jews' College, only experience could teach us how to match our vocational ideals to the expectations of our communities. From the beginning, I was assigned a special responsibility for youth. I was deputy head of the Sunday morning classes. It wasn't so easy organising activities for young people; most of their families lived at a distance from Lauderdale Road or Bevis Marks or they were in boarding school, which could make it impractical to arrange something for Shabbat afternoons, for example. One evening a week, I went up to Hackney to work at the Victoria Youth Club – which was supported by one of our leading families, the Nabarros – under the direction of Alan Greenbat, who knew everything there was to know about Jewish youth work.

One of my duties at the synagogue was to interview marrying couples before their wedding. I remember one middle-aged man who was terribly nervous about the ceremony. "Look here, Mr Levy, I need your help," he said. "I am scared stiff about meeting the rabbi who is going to marry me and I want you tell him to put me at ease." I was only too happy to oblige him. "Don't worry, I am going to marry you," I reassured him. At which point, as he surveyed my beardless chin and unfurrowed brow, his expression turned to one of disgust. "You, a kid, you are going to marry me?" Despite that incident, I was never tempted to grow a long beard in order to look more rabbinical. As I once told an interviewer, "a beard is a barrier when communicating with others."

My appearance was sufficient, at least, to make a positive impression on one section of the congregation – the children. I used to take the children's services on Shabbat and I would always be dressed in my top hat and gown. One week I was away and a mother told me that she had asked her daughter if she had enjoyed the service. "Yes," the little girl had replied, "but God wasn't there."

There are some who disparage the very idea of a children's service, believing the children should be with their families in the main synagogue, but I always felt it gave me valuable time with the youngest members of the community. I once had to write to the *Jewish Chronicle*, however, to correct any misperception that we were child-unfriendly. The paper reported that Estelle had organised a crèche over Pesach and, under the heading "Passover without babies", I was quoted as saying, "Small children are not allowed into the synagogue because we are very particular about decorum." Now it is true that Lauderdale Road was not the place for infants to be running noisily up and down the aisles but, as I explained in a letter that was published by the paper the following week, we had arranged the crèche because the Pesach services, at four hours, were particularly long and a small child couldn't reasonably be expected to sit quietly for that length of time. I made it clear, "No child, however small, can or ought to be refused entrance into a house of God."

Every rabbi has his store of theological posers, which children innocently pitch at him. I remember one mother trying to explain to her daughter why she only had one grandmother. "Your other granny has gone to Heaven so she can help God," she said. "But doesn't God have an *au pair*?" the little girl replied. Another time a boy was being told by his mother that God was his Father. "But if God's my Father," came the puzzled response, "who's His wife?"

I gave my first sermon at Lauderdale Road on Shabbat Chanukah 1960, when I was twenty-one and still a student minister. Whereas a rabbi now is expected to address his community pretty much every Shabbat, sermons were far from a weekly fixture in those early years and when I first came, may have been no more frequent than once a month. Apart from our homiletics training at Jews' College, I was offered extra guidance by someone who was well-versed in public speaking, Neville Laski. A barrister and judge who had also been president of the Board of Deputies, he was a Sephardi by marriage, so to speak, having married Haham Gaster's daughter Sissie. On one appearance in court when he was defending a hopeless case, the judge told him, "Mr Laski, I fear you are trying to make bricks without straw." The advocate was undeterred, "Your Honour, my ancestors managed to do so 3,000 years ago in Egypt, so let me have a try." He once told me that his father-in-law Haham Gaster, when reviewing a book by Chief Rabbi Joseph Hertz, had said, "You know the best part is the two covers at each end." He asked if I wouldn't mind sending him copies of my sermons after I had delivered them and he would return them with improvements to my English, marked in green ink.

I was not inhibited about speaking my mind from time to time. In one of my earliest sermons on Simchat Torah, when I was still a student rabbi, I stressed that it was far more important for the synagogue to be a place to rejoice with God than a fashion show, whereupon one or two women in the gallery may have shifted uneasily in their fur coats. Looking back, I might have counselled my younger self to be a little more circumspect. Still, a congregation will tolerate a pointed remark from the pulpit if its members feel the rabbi has their best interests at heart and has proven so by being there when they need him.

In a sermon I gave in 1977, I reflected that a rabbi can only be effective in his work if he is prepared to identify with congregants in their times both of "joy and festivity" and "of sorrow and calamity". A rabbi could not be a detached spectator. "This makes the work of the rabbi fascinating but at times somewhat difficult for he is often asked to change his mood from hour to hour as he proceeds through his difficult task in any one day."

Although I tried to give congregants the personal attention they sought, it was sometimes hard to persuade someone that I could not be in two places at once. One busy Sunday, I was attending a wedding lunch, having conducted the ceremony. After the first course, I got up from the top table where the rabbi always sat, and made my apologies to the mother of the bride, "I'm sorry, I have to leave now, because I have to go and do a funeral", but the mother responded reproachfully, "Rabbi, have you any idea how much I paid for your meal?"

To join with families in their celebrations is one of the privileges of the job. In our garden, Estelle has planted some of the plants given to us as thank-yous, which remain as mementoes of particular *semachot* over 40 years. None the less, whatever you do to make sure proceedings run smoothly, you will sometimes have to confront the unexpected. I was once marrying a couple whose families came from Iraq. As there was no civil marriage in Iraq, the only legal document was the *ketubah* and it was the practice for that to include all the financial agreements. In this instance, the dowry had not been settled and the haggling went down to the wire. The expectant guests were waiting in the synagogue for the ceremony to begin but behind the scenes the fathers of the couple were locked in negotiation. The *chuppah* had to be delayed for half an hour until we could finally go ahead.

And then there was the glass that wouldn't break. From the 17th century, it has been our custom for the *hatan* to pay £1 to the synagogue – thirteen shillings to write two copies of the *ketubah* and seven shillings for the *shamash* to buy a glass to break under the *chuppah*. On one occasion the *shamash* had a glass at home which he couldn't use any more and thought it would be a shame to waste. The dish happened to be Pyrex, which, in mainstream Sephardi tradition, is perfectly acceptable to be used for both meat and milk. However, the *shamash*, who was very religious, considered the glass fit only for one or the other, not both; when his wife got mixed up, he would no longer keep it. At the end of the ceremony, the groom brought his foot down on the package containing the glass. Instead of the crack, there was silence. "Try harder," I whispered. Three or four times he lifted his foot, only for it to bounce off the resistant object. "I can't any more," he pleaded, "my foot is hurting." "Sorry," said the *shamash*, exiting to find another glass.

There was never a more dramatic moment when, as I was addressing the couple beneath the *chuppah*, the bride simply crumpled and fell to the floor. Shocked, I wondered it if it was because of anything I had said. "Don't worry," her husband reassured me, "she is having an epileptic fit." When she came round, we resumed the service but I have never completed one as rapidly.

As a rabbi, it was my duty to explain to a couple the meaning of the rites in which they were participating, knowledge not always available to their guests. I was once officiating at the marriage of Charles Corman, a solicitor who is well known in the Jewish charity world and who attended the study circles I held in my home. Before the *hatan* places the ring on the finger of his bride, I formally ask him, "Is this ring your own property?" This is because if he had borrowed and not bought the ring, the marriage would not be valid according to *halachah*, Jewish law. One of the guests was Michael Heseltine, the Conservative politician, who was a client of the groom, and at the reception he came up to me with a slightly quizzical look and remarked "Rabbi, do you really think my lawyer would get married with a ring that didn't belong to him?"

Some years into my rabbinate I adopted the practice of inviting each of the marrying couple to write to me to say why they had chosen their partner in order to help me get to know them better. I had heard about the idea from someone in America and it worked well when I introduced it here. While one or two were content with a list of bullet points of their intended's qualities, I was often touched by the heartfelt, handwritten letters some gave me. One woman recalled how her fiancé had left Iran as a young teenager without his parents and had lodged with a family in Amsterdam for a few months until he was able to come to Britain. As he discovered later, the Dutch family happened to be related to his wife-to-be. "I know that G-d had the perfect person for me," she wrote.

Another woman told me how her fiancé always used to quote the advice he had heard given by a rabbi to another couple under the *chuppah*, "Never end the night angry with one another." One night, after they had had an argument, she said, she had just wanted to go to sleep but her fiancé had reminded her of the rabbi's words, so they kissed and made up.

I felt gratified if I could put them at ease enough to be open with me. If you are a rabbi in a mainstream congregation, of course you can hardly pretend that you don't know that many couples set up home before marriage but when the bride went to the mikveh before the *chuppah*, I took heart from the fact that by having a Jewish marriage at all, they were looking to inject a spiritual component into their relationship.

I was chatting once to a senior Christian cleric who was sitting next to me at a dinner. "Tell me, do you feel that with most of the weddings you do, the couple are living together?" I asked him. He replied, "I put it this way. They do all the right things – but in the wrong order!"

I have always enjoyed the elegant restraint of our wedding ceremonies. The philosopher Sir Isaiah Berlin, who attended the marriage of his stepson Peter Halban to Martine (the publishers of this book) in 1983, wrote afterwards to thank me for a service which was "unselfconsciously traditional and at the same time natural in exquisite taste". My experience as a marriage officiant was recorded for posterity by one of the leading Jewish artists of the time, R.B. Kitaj, who painted me performing one that same year – although I remain unrecognisable for a reason which I shall explain.

Kitaj had been looking for a beautiful synagogue to marry his second wife Sandra Fisher. His friend, the former *Jewish Chronicle* editor William Frankel, who knew my father (who had been the paper's honorary Gibraltar correspondent), called me and said, "You've got to give him Bevis Marks." When I met the couple, I did what I always do before the marriage can proceed, which is to authenticate their Jewish status. The famous artist took offence at my enquiries. Here was someone who reflected on Jewish identity and the Holocaust in his art. Who was I asking to see bits of paper to determine whether he was Jewish? After some research, we found the requisite proof but Kitaj exacted revenge for what he saw as my rabbinical impertinence. He painted a picture of his wedding, portraying a number of some of his famous artistic colleagues beneath the *chuppah* including David Hockney, Leon Kossoff and Frank Auerbach. And with them is the rabbi too, rendered anonymous, in a top hat but without a face!

Kitaj did not hold a grudge against me and we became quite friendly afterwards. He invited me to put up a mezuzah in his studio, buying kosher cakes for the occasion. Sadly, he and Sandra had little more than ten years together. He was convinced the negative reviews he received for his exhibition at the Tate contributed to her death in 1994. On the occasions I saw him after, he seemed depressed without her.

While we are called on by our ministry to act as the public face of Judaism, often our most valuable work is done in private. The long-term effect of our sermons we might never know, but we could sometimes take quiet satisfaction from seeing the more immediate results of our pastoral care: finding assistance for someone in financial difficulty, for example, or sorting out a family dispute. A couple who were getting on badly came to see me about their son's barmitzvah. He was Sephardi, she was Ashkenazi and the forthcoming *simchah* only exacerbated their differences. The father wanted his son to have a Sephardi barmitzvah ceremony, the mother an Ashkenazi one. Caught in the middle, anxiety was written all over the child's face. I asked the boy to leave the room for a moment. Then I turned to his parents. "I don't mind whether the ceremony is Ashkenazi or Sephardi, I only want what is best for the child. Are you prepared to abide by my decision?" They agreed. It didn't require the wisdom of Solomon. I took out a coin. "Heads or tails," I said. The mother won, leaving the boy free to begin his barmitzvah preparations.

Inevitably, there were some people I was unable to help. I was once visited by a young man who wanted to see if his non-Jewish fiancée could convert. His grandmother, however, was deeply worried that her grandchildren were assimilating and feared that if we enabled him to marry a convert, it would set a precedent. When I met her subsequently at a function, she berated me for trying to assist her grandson, saying "You are the cause of all my troubles." I could see her point.

The most difficult decision I had to take during my whole rabbinic career occurred at the funeral of a little boy of six or seven, who was the son of a Moroccan Jew. He died after falling into a pit. A large crowd of several hundred people had gathered at the cemetery. Shortly before I was to begin the service, someone took me aside. "Rabbi, I want you to know that the mother of this child is not Jewish," the informant said. "You cannot bury him in a Jewish cemetery." I couldn't think what to do; to call off the funeral would have added to the distress of the bereaved family but if I turned a blind eye, I would betray my rabbinic position and my duty to the congregation. I went over to the father, hoping that the information I had been given was wrong. "I took my wife to Morocco," he explained, "I paid the rabbi and he put her in the mikveh." If she had undergone ritual immersion in the mikveh, then as far as I was concerned, that was enough to fulfil the religious requirements for conversion: she was Jewish. And so was her poor boy. So we buried him. Not everyone agreed with what I had done; one or two dissenting voices in the community felt I had been overly lenient.

One touching story concerned a very old man who used to be visited by a number of young boys from the congregation. He did not ask for much but he had long wanted to have a little gold chain with a Magen David. So the boys started collecting in order to buy him a chain but on the very day that they were finally able to go out and get it, he died. The boys came to his funeral and they asked me to put the chain in his coffin. I told them that it was a lovely gesture but I could not do what they asked, because we do not bury people with any kind of adornment or jewellery. I suggested instead that we should sell the chain and buy some prayer books in his memory, which they happily did.

While finding the right words to say in a eulogy can be one challenge for a rabbi, sometimes preventing a relative saying the wrong words is another. I once conducted the funeral of the father of a man who was professionally very successful and highly educated, but he could not read Hebrew. It is always poignant for a rabbi to see a person who has achieved much in the secular world yet has been denied a basic Jewish education, particularly when it makes them feel awkward at a difficult moment in their life. I made him a phonetic Kaddish, the mourners' prayer, in English letters but he remained self-conscious and, before he recited the Kaddish, he wanted to announce that his father had never taught him Hebrew. He was used to doing everything with such a high degree of accomplishment that he wanted to apologise in advance for what he anticipated would be his halting delivery of the prayer but I prevailed on him not to say anything in order to spare him embarrassment.

During my rabbinate, I ushered in one small change in funeral practice. It had long been the custom for women to remain in the prayer hall and not to accompany the body to the grave. Among some Orthodox groups it is not the done thing for women to go to a funeral at all but as the position of women in society generally began to shift, they became less prepared to put up with what they regarded as obsolete restrictions. One forthright member of the community left me in no doubt that she was not going to be bound by the status quo. "Abraham, my father has only two daughters," she said. "I'm telling you that when he dies, I'm not going to stay behind in the hall and I am going straight to the grave and I am going to put earth on his coffin." When the time came, I allowed her and the precedent was set. It hardly seemed a radical innovation, yet some in the Sephardi rabbinate continue to disapprove.

In one area of our burial policy, we certainly led the way by introducing two-tier interment in deep graves. A husband could be buried on top of his wife: a man above another man, or a woman above a woman but a man and a woman with no relationship could not be buried above one another. Some years ago the government proposed that the practice be adopted widely, given the acute shortage of cemetery space in certain parts of the country, although acknowledging it remained a "political taboo". As far as I am aware, we are the only Orthodox community in the country to permit it, although some Progressive cemeteries later followed suit.

The policy nevertheless met some opposition within our ranks, particularly from among our Oriental – or Mizrachi – congregants. Alan Nabarro, who was on the Mahamad and a strong-willed character, was determined to see it through. So we agreed that anyone who did not wish to be laid to rest in a double-depth grave should make sure to write to the congregation before their death and express their desire for a single one. Still, we had to exercise sensitivity on occasion after the event. There was a man who died relatively young and was buried in a two-tiered grave above another man with whom he had no connection. His brother, an official in the Israeli government, was upset and wrote to me to say that his brother had wanted to be buried in a single grave, even though he had neglected to put that in writing, and could we arrange it. He urged me to "bring this very painful matter to a positive conclusion and allow me the peace of mind in fulfilling my late brother's will". So we did what we could to accommodate him. In another instance, we had to dig under one grave to exhume the body of another person for reburial in Israel without disturbing the one on top.

An even more delicate time than a funeral can be attending to someone who is close to their end. When I go to a hospital to visit someone who is dying, if they are reasonably conscious, I am careful not to say the Shema too loudly because I don't want to frighten them. On one occasion I was summoned to the bedside of an old man who was originally from Egypt. His whole family had come from France to be with him in his final hours. He had lain motionless for a day or two. In these circumstances, I will say the Shema out loud and I began to recite the prayer but, as I did so, the man began to tremble and shake. He must have heard me and he was not resolved to go just yet. He lived another six months. Another time a call came in the middle of the night, "Rabbi, my husband is dying, my husband is dying." I rushed to the hospital to be with the poor man. His wife brought some rosewater with her and began sprinkling it over him. "Haim, Haim," she cried, "you can't die." And he didn't. He held out for a few more weeks.

For a rabbi, there is no more taxing question than when someone who has suffered serious loss or misfortune asks you point-blank, "Why me?" It is a question to which I have no answer. I often found it helped when I told them that there are people who have got through worse. It has made me admire all the more those I have come across who, in different ways, showed resilience in the face of adversity.

There was a young woman in the community, Nicole Davoud, who enjoyed a comfortable life; she was intelligent, successful and happily married. Suddenly her world was thrown into turmoil when she was struck by a disease that left her virtually immobile. Many of the things she had once thought important were denied her but she did not succumb to the depression that

1 My mother, Rachel, on her engagement.

2 My parents' wedding, Gibraltar.

3 With Solomon (Momy) and Nita, my elder brother and sister, in Madeira during the War.

4 Purim with sister Nita, 1949.

5 Tu Bishvat. I am the first child on the right, Madeira, 1942.

6 Estelle's parents on their wedding day, Holland Park, 1940.

7 With two friends at Carmel College: Kim Chiswick from Israel and Theo Hirshfeld from Kenya.

8 Friends at Holland Park Synagogue many of whom Estelle is still very close to.

9 Our engagement party, 1962.

10 Our wedding day, Lauderdale Road Synagogue, June, 1963.

11 Multi-tasking at home.

12 On holiday at Sotogrande.

13 In the kitchen, 2000.

14 With my family after receiving the OBE, 2004.

15 The four Isaacs (from left): Isaac Corré, Julian Isaac, Rabbi Isaac (Levy) and Isaac Levy.

16 With my brothers and sisters, Gibraltar.

17 Wearing the insignia of Spanish Knight Commander, Spanish Embassy London, 1993.

18 In the State Bedroom, Mansion House, 1998.

19 In Eze, South of France.

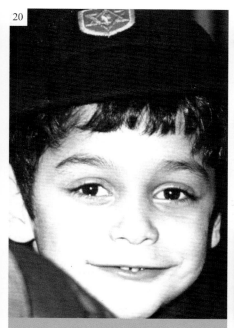

20 Julian, 1970.

21 Julian's surprise fortieth birthday party, 2004.

22 With Julian and Sian on their wedding day, 1998.

23 With Avi and Jamie, my grandchildren, handing over MDA ambulance, December 2003.

24 The grandchildren on holiday

25 and in Naima uniform.

understandably she fell into at first. She re-evaluated her life and decided to use her talents in a different way, starting a movement to bring comfort and help to others suffering from the same disease as her. As I recalled in a sermon, when I visited her, I left "by thanking her for seeing me, for I know that she has given me much more than I could ever give her".

We had in the community a brother and sister from Greece, who had once been wealthy but who were unable to take their money out of the country. I tried to intercede with the Greek embassy on their behalf, without success. As their resources dwindled, their life became harder but they would accept no charity. They had been people used to giving, not receiving. After their death, the porter who was clearing their flat called me as they had no children. He had found hundreds of pounds in cash stuffed under the mattress. The brother had been putting away a pound here, a pound there, for them to live on, so determined he was to maintain their independence. I am not suggesting at all that people shouldn't seek help when they fall on hard times – our congregation prided itself on its charitable services – but I was moved by the lengths to which the brother and sister had gone to preserve their self-esteem.

Invitations to preach at other synagogues or to talk to university societies enabled me to venture beyond the precincts of the Spanish and Portuguese. As the '60s rolled on, one subject I was increasingly asked to address by students was the Jewish attitude towards sex. Whereas Catholicism tended to view sex as a sin, I told them, Judaism considered it, in the right circumstances, a mitzvah; a Spanish kabbalist even wrote a prayer asking God that his union with his wife should be spiritual, blessed and unifying.

My educational outings occasionally took me off the beaten track. A few times I went to speak about Judaism to Beshara, the universalist movement founded in the early 1970s in the UK by

Bulent Rauf, the brother-in-law of King Farouk of Egypt. Its Arabic name, meaning "good tidings", is similar to the Hebrew word in Isaiah announcing the advent of a messianic age. Beshara appealed to idealistic young people seeking respite from the rat race and a more spiritual path. "They come from all walks of life – architects, lawyers and businessmen," I recalled in a sermon after a visit to one of its communities, a dilapidated mansion in the Cotswolds. "They grow most of their own vegetables, look after a few chickens and they are in the process of converting an old barn into a room of prayer and meditation – trying their hardest to lead a godly life." They embraced a humble lifestyle and did not care about such fripperies as furniture; every chair there was of a different design.

Since they were not trying to start their own religion and seemed generally interested to hear what the monotheistic faiths had to say, I saw no problem and had some admiration for their quest. I even joined in a little meditation with them – which was a struggle because I find it difficult to sit still for long. Estelle came with me on one visit to the Beshara centre in Scotland, where we stayed overnight. As I noted in my sermon, a spiritual retreat, from a Jewish point of view, can "only be a temporary measure" and we must return to society in order to try positively to influence it.

However fleeting, my encounter with this alternative lifestyle did result in an angry letter to the Chief Rabbi. The mother of a Jewish girl who was in Beshara wrote to Rabbi Jakobovits, protesting at my association with what she saw as a bunch of hippies who had ensnared her daughter and demanding that I be defrocked. I was not under the authority of the Chief Rabbi, of course, even if he were to object to my activities. Generally, I could go and talk where I pleased.

I saw a different kind of asceticism in the tutor with whom I learned Talmud weekly for a number of years, Rabbi Joseph Lieberman, the head of a yeshivah in Golders Green. He was a deeply pious man of meagre means, who lived frugally. One time we were talking about a rabbi so poor that he had to write his commentaries on the wall because he couldn't afford paper. Rabbi Lieberman turned to me and said, "And we complain, with all our luxuries!" I looked around the room with its bare furnishings. His son recalled his father once saying to him, "Imagine if you could have Coca Cola and chips every day, wouldn't that be tremendous?" That was his idea of abundance.

I could never have served my community to the extent that I did without Estelle's support and forbearance. She had not sought the role of a rabbi's wife nor envisaged the use of her home as a kind of religious consulting rooms. We entertained guests regularly for Shabbat meals and then on Saturday afternoons I would have a group of youngsters round for tea. A pastoral rabbi has to be ready to sacrifice some of his family life to the needs of his congregants. Nevertheless, the demands of the Mahamad at times would have tried the patience of a *tzaddik,* or righteous person.

In 1964, when our son Julian was born, Estelle was in labour on Shabbat. Nonetheless, I was expected to carry out my official duties leading the morning service at Bevis Marks Synagogue before I could make the long walk to be with her at the hospital in Paddington. It was an anxious time; Julian was premature and weighed only three-and-a-half pounds at birth. As a result he spent the first few weeks of his life in hospital.

For the Mahamad, loyalty to the synagogue was all and nothing could be allowed to interfere with its orderly running. I can't imagine any rabbi these days being willing to tolerate such conditions. The Mahamad, at least, did make some provision for visiting ministers to have a meal at Bevis Marks, although the woman charged with catering it wondered how on earth she was supposed to do so within a budget of two shillings and sixpence (twelve and a half pence) for a meal.

Five years after I gained my ministerial diploma, I was able to call myself "rabbi" when I qualified as the first student to receive *semichah* from Chief Rabbi Jakobovits, a month after the Six Day War in 1967. It wasn't easy managing on a ministerial salary. At the time, we were living in a flat provided by the synagogue in Rodney Court, Maida Vale, but we wanted something larger with a garden where Julian could run around and we could have a succah. We found an attractive house with a cottage-like façade close by in Biddulph Road. The only problem was that the Mahamad had given us a budget for £18,000 and the house cost £21,000. This difficulty was overcome when Kenneth Rubens, one of the upcoming leaders who was well disposed towards us, ignored the limit and authorised the purchase of the property, which has been our home now for some forty-five years. Although ministers were not well paid, it was within the congregation's gift to at least offer them the security of housing for life. It was some years later that we successfully claimed the right to tenure, with the assistance of Charles Corman and a distant cousin of mine, David Blackburn.

Not long after Julian was born, Estelle embarked on the degree she had postponed because of marriage and graduated in social work. For many years she worked with the Jewish Blind Society (which became part of Jewish Care) but after qualifying, she first wanted experience outside the Jewish community and took a job with the local authority. An only child, she had grown up as, by her own admission, "a little princess". Now she found herself on tough council estates dealing with family crises and issues from which her sheltered childhood had protected her. "There was a problem behind every door;" she said. One of her responsibilities was to register childminders so the authorities could keep an eye on those looking after children and help reduce the risk of abuse. She encountered children who had been forced to sit idly on a square rug all day and would bring toys to provide them with at least some stimulation.

Her expertise and understanding proved an asset when congregants came to see us with their problems. She knew her way around the Jewish social services so she could advise which was the best organisation for them to go for specialist help. Compared with what she had come up against in her professional life, there was nothing at Lauderdale Road that could surprise or shock her.

I would not have progressed in the synagogue had I not been taken, from an early age, under the wing of the Haham. When we were still schoolboys, my brother Momy and I would regularly eat at Dr Gaon's home in Maida Vale during our Carmel half-terms. The Haham encouraged the Mahamad to recruit me as a student hazan. He was widely regarded as having re-energised the congregation during his early years in office and was still in his thirties when he was appointed Haham. After a while he set his horizons further than London and by the time I had become a rabbi in 1967, he had begun his love affair with America. It so happened that the oldest Spanish and Portuguese congregation in New York, Shearith Israel, was being led by the Reverend Dr Louis Gerstein, a graduate of the leading Conservative academy, the Jewish Theological Academy, and an Ashkenazi. A number of influential families feared that Shearith Israel would slide towards Conservatism and invited the Haham to take a closer interest in its affairs to ensure that it remained within the ambit of Orthodoxy.

It was an opportunity he naturally leapt at. His trips to New York became more frequent and more prolonged. At one stage he asked me to send him over an educational curriculum which I had developed for our Sunday classes at Lauderdale, to use at Shearith Israel. By 1976, he had also become a professor at Yeshiva University in New York. They say absence makes the heart grow fonder but the Haham's transatlantic excursions did not endear him to everyone in his London community. He did not wish to relinquish control but he was not always around to make decisions.

For many years, I assisted the Haham in his congregational business, drafting letters for him to sign. When he was abroad, I would open his post for him, although eventually his wife Regina decided that she would do this herself. But he did not hesitate to make his views known if he thought I was overreaching myself.

What created problems in my relationship with the Haham was Sir Alan Mocatta's active promotion of me as a potential successor. He wrote a letter to Dr Gaon to suggest that he should train me as a future Haham – a suggestion which did not go down at all well with its recipient and which, in view of all that later happened, I wish that Sir Alan had never made. That, and the murmurings among some about the time the Haham was spending in America, had made life more difficult when I was appointed rabbi of Lauderdale Road in 1975. When, later that year, a small advert in the *Jewish Chronicle* announcing that I would be speaking one Saturday night at a *melaveh malkah* at a South London synagogue mistakenly referred to me as "Deputy Haham", it aroused Dr Gaon's suspicions.

The politics of the congregation were complicated by an additional factor – the arrival of Rabbi Pinchas Toledano. Moroccan-born, he had received *semichah* from the Etz Chaim Yeshivah in London in his early twenties and was an halachic scholar – which I could never claim to be – who wrote a beautiful and poetic Hebrew. The congregation had lacked a local halachic authority since the death in the early 1950s of Rabbi Shemtov Gaguine, who had headed the Judith Lady Montefiore College, the theological academy founded by Sir Moses Montefiore, in Ramsgate. From a Moroccan rabbinic dynasty, Jerusalem-born Rabbi Gaguine had served in Egypt before coming to Manchester. It no doubt suited some elements within the community, who did not regard him as English enough, for him to remain out of the way in Kent. Anyhow, Dr Gaon took on some of the halachic decision-making himself, including handling divorces, which was brave of him since it wasn't his forte. Nonetheless, he realised that he could do with more of a specialist in Jewish law.

Rabbi Toledano joined us from the Eastern Jewish community in Golders Green and became rabbinic assistant to the Haham. He later moved to Wembley to preside over the new Spanish and Portuguese synagogue, started for the Egyptian Jews who had begun arriving after the Suez Crisis in 1956. Its first rabbi, David Kamhi, a man I particularly liked and respected, had quarrelled with the Mahamad and left to found a rival congregation, prompting some even to call for his excommunication. He died tragically young from cancer. Under the tutelage of one of our most erudite members, Raphael Loewe, who became professor of Hebrew at University College London, Rabbi Toledano consolidated his standing within the Spanish and Portuguese by studying for a BA in Semitics and then a doctorate. He was appointed a dayan of our community in 1974.

It was no secret that Dayan Toledano and I never personally hit it off but the tensions that arose between us were largely due to the consequences of our situation. I had the brief for education, he for ruling on *halachah*. But our roles were not clearly delineated and inevitably there was some overlap. With the Haham often in America, decisions needed to be taken. Both of us wanted to make them but neither could always be sure who had the prerogative. A charitable interpretation might be that two heads seemed better than one. But, from another angle, it seemed like a case of divide and rule, which left the Haham, even if he were off stage, to retain his authority from afar.

Matters finally came to a head a year before the Haham's official retirement date at the end of 1977. Many rabbis might happily step down on reaching the age of sixty-five to enjoy some peace and quiet after years of loyal service: some no doubt, like the prophet Samuel, having grown grey before their time. But in much of the traditional world, one did not simply show the rabbi the door if he were willing to continue. In Charedi communities, rabbis often did not retire until they drew their last breath. The Mahamad felt the time had come for Dr Gaon to go but some of his supporters had other ideas and launched a campaign for him to be invited to remain. The Spanish and Portuguese do not do disputes by halves. Haham Gaster clashed with his lay leaders over Zionism. The most illustrious of all Hahamim, David Nieto, was accused of pantheism. The controversy over Haham Gaon's retirement was more about personality than religious or political principle but it was enough for the *Jewish Chronicle* to describe it as the worst conflict within the Sephardi community since the breakaway of the West London Synagogue (which led to the birth of the Reform movement in Britain) back in 1840.

An extraordinary meeting of the congregation was arranged in late January at Porchester Hall in Westminster to approve Dr Gaon's retirement. I could only sit on the sidelines since the clergy was not allowed to attend. And I could only be glad that I did, in view of the "acrimonious, highly emotional and undecorous [sic]" atmosphere, according to the report in the *Jewish Chronicle*. The result of the three-and-a-half hour meeting could hardly have been worse, for it left the congregation riven down the middle. When the votes were counted for a resolution to accept the Haham's departure, they were tied at seventy-five for and against. In the end, it came down to the chairman of the meeting, Roderick Romain. From one of our oldest families, he cared deeply about the congregation and had helped to found the Wembley Synagogue. He was a man of great integrity who felt that it was in nobody's interest, not least Dr Gaon's, for his tenure to be prolonged. By his single casting vote, the resolution was carried.

If such a meeting took place today, someone would no doubt

tweet a blow-by-blow account by mobile phone. But I had to wait until the following day to hear what had happened. It was clear that a difficult period lay ahead and, while we could not reunite the community overnight, we had to take care not to deepen the divisions. A few weeks after the Porchester Hall meeting, it was announced that Dr Gaon would bow out as religious leader of the congregation at the end of the year but that he would keep the title of Haham as head of the newly formed Association of Sephardi Synagogues.

The post-Haham arrangements did little to address the latent tensions between Dayan Toledano and myself and our respective spheres of responsibility. We each had our own champions who hoped that their favourite might eventually gain the upper hand. But if the politics could be dispiriting, I tried not to get enmeshed in them. Apart from attending to congregants, I busied myself with my educational interests, most notably the launch of the Young Jewish Leadership Institute in 1978. The same year I completed my London University doctorate under the guidance of Chimen Abramsky, a remarkable, self-taught scholar who moved from running an East End Jewish bookstore to becoming Goldsmid Professor of Jewish studies at UCL. My subject was medieval court rabbis. Whereas Ashkenazi rabbis generally regarded contact with kings and queens as corrupting, their Spanish counterparts offered a different model, successfully combining spiritual leadership of the Jewish community with influential roles at court until Don Isaac Abarbanel and the expulsion of 1492.

I was fortunate in the loyalty shown me by friends. One of those who helped keep up my morale was Cesare Sacerdoti, who particularly understood the tribulations of being a rabbi because he was the son of a rabbi himself. His father had been Chief Rabbi of Ferrara in Italy. During the Second World War, their father entrusted Cesare and his younger brother to the care of nuns to shield them from the Nazis. Cesare later successfully campaigned for his protectors to be recognised as among Righteous of the Nations by Israel's Holocaust memorial centre, Yad Vashem.

Whatever the frustrations, I was never seriously tempted to leave the community. When my Jews' College contemporary Raymond Apple returned to his native Australia in 1972, Hampstead Synagogue asked if I would be interested in succeeding him as rabbi. It was then the last United Synagogue to maintain a mixed choir and the lay leaders wondered how I felt about it. I said that as I had preached there on several occasions, I had no objections to visiting the synagogue. But I would not want to be the rabbi of an Orthodox synagogue where a mixed choir sang in case that put off anyone who might think of attending it. Another United Synagogue, St John's Wood, approached me, when Rabbi Solomon Goldman retired in 1976. When I received overtures from the Spanish and Portuguese synagogue in Philadelphia, I asked Rabbi Nahum Rabinovitch, then dean of Jews' College, if it would be ethical to fly across at their expense if I was unlikely to take the job. He said go, but I found nothing on offer in Philadelphia to prise me from Lauderdale Road.

One step I took in planning for the future was to commission a piece of market research, which then was a fairly novel thing for a rabbi to do. It was done for me by Nicole Davoud's husband, Raymond. We looked at men in the thirty-five to fifty age group who were not regular attenders of synagogue, in most cases putting in an appearance only on the High Holy Days. Even though not especially observant themselves, they were not looking for Judaism to change with the times. They respected Judaism for representing timeless standards which, even if they could not always reach themselves, were nonetheless something to aspire to. I was encouraged that, opposed to religious extremes, they felt that the Spanish and Portuguese tradition struck the right balance.

But the thing that struck me most was their feeling that if the rabbi helped them, they should offer him a gift: and if he did not accept a gift, then they owed him a favour should he, in turn, call on their support.

In 1980 Dr Gaon decided to call it a day and resigned from his office with the Association of Sephardi Synagogues. All too aware of the contention the Haham's exit had caused, the Mahamad were not going to reopen old wounds by rushing to appoint a new one. In the *Jewish Chronicle*, Chaim Bermant teasingly floated the thought of Dayan Toledano and myself serving as a double-headed Haham, "with one functioning as Ha and the other as Ham", before he went on to say that the Sephardim "need a Haham like a hole in the head" and he could not understand, "why they would perpetuate an office which has often been the cause of division and is more becoming a source of derision." The Mahamad hit on a compromise, to create a "joint ecclesiastical authority", whereby I would be spiritual head and Dayan Toledano head of the Sephardi Beth Din. It was not an ideal solution but one we would have to try to live with. It still left room to tread on each other's toes, however, and it took another year before we were able to find a modus vivendi, thanks to the intervention of Rav Ovadia Yosef, the Sephardi Chief Rabbi of Israel. Rav Ovadia paid a visit to London in 1981. He was well aware that the community had been going through a rough patch. On his way home, Dayan Toledano and I accompanied him to the airport, where he asked us to come with him to the VIP lounge. On the spot, he drafted a memorandum which set out our responsibilities: I would be in charge of education and inform Dayan Toledano of what I was doing, Dayan Toledano would make halachic decisions and consult me before they were implemented. Rav Ovadia was the greatest Sephardi religious leader since the Second World War. His word was final.

When I came to give my twenty-fifth anniversary sermon at Rosh Hashanah in 1987, I did not shy away from mentioning that while there had been quiet and productive years, a few had been "tempestuous and unhappy". I compared the role of the rabbi to that of a shofar. The protracted single blast of *tekiah* was a wake-up call, urging people to think what more they should do to improve the religious lives of themselves and their children. It didn't always make the rabbi popular. "I always say that if I want an easy rabbinate, that is the easiest thing to achieve; ask no questions, do not initiate, turn a blind eye," I declared. The broken three-note sequence of *shevarim*, the sound of lament, represented the rabbi's sharing in the troubles of his congregants and holding their hand in times of need. The staccato burst of *teruah* – blown in biblical days as a rally to war – was a summons to action. "For if I believe that something needs doing," I said, "I will continue to blow the notes of *teruah* into everybody's ears until hopefully it gets done."

In that sermon, I described myself as "an incorrigible missionary". My philosophy was simple and let me give this example to illustrate it. The publisher Anthony Blond grew up in an ultra-assimilated family without any Jewish upbringing. I was introduced to him through my father-in-law Leon Nahum, who worked in the book trade. Blond told him he wanted to meet a rabbi. He started coming along to synagogue, taught himself Hebrew and used to put on tefillin daily, after I showed him how to. In a letter he wrote to thank me for letting him read my sermons, he told me in a lovely phrase, "drops of Judaism are gently entering my veins". There was just one thing: he was bisexual and open about his relationships with men. After one service, one of our members accosted me. "Rabbi, I'm disgusted with you." "Why?" I asked her. "How can you let someone like that come to our synagogue?" she said. "Do you keep Shabbat strictly?" I asked. "No." "Or kosher?" "No." "So who am I to judge which of you is the better Jew?" I replied.

When Blond decided to marry his second wife, Laura Hesketh, from an old English family, he wanted me to fly to Sri Lanka to bless the wedding, but I had to explain that I could not officiate at an intermarriage. "So what advice can you give us?" he asked. To Laura, I said that she should be as good a Christian as possible and to Anthony, I said he should be as good a Jew. No, I didn't get him to become a *ba'al teshuvah*, someone who returns to a fully religious lifestyle. But if a rabbi can nudge, cajole and even inspire as many Jews as possible to admit more Judaism into their lives rather than less, he is making progress. Who is a good Jew, people sometimes ask me? My answer: someone who wants to be a better Jew.

3

New Blood from the East

WHEN THE SIX Day War broke out in June 1967, British Jewry held its breath as the young Jewish state fought for its life. While there may have been a few within the Spanish and Portuguese Community who still harboured the anti-Zionist sentiments of the communal elite in the earlier part of the century, the overriding feeling was of concern for the fate of our co-religionists in Israel. A solidarity meeting was hastily convened one lunchtime at Bevis Marks Synagogue and it was packed. There were two speakers. Sir Alan Mocatta, in his customary measured tones, said something like this: "Ladies and gentlemen, while we may not have always agreed with everything which Israel has done over the past few years, today is a time when we feel that it is right to come together to support and protect our fellow-Jews." The second figure was far less restrained. When the businessman and philanthropist Leon Tamman rose to his feet, he launched into a tirade against the Egyptian leader. He might have been talking of Haman: "Nasser, may he be cursed. Amen v'Amen. May there be nothing left of him." And he continued in that vein for several minutes.

I first met Leon Tamman three or four years before. I had come to Lauderdale Road one morning to practise my Torah reading and I saw a man alone in the synagogue. He was reciting Psalms and crying. I had no idea who he was. I went up to him and asked him what was the matter. His wife, he told me, was having an operation in a nearby hospital. So I invited him and his children to come to our house. His family, of Iraqi origin, had established a successful business in Sudan and moved to Egypt. But as the Egyptian government turned on the country's Jews in the wake of the Suez War of 1956, the Tammans were forced to leave. His commercial enterprise knew no borders, however; he set up a pharmaceutical company and became a major investor in Israel, with a wider portfolio which included luxury hotels. His central London home was a portrait of opulence but he was generous with his wealth. Early on, Dr Gaon spotted him as a man of the future, who was to prove instrumental in the revival of the World Sephardi Federation. His appearance alongside Sir Alan at the Bevis Marks meeting announced his arrival as a person of influence. But I felt there was a larger significance. It marked a moment of transition, when the leadership of the Sephardi community in Britain passed from the old Spanish and Portuguese families to a newer generation of immigrants from the *Edot Hamizrach*, the Oriental Jews.

The majority of Jews who settled in Britain after the Second World War came from the Middle East or North Africa, from Egypt, Morocco, Algeria, Iraq, Libya, Aden, Iran. Some were driven from their homes; others fled, fearful of their future under a more aggressive Arab nationalism. At a meeting a few years ago I suggested that they were being too self-effacing by calling themselves "Sephardi", which historically applies to Jews of Spanish origin. The Iraqi community was much older than the Spanish. "I hate the term Mizrachi Jew," one of the audience objected. "I prefer a Babylonian Jew." "But a Moroccan Jew is not a Babylonian Jew," I pointed out. "No, no, he's a Sephardi," someone else piped up. "So let's stick with Oriental," I said.

While most Jews from the Middle East came here in the backlash after the creation of the state of Israel, they had been preceded by a few earlier migrants. Joseph Smouha, who was born in Baghdad, was already established in textiles in Manchester by the outbreak of the First World War. But he prospered even more after he went to Egypt in 1917 at the invitation of the British government. His masterstroke was to buy an area of marshland which had been created by the diversion of a river ahead of the clash between Napoleon's and Nelson's fleets at the Battle of the Nile. Smouha had done his homework. Once he acquired the land, he re-diverted the river and ended up with a prime development site. He called it Smouha City.

Joseph Smouha was typical of the immigrant who believed that the best way to make good in England was to leave the past behind him and to become as English as possible. His sons went to Harrow and they and his daughter served with the RAF during the Second World War. One son, Edward, ran for Britain in the Olympics. The early exiles from Iraq, such as Nathan Saatchi or Elie Kedourie, showed a similar willingness to adapt to their new home. The Iraqis, in particular, had a single-minded determination which enabled them to excel in their chosen fields, whether business as with Saatchi or academia in the case of Kedourie, a distinguished historian of the Middle East who was a leading professor at the LSE and received a CBE. Kedourie was a wise and prescient man. I will never forget when I had dinner with him shortly after Israel's spectacular victory in 1967 and its capture of the West Bank and the Sinai, how he said to me, "Abraham, we may have taken all these lands – but what are we going to do with them?" His wife, Sylvia Haim, also from Iraq, was an accomplished scholar in her own right who edited the journal *Middle Eastern Studies*. Sylvia, who died last year in 2016, was a regular at our Pesach Sedarim.

Another of those émigrés who contributed to the cultural and intellectual life of Britain was Nessim Joseph Dawood. He arrived in 1945 as a student to take a degree in English literature at the University of London. He established himself as a translator from Arabic and translated an edition of *One Thousand and One Nights* for Penguin. But his most famous English translation was of the Koran which first appeared in Penguin in 1956 and was so highly regarded that the latest revised edition came out in spring 2014, a few months before his death. I could spend hours talking to Nessim. He had a sharp intellect and he taught me a lot about the Koran. Apart from his command of Arabic, his English was masterly. He was a great lover of Shakespeare and had a cottage near Stratford-on-Avon so he could go and see the plays.

Another notable man of letters was the last president of Iraq's Jewish community, Meir Basri, who came here much later in 1974, when he was finally allowed to leave by Saddam Hussein's regime. He wrote widely on history, economics and literature and composed romantic poetry in Arabic. He was so admired by the expatriate Arabic community here that at his memorial service in Lauderdale Road half of those present must have been Muslims.

Jacques Ohana, who was from Morocco, carved a niche in the art world as an expert on Picasso. Whenever he put on an exhibition, the legendary artist would do a drawing dedicated to him in the catalogue. The drawing alone would be worth a small fortune, Jacques would tell me. He happily lent me his West End art gallery to run activities for Sephardi youth. Sometimes rabbis have to make do with drab synagogue halls as a venue but there we were surrounded by the works of the modern Spanish master. "Abraham, here is the key," Jacques would say when we arrived. "Lock up when you are finished." I can't imagine anyone being quite so relaxed in these more security-conscious times.

The desire of the newcomers to integrate extended to their Jewish affiliation as well. Since the Sephardi tradition was the nearest to their own, they naturally gravitated to the Spanish and Portuguese and accepted the congregation as the established institution of Anglo-Judaism. The Spanish and Portuguese Congregation was happy to accommodate them, as long as it was on its own terms. Shortly after I returned from honeymoon, I was drafted in to help with organising services for the fledgling Egyptian community, which had settled in Wembley. We rented a church hall until we were finally able to open a synagogue for them in 1977. If they came under the patronage of the Spanish and Portuguese Jews' Congregation, they were expected to abide by our customs and ways. Chaim Bermant once imagined a notice posted above the door of Bevis Marks, proclaiming "Purveyors of Judaism to Her Majesty's Sephardi Subjects since the Days of Queen Anne." Whatever regional variations the Jews of North Africa and the Middle East might have wished to introduce into the service were considered irrelevant by the Sephardi elders. While cultural diversity might be treasured today, conformity was the watchword then.

On High Holy Days, Oriental newcomers made up the bulk of the worshippers at the overflow service in the Montefiore Hall at Lauderdale Road. We relied on the assistance of students from the Judith Lady Montefiore College in Ramsgate, which had been a ministers' retirement home but which Dr Gaon had revived as a teacher training institute whose recruits came from the Middle East and North Africa. I often officiated there but one year I was delayed in the main service and didn't arrive in time for the recitation of the Prayer for the Royal Family so one of the Montefiore students had to recite it instead. The prayer book he was using was so old that it contained the blessing for King William and Princess Charlotte, which, none the wiser, he duly read out. It was apparently an act of treason to bless the wrong sovereign, Professor Raphael Loewe informed me – though we escaped the Tower.

Only slowly did the Spanish and Portuguese congregation make any concessions to the cultural background of the Oriental Jews. In our community, those who are awarded the honour of being Hatan Torah or Hatan Bereshit at Simchat Torah are expected to be able to read the appropriate portion from the Torah on the day themselves. Eventually, people such as Nathan Saatchi, who had a fine singing voice, were allowed to chant it in the Iraqi style of cantillation they had grown up with rather than have to adjust to the Spanish style. As the Middle Easterners became more numerous, a little more latitude crept in. Whereas *Bircat Cohanim*, the Priestly Blessing, used to be reserved for festivals, I agreed to it being said every Shabbat – a decision which was duly ratified, as it had to be, by the *Yehidim*.

We reintroduced *tashlich*, going down to the river to cast out your sins, on the afternoon on Rosh Hashanah – which, though common among Ashkenazi congregations in Britain, had long been absent from our own repertoire. The practice has kabbalistic overtones and back in the 17th century the first Haham Jacob Sasportas had removed anything that smacked of Kabbalah from our prayerbook. Sasportas was a vehement opponent of the False Messiah, Shabbetai Zvi, and downplayed Kabbalah because Zvi had used it to bolster his claims.

Another rite that had been deleted from our liturgy, for an entirely different reason, was the *hakafot*, the ceremonial parade of the Sifrei Torah around the synagogue on Simchat Torah. That was due to the notorious visit to a synagogue in the 1660s of the diarist Samuel Pepys, who was curious to see the recently established Jewish community at worship. Unfortunately, he chose Simchat Torah and was so appalled by the "disorder, laughter, sporting" he witnessed that he wrote that he could never imagine "there had been any religion in the whole world so absurdly performed as this". As a result, to protect the reputation of Judaism in the outside world, its leaders abolished the *hakafot*.

The circuits did not return until the 1960s when they were reintroduced in the evening service. But the ceremony was more like a dirge than a rejoicing. There were no children other than my son Julian, who was three or four. You would be handed a card, "the Parnas Presidente presents his compliments and asks you to take the third Sefer of the fifth circuit", and then the Torahs would proceed around the synagogue in a slow march. Gradually, the *hakafot* became a little more animated and for a brief spell we had them in the morning as well.

At the conclusion of a *chuppah* today, you will often see a boisterous hora break out around the bride and groom. This, too, reflects the changing complexion and tastes of our community. Not so long ago dancing in the synagogue would have been thought an unseemly breach of etiquette. So stately had been our wedding ceremonies that a groom used to break the glass to a hushed audience rather than to a chorus of "Mazaltov".

Not all the new immigrants wished to be clasped to the bosom of the Spanish and Portuguese congregation. The war that followed India's independence brought an influx of Jews in the late 1940s and early 1950s, mostly of Baghdadi origin, who had settled there to enjoy the trading opportunities afforded by the British empire but who felt too uncertain to entrust their future to the new state. Dr Gaon worked hard to assist them and we held weekday religion classes in the Bet Cholim, the Sephardi old age home, in the East End of London. I did many of their weddings and I taught their children. Still, they preferred to remain independent and set up a number of synagogues of their own, in Golders Green – in what had been the home of Munk's, one of the oldest strictly Orthodox synagogues in the UK – Stamford Hill and Ilford. They were fortunate to be led by the indefatigable David Elias, who acted as a father to his community and kept open house for all who sought his help.

Some of the Indians brought the ways of the old country with them. I was once called to help a newly married couple who were quarrelling. The mother of the bride demanded to see the bed sheets to prove that her daughter was a virgin. I had to calm her down and ask her to show a little patience. Others were affluent and highly anglicised. There was a lovely man called J.R. Jacobs from Calcutta, who was one of the donors to the Indian synagogue in Stamford Hill. "Rabbi," he would say to me, "whenever you want to go to India, I still have my house there with seventeen servants. You can go and enjoy yourself there." He was living in St John's Wood but he did not want his servants back in India to be impoverished, so he retained their services.

Religiously, the Indians were steered by Rabbi Solomon Sassoon, who himself hailed from a Baghdadi Indian family which had come to Britain some years before. He was the only one of them to remain truly religious and must have been conscious of the way others had assimilated into English society. One of his relatives, Reuben, had been a friend of Edward VII and there is a portrait of him, cigar in hand, looking exactly like the pleasure-loving king. Rabbi Sassoon was a noted scholar who had inherited a magnificent collection of Hebrew books and manuscripts from his father. He swam against the mainstream, living in Letchworth, where he led a small synagogue and community. Although he was a member of the Spanish and Portuguese, he came to pray with us only on Tishah b'Av, when he was able to drive. Indeed, he worried that spiritually we were too tepid and he kept a watchful eye on Dr Gaon lest he veer too much to the left. More sympathetic towards a Charedi way of thinking, Rabbi Sassoon presaged a trend that became more marked in subsequent years. One of his disciples was a young artist who was persuaded to go to Gateshead and went on to build a reputation as a kabbalist in Israel: he was Rabbi Yaakov Hillel. In the early 1980s, Rabbi Hillel helped to found a new Indian community in Hendon, Od Yosef Hai, the largest of a number of independent Oriental synagogues which sprung up in the area but which chose to keep their distance from the Spanish and Portuguese Community.

Had the Spanish and Portuguese adopted a more flexible approach, we might have stood a better chance of wooing some of the new communities to accept a closer relationship. They must have thought the formality of our services cold and they might have responded more favourably if we had incorporated some of their customs earlier rather than adopt the attitude, "When in England, do as the English Sephardim do." But the various Oriental synagogues were always too disparate to be coaxed under one umbrella. Dr Gaon tried gamely in his time to make a success of the Association of Sephardi Synagogues but even Moses would have struggled to unify these different tribes.

As the number of Oriental Jews who settled in Britain grew over time, conditions for those who remained in the Middle East became more difficult in the wake of the Arab-Israeli conflict. The net tightened around them and made escape near impossible unless they could arrange to be smuggled illegally out of the country. Occasionally, they were allowed to leave temporarily to receive medical treatment here. A little girl from Syria came to London with her father to have an operation on her leg which could not be carried out in her home country. The father had brought with him a letter to me from the Chief Rabbi of Syria, Ibrahim Hamra, who wrote, "We warmly beg you to render all possible help." When Estelle and I went to the poky little hotel in Bayswater where they were staying, I asked how they managed to get permission to travel. The father explained that his wife and other children were still behind in Syria; they were, in effect, hostages. Our synagogue responded generously when I appealed from the pulpit for assistance for the child. A couple of Arabic-speaking doctors in the community, Victor Dellal and David Sopher, looked after her. Estelle went to buy new clothes for her. She came back a second time and her treatment proved successful.

I had been involved in some of the protests on behalf of Syrian Jewry that gathered steam in the 1970s, reciting prayers on a march to Downing Street and outside the West End offices of Syrian Airways. A community of 30,000 before the establishment of the state of Israel had dropped to around 4,500. But public activism had to be balanced with quiet diplomacy. At the inaugural meeting of the UK branch of the International Committee for the Rescue of Syrian Jewry in 1985, I suggested that it would help to invite on to it a former Syrian Jew who was now in the UK. But it was pointed out this was too risky, as all of them had relatives remaining in Syria.

In another case, a little boy with a terrible heart condition was sent here from Iraq with the assistance of the charity now known as World Jewish Relief. We put him and his sister, who had accompanied him, up in our house. Their father had given money to his brother, who was living in France, to pay for the operation but it never arrived – the uncle had pocketed it himself. So we had to raise the funds instead. The boy lived into his forties in Israel, and when we go to Israel, we still call on his sister, who remains grateful for what we did.

One of our members, Ellis Douek, a distinguished ENT surgeon whose family had come from Egypt, was once invited to Iraq to demonstrate some surgical procedures. After completing an operation in Baghdad, as part of the normal post-operative care, he called on the patient to make sure he was all right. It was only then that he realised that there, before him, was none other than Saddam Hussein. It might have been better for the Middle East if Saddam had never got up from the operating table but Mr Douek – who happens to be the brother of the food writer Claudia Roden – was too good a surgeon.

No event did as much to draw attention to the dangers faced by our co-religionists in the Middle East than the execution in early 1969 of nine Jews in Baghdad – the majority in their teens –

on spurious charges of spying for Israel and the public hanging of their bodies the next day to whip up hatred among the baying crowds. Saddam Hussein had taken control in a coup only a few months before. The horror and grief was all the more immediate for us because some of the men had relatives among our own congregation. I visited the home where a brother of one of the victims, Ezra Naji Zilkha, was sitting shivah.

At a large protest outside the Iraqi Embassy in London, where British Jews gathered to express their outrage, I blew the shofar. It was a "solemn affirmation against persecution on earth, a cry of anguish to heaven", as I recalled ten years later at a memorial service at Bevis Marks for the nine martyrs. For all the bitter experience of recent times, I counselled then against dwelling only on enmity between Jew and Arab and ignoring the periods of co-existence between Jews and Muslims, which might instead point the way to the future. "If we can, as we do, live happily with our Christian fellow beings even while forgetting the many calamities which we suffered in the name of Christendom," I said, "then surely we can do as much with Islam also." I asked the congregation to pray that what happened in Iraq was not repeated in Iran.

But the turbulent currents of Middle Eastern politics that swept Ayatollah Khomeini into power in Iran in 1979 did not leave the community of that country unscathed. Iranian Jewry had been led for many years by Habib Elghanian, the founder of a plastics business and a philanthropist who supported Jewish schools and other causes. In the 1960s, he built what was then Tehran's tallest building (which collapsed in a fire early in 2017). He and his brother also had business interests in Israel, erecting a skyscraper in Ramat Gan. While members of his family were among those who packed their bags and came to the UK after the regime change, he remained in Iran both out of a sense of duty and a belief that his prominent status would protect him. But he was arrested in 1979 on account of his connections "with Israel and Zionism", hauled before a revolutionary Islamic court and shot. He was a scapegoat whose killing was intended to send a warning signal to the Jewish community to keep its head down. Three months after the service for the Baghdad victims, I conducted a memorial service for him at Lauderdale Road, the first but sadly not the last for an Iranian Jew. A year later I had to do the same for a compatriot who suffered a similar fate, Albert Danielpour.

The shock of Elghanian's death spurred an increasing Jewish exodus from Iran. The service we held had the effect of drawing attention to the fears of Iranian Jewry and at first the Israeli Embassy encouraged me to raise their plight. But then word came from the Embassy to avoid any public condemnation of or demonstration against Iran. As I later discovered, the Israelis were covertly selling arms to Iran during its war with Iraq and did not want any diaspora rabbis rocking the boat.

In the meantime, we worked quietly to bring here as many Iranian Jews as we could, while trying to support those who remained. I held *shiurim*, religious classes, in a house of the Chitayat family for a group of them in London and they told me that they had gained more Judaism in three months than in their entire lives in Iran. Some of them did venture back to retrieve their assets, despite more than one meeting in my home to discourage them from taking the risk. The Iranian authorities later gave us permission to send prayer books and other religious items to the country, which we have continued to do over the years, thanks to an anonymous donor in Switzerland. Once or twice a year I despatch pairs of tefillin. Sometimes I would receive a gift in return – I have a *luach*, a Hebrew calendar, with the picture of Ayatollah Khomeini at the top, a revealing detail of their delicate situation.

At one stage, I even started getting invitations to visit Iran but I was dissuaded from accepting by a senior member of the

Oriental community in London. He thought my visit would serve no purpose other than a PR exercise to create the impression of Iranian goodwill towards the Jews, as opposed to hostility to Israel. Some years later, when we began a training scheme for rabbis, a request came from the Iranian community to send them a couple of rabbis. That being hardly a realistic proposition, instead I suggested they send a couple of young men to train with us in London – an offer which was not taken up.

While the 10,000 or so Jews of Iran – some Iranian Jews in the diaspora put the number as double that – now represent the largest Jewish population left in the Middle East outside Israel, the historic community of Iraq has gone. As that country plunged into chaos after the fall of Saddam, we received a request for money from a Christian minister in Baghdad, who wanted it to help secure the freedom of some of its last remaining Jews. It so happens that one of our communal offices remains that of the *parnas dos cautivos*, created in 1670 to ransom the hostages of pirates. Every year we dutifully appointed a member of the congregation to fill it but it was a purely honorary title which must have been inactive for most of the previous 200 years. Now I could tell its holder, "We have got something to do."

In London, the émigré Iraqi-Jewish community gradually moved from the margins of Anglo-Jewish life to a more visible role. In no small part this was thanks to the leadership of Sir Naim Dangoor, who at 101 became the second oldest person to be knighted when he received the honour in June 2015, a few months before his death. Educated at the University of London, he had prospered on his return to Iraq by winning the franchise to bottle Coca Cola. But like many Iraqi Jews, he had to leave his assets behind him when life became too precarious and he eventually made his home here in the mid-1960s. Whereas other Iraqi Jews were content to melt into the wider Jewish community, as the grandson of a former Chief Rabbi of Baghdad he took special pride in his cultural heritage and was determined to preserve it. He persuaded some of his compatriots to join him in opening a social and cultural club in West Kensington which operated as a centre for Iraqi Jews for many years. Had he not done so, I believe many might have drifted away from organised Judaism altogether. In 1971, he started a magazine called *The Scribe* to ensure the survival of Iraqi-Jewish traditions, penning articles under the *nom de plume* of "Exilarch", the traditional title of the leader of Babylonian Jewry since talmudic days. It was also the name he gave to his charitable foundation, which was funded by the substantial proceeds of the property business he set up in London. A big sponsor of education in particular, he supported causes ranging from university scholarships for students from disadvantaged backgrounds in Britain to Jewish studies in China.

I was only too happy to encourage Sir Naim's cultural ventures and the desire of the Iraqi Jews generally to play a greater part within British Jewry. Others such as Dr Davide Sala were also becoming known inside the community. From a family in Iraq which had among other things been agents for Gordon's Gin, Dr Sala had run an underground Zionist movement during the Second World War and was one of the committee of five tasked with organising the exodus of the Jews after the establishment of Israel. As life became more dangerous, he left for Italy before settling in the UK. This "self-effacing millionaire", according to the *Jewish Chronicle*, became a leading supporter of the JIA, the forerunner of the United Jewish Israel Appeal.

In 1985, the Board of Deputies recognised their efforts when it agreed to give three seats to the Iraqis as a group, although they did not form a separate synagogue congregation. As one of the two ecclesiastical authorities of the Board – the other being the Chief Rabbi – I readily certified their application for representation. As far as I was concerned, the Iraqis were a rejuvenating force within our congregation. But others did not see the positive side of their membership of the Board in the same way.

Once again our congregation displayed its gift for disputatiousness. In early January 1986, I received a curt note from the Mahamad, informing me they had written to the president of the Board of Deputies, Lionel Kopelowitz, to say that my ratification of the Iraqi application had been taken "without the prior knowledge or consent of the Mahamad". The previous month, one of our deputies at the Board had openly objected to the independent affiliation of the Iraqis.

Naim Dangoor was outraged. In a letter to the president of the Board of Elders of the Spanish and Portuguese Community, Eric Nabarro, he emphasised the Iraqis' sense of being "a unified congregation with our own tradition which we try to uphold by conducting, for instance, communal Seders every year and also in celebrating Chanukah and Purim". He also referred to the High Holy Day services according to Iraqi custom which I was trying to arrange for them. He noted that opposition to the Iraqi membership of the Board had been voiced by the deputy of a congregation in which they formed the majority. "I find this attack very hard to take, coming as it does from fellow Sephardim," he said.

Blessed indeed is the rabbi who does not have to negotiate the obstacle course of synagogue politics. The row blew over and the Spanish and Portuguese Community had every reason to be grateful to the largesse of the Iraqis in subsequent years. I had long nurtured the ambition of having somewhere that could act as a broader educational base for disseminating the Sephardi tradition and its values of synthesis and tolerance. But it took many years to accomplish. In November 1994, we were finally able to open the Sephardi Centre at Lauderdale Road, the centrepiece of which was a magnificent new library. Its activities would include a programme one evening a week aimed at the under-thirty-fives. It would be a place, I said at the launch, to display "a culture that has never been studied or appreciated properly in this country".

The new library was named in memory of K. C. (Khedouri) Shasha, an Iraqi businessman who had settled in Manchester in the early years of the 20th century, and his wife Jeanne, whose charitable foundation made it possible. I had been giving a talk on Jewish education at Wembley Synagogue and when I mentioned my dream of a centre, my frustration that nothing had come of it so far must have showed. In the audience happened to be Dr David Sopher, one of the sons-in-law of K.C. Shasha (who had died in Nice in 1988). He came up to me after the meeting and suggested, "Why don't you go and speak to my son, Rick?" Rick Sopher is a financier with close links to the Rothschild family. When I outlined my plans to him, he readily offered backing. The Shasha Foundation agreed to make available a substantial sum for the project as long as it was under my direct control. But the Board of Elders did not like the thought of the rabbi having so much money to spend and at first voted to turn down the grant. Others, led by Cesare Sacerdoti, thought the idea of spurning such an offer nonsensical and the elders were persuaded to retract their rejection.

A rabbi has to be many things – teacher, preacher, pastor. But one role you won't find in the traditional job spec is that of fundraiser. Since synagogues generally do not sit on endowments, if you want to develop your congregation, you have to be able to secure the means to do so. I have my father to thank for the good fortune of having inherited at least a little of his business skill. Among the donors who contributed to the community were Charles and Maurice Saatchi, whose advertising agency had helped the Margaret Thatcher-led Conservatives to power. The boys were not religious but their parents, Nathan and Daisy, had been regulars at the synagogue for many years. Nathan was one of the first Iraqis who had served on the Mahamad. When I met Charles and Maurice, I told them: "Your mother and father are getting on. Why not give them pleasure and let's do something to honour them." They were only too willing and agreed to help.

We were doing some renovation of the Montefiore Hall at Lauderdale Road at the time and I went to see one of the family, Denzil Sebag-Montefiore, to see if they would contribute. "Abraham, we don't have the money to give you," he said, "and even if we did, I don't know whether we would give it to the synagogue. You have every right to take away the name Montefiore and call it the Saatchi Hall." In my mind, I began to plan some event where the Montefiores would officially hand over the hall to the Saatchis. There was some pleasing historical symmetry. In his day, Sir Moses Montefiore had been a friend of Benjamin Disraeli, the Conservative Prime Minister of Jewish origin. The Saatchi brothers had connections with the modern-day Tories.

Denzil's wife Ruth wrote to me to suggest that if we put a plaque formally recording the transition from "Montefiore" to "Saatchi", that should soothe any "ruffled feelings". But not all the Montefiores shared Denzil and Ruth's equanimity about relinquishing their title to the hall. A story in *The Times* Diary which reported that the Montefiores and Saatchis were at loggerheads helped to scupper my plans. The historian Simon Sebag-Montefiore (a former barmitzvah pupil of mine) was quoted as commenting that it was "as wrong as renaming the Albert Hall as the Philip Hall after the Duke of Edinburgh". A few days later he told the *Jewish Chronicle* that "it would be nice if there is a way to keep the name Montefiore. I feel the hall should be called the Montefiore-Saatchi Hall." I had to find an alternative solution and, as you will see in the next chapter, fortunately I did not have to wait long.

Not only do we have the Shasha Library but the small synagogue we use for weekday services at Lauderdale Road is called the Dangoor Synagogue. There is also the Simon Fattal Succah, endowed by his sons William and Elias Fattal. Without the generosity of the Oriental Jews, we would have found it hard to move forward. The Spanish and Portuguese Community resembled an old English aristocratic family who lived in a grand country house but struggled to afford it. We were like the Duke of Marlborough, who in the late 19th century needed the new money that came with his wife, a wealthy American heiress, to maintain his estate. I became aware, too, that were it not for the many hours I had invested in my pastoral work, holding people's hands when they needed it, they would not have been so forthcoming when the community sought their support. The Iraqis were certainly indispensable to achieving what I believe to be the single most important project in all my years as a rabbi: the Naima Jewish Preparatory School.

4

The Gates of Hope

WHENEVER I CAME home to Gibraltar for the holidays while a student at Carmel, I returned to a community that was generally more observant than the Anglo-Jewry in which many of my school contemporaries had been raised. Jewish businesses in Gibraltar were invariably closed for Shabbat and Yom Tov. Superficially, it appeared that little had changed since before the War. But the intervening years had disrupted our religious continuity. The marriages made by young men who had taken non-Jewish partners, when the evacuation had led to a dearth of young Jewish women, and the easy conversions they obtained in Tangiers, had altered the complexion of the community. Established families frowned on such matches. Jewish education lacked depth and even the primary Jewish school my father had helped to open was not enough on its own to make up for it. But anyone who worried about the future need not have done so; Gibraltarian Jewry was about to undergo a revival.

Its architect was a young rabbi from Italy, Josef Pacifici. He grew up in a patrician family: his father was a judge who had once been friendly with Mussolini but eventually severed his connections with Il Duce and became more Orthodox. The young Josef was sent to Gateshead Yeshivah, whose importance as a centre for preserving the more rigorous traditions of East European Judaism had increased post-War after the ravages of the Holocaust.

Rabbi Pacifici was a first-class educator who transmitted his passion for Judaism to his young acolytes. He chose three of the cleverest boys and three of the cleverest girls and devoted a disproportionate amount of his time to them. One was a cousin of mine, Abraham Hassan, who became a rabbi, and another my sister Loli. When they were ready, he encouraged them to go off to yeshivah or seminary. The example of these model pupils spread. Today there is hardly a boy or girl in Gibraltar who does not go off to yeshivah or seminary after school. As a result, Gibraltar began to look a little more towards modern Gateshead than old Andalucia for its Jewish bearings. My younger brother Hayim, James, also grew up under the influence of Rabbi Pacifici and leans more to the yeshivah world than my elder brother Solomon or me. Hayim was instrumental in strengthening the educational infrastructure by co-founding both the boys' and girls' Jewish high schools and also a *kollel* – no mean feat for a community of 800. Gibraltar nevertheless retains some of its worldlier outlook; if its children now receive a more intensive Jewish education than the pre-War generation, many still go to university and study for the professions.

When I was a Jews' College student and went back to Gibraltar, I would always be invited to give a sermon. Rabbi Pacifici would tell me, "You have learned the most important thing that Jews' College is able to teach you – which is how to speak. So now you can speak, why don't you let me take you to Gateshead?" I was far too ingrained in the customs of the college to take up his offer. Despite my preference for *Minhag Sepharad*,

Sephardi custom, in London over talmudic immersion in Tyneside, we remained close. When I became a rabbi, he counselled me to "devote most of your energy to the young". It was advice I gratefully took.

By that time I was head of the Hebrew classes at Lauderdale Road, having been conscripted to teach years earlier as a student. The headmaster then, Daniel Mendoza, who shared the name of the renowned 18th-century boxer, was a kindly English gentleman who had been headteacher of the Solomon Wolfson School. He felt I had the makings of a good teacher and he didn't often make mistakes, he said. We did our best to lay what foundations of Jewish knowledge we could in the limited time available, which in most cases was little more than two hours on a Sunday morning. While midweek classes were held twice a week, they were sparsely attended. On Shabbat afternoons I used to hold discussion groups in my home for youth who showed greater interest such as Sylvia and Elie Kedourie's son, Michael, who eventually became a rabbi. I was less successful in another case, for while the boy also opted for a spiritual path, it was as a spokesman for the Dalai Lama.

I also tried to supplement what we did in our religion classes by holding Jewish days in the holidays when we would mix learning with entertainment: I would show them a film like *The Ten Commandments* and they would carry out the kind of activities that are now called "informal Jewish education".

A roll call of our pupils would include the BBC's Alan Yentob and the head of the Supreme Court Lord Neuberger. The Neubergers were not Sephardim, but the father, Professor Albert Neuberger, believed we offered a sensible approach to Judaism. I can't recollect Alan Yentob ever showing much interest in religion, whereas his twin brother Robert became a stalwart of the community and served as its first representative on the Jewish Leadership Council and the chairman of the Jewish Preparatory

School. Siblings might display differences in religious attitude even at a young age. I remember one spiritually-minded boy who, when he was six or seven, came home one day agitated from a party. He told his mother that he had seen his younger brother scoffing non-kosher sausages. "What did you do?" she asked him. "I said the Shema every time he ate one," he replied.

For many years I took personal responsibility for preparing boys for their barmitzvah. It is not uncommon now for a family in London to have to engage a private tutor to teach their son his barmitzvah portion at considerable expense. But I saw it as an important part of my rabbinical duties and there was no question of charging for it. We also wanted boys to do more than the bare minimum of simply being capable of reciting their portion on the day. We wanted them to be familiar with the prayer book and from an early age to know how to lead prayers such as the *Zemirot* or *Musaf* on Shabbat morning.

Among Sephardim it is also the tradition for boys to learn how to chant a *haftarah* when they are as young as six. When my own grandsons, Julian's children, Avi, Jamie and Daniel, reached that age, I taught them myself. I had a reproduction made of an antique *yad*, a Torah pointer, from a Gibraltar synagogue and I gave them a copy inscribed with their name and the year in which they said their first *haftarah*. Every boy in our community who recites his first *haftarah* also receives a gift of £25. There was a member of the congregation who, although he was a man of limited means, left me £100 in his will to reward boys for learning their *haftarah*. Though his fund quickly ran out, I have used another charitable trust to honour his wishes since. One father, in a letter thanking me for our policy, said, "Your insistence in pushing children to do parts of the service by making David do a *haftarah* last year does make a difference... you help us realise what our children are capable of achieving."

I also became known as something of a tefillin pusher, stressing the importance to boys coming up to their barmitzah of a mitzvah which literally binds them to daily Jewish practice. I would impress on them that I had never missed a day in my life, putting on tefillin in buses, planes and all kinds of places. My son once got a call from his son Jamie in an anxious state. He had gone on a day trip with his school, City of London, to Paris, but they were stuck there and had to stay overnight. He and a couple of his friends had not taken their tefillin with them and didn't know what to do. Julian started ringing round Paris until Lubavitch came to the rescue with a pair of tefillin, which they brought to the boys at the Arc de Triomphe.

One former pupil of mine, Daniel Jackson, now a professor of computer science at MIT, told me recently how much he had taken my words to heart. When he had sought guidance from his own rabbi on how to say his prayers on a long flight to Asia and was told that if he felt uncomfortable, he could skip tefillin that day, he said he was "frankly astonished" to hear such a suggestion. "I have certainly missed a bunch of days, but by my reckoning only about two in each decade," he said. Mentioning his gratitude too, for having been taught how to lead prayers, he added: "The Spanish and Portuguese music is still to me the very centrepiece of my experience of *tefillah* [prayer], inseparable from the words and their meaning." Whenever he looked up from the reading desk at the motto in Hebrew above the ark, "Know Before Whom You Stand," they would remind him to "temper any sense of importance because it wasn't a performance in front of human beings, and second, that I should forgive myself when I messed up, since it's the *kavannah* [intention] that matters most."

Personally tutoring the boys helped me to get to know them before the actual day of their barmitzvah. One of the moving addresses I gave to a barmitzvah was to a boy who was profoundly deaf. I placed him near to me on the *tebah*, the bimah, so he could

86

lip-read what I said to him. Every so often, if he could not follow, he would raise his hand and I would repeat the sentence. Many had tears in their eyes.

Although too many of the descendants of our historic families may have been lost to assimilation, some of our congregants could trace their origins back to the 18th century and even earlier. When I addressed Mark Pacifico, a Harrow pupil, on his barmitzvah, I reminded him of an extraordinary episode involving one of his ancestors. Don Pacifico was a Gibraltarian Jew who was living in Athens in the mid-19th century – and also an ancestor of my maternal grandmother Hassan. One of the Rothschilds was due to visit Greece and to forestall any trouble during his visit the authorities had banned the locals from performing their custom at Easter of burning an effigy of Judas Iscariot. Incensed, a mob found an alternative outlet and burned down Don Pacifico's house instead. When the Greeks delayed payment of restitution, Lord Palmerston, the British Prime Minister, despatched a gunboat to prompt them. Don Pacifico's money is still lying in Chancery, waiting to be legitimately claimed.

From time to time a photograph of me in clerical garb would crop up in the *Jewish Chronicle*, among a group of smartly dressed girls in white blouses and hats. We would prepare them for the annual confirmation ceremony – we did not call it batmitzvah then – which we held for them on a Sunday afternoon. As the Orthodox community in Britain gradually became more conscious of the religious needs of girls, the group services became unpopular and we instead offered individual ceremonies for a batmitzvah on Shabbat morning.

All this time I was mindful of what Rabbi Pacifici had achieved in Gibraltar and tried to emulate him by devoting special attention to the pupils who seemed most promising. There is a famous saying in *Ethics of the Fathers*, "find yourself a teacher". For a rabbi, you might add also, "find yourself disciples".

Nurturing future leaders is one of the most important investments you can make for the next generation.

I encouraged those who were keen to pursue their Jewish studies to come to me for extra, one-to-one tuition. A number of those dedicated students went on to become rabbis themselves, like Michael Kedourie, Jonathan Cohen and Jonathan Rietti. Jonathan Rietti, the son of the actor Robert Rietti, once came to see me when he was around thirteen and told me that he was praying to God for his mother to fall pregnant and have a boy; what's more, the baby should be born on his birthday. I said he was asking for rather a lot. His mother did become pregnant and gave Jonathan a brother but there were a few days' difference between their birthdays. "I didn't get all my prayers answered," he said sadly. "What calendar are you using?" I replied. "The ordinary calendar," he said. "Shouldn't we try looking at the Hebrew calendar?" I suggested. When we turned to that, we saw that both boys were in fact born on the same date.

I fancied I could spot a potential rabbi from among my barmitzvah boys but while I was right in some instances, I was way off the mark in others. If I came across a pupil with an unusually strong spiritual inclination, I'd ask the parents about their background and more often than not they would tell me that one of their grandparents or great-grandparents had been a rabbi. There must be such a thing as rabbinic genes. They might skip a generation or two but eventually they will out. Another factor I noticed with the boys who became rabbis was that they invariably had a mother who was religiously sensitive and cared for their spiritual welfare.

Jonathan Cohen and another of my pupils, Daniel Halfon, who both now live in Israel, became experts in our hazanut, our liturgical traditions, and now promote it to a younger generation through Facebook and YouTube. Jonathan's two brothers also became rabbis. I once asked their father, who was high up in the advertising world, if he could design us an advert to highlight the importance of kashrut. He came up with a catchy poster which I still use today, "Eat kosher to keep body and soul together."

For all my efforts, I would have to admit that in one respect I did not succeed. Once my star pupils headed off to yeshivah, they were taken over by the Charedi world. They fell under the spell of a more uncompromising brand of Orthodoxy which had little time for the middle-of-the-road traditionalism represented by the Spanish and Portuguese synagogue. As they became more observant, they mixed with religious Ashkenazi boys who suggested which yeshivot they should attend, such as Dvar Yerushalaim in Israel. I was rather naïve in those days and did not appreciate how influential such places had become in both inculcating a Charedi outlook and undermining any alternative. They were too young for Jews' College, which now only took students for degrees. The Montefiore College catered primarily for young men from Tunisia, Morocco and Algeria, starting with English classes.

My students remained grateful that I had helped them. A few years ago I received a letter from Jonathan Rietti, now a leading Jewish educator based in the Charedi stronghold of Monsey, thanking me for "being the first one to ignite the light under my soul and set it on its journey to the service of God". But if I did not lose touch with them altogether, I was no longer their mentor.

In truth, there was not a great choice of institutions upholding the Sephardi ethos to which they could have gone, even if they had wanted to. I had been made all too aware of that when I spent a few weeks on sabbatical in Israel some years earlier, in 1970, after being granted a Sir Robert Waley Cohen Travelling Scholarship by the Jewish Memorial Council. In the resulting booklet, *The Sephardim – A Problem of Survival?*, I expressed my worries about the prospects for a distinctive Sephardi outlook, at least one committed to the traditions of synthesis and halachic leniency with which I sympathised. "Unless Sephardi education can be drastically improved, Sephardim will continue to fail to exert any influence at all on the religious, cultural and social life of Israel," I wrote. The typical Sephardi seemed "more passive and retiring" than his Ashkenazi fellow and the current state of Sephardi institutions was bleak, though I added, "not desperate".

One student who remained closer to modern Orthodoxy was Gideon Sylvester, now Israel Rabbi for the United Synagogue, who was some years younger than the others I have mentioned. Rather than Gateshead, he opted to do his rabbinic studies in one of the newer Israeli yeshivot which became popular with English-speaking Jews. Gideon was the son of Sam Sylvester, a solicitor whose clients included Sir Paul McCartney and The Who. Sam had crossed over to us from Hampstead Synagogue and become one of my most loyal allies. When Gideon announced that he was going to enter the rabbinate, his father said, "I told you to take Rabbi Levy seriously – but not that seriously."

For the vast majority of our youngsters, yeshivah was never on their horizon and their formal Jewish education effectively ended at bar- and batmitzvah. Like most congregational rabbis, I ran *shiurim*, classes, for small groups in my home on Maimonides and other texts. But in mainstream British Jewry at the time, adult education was a barren landscape. It was only in the late 1970s that Robin and Nitza Spiro began their pioneering courses in Jewish history and Kopul's son, Rabbi Michael Rosen, who believed he could offer a more creative approach to Orthodoxy outside the establishment, founded his independent Yakar centre.

I realised we could not allow this vacuum to continue. If Jewish organisations were not led by people with a mature appreciation of Jewish civilisation, how could we expect the community to prosper? In 1978 I launched the Young Jewish Leadership Institute with a former Jews' College contemporary, Rabbi Moshe Edelmann, who was from Denmark and who had come here as a *shaliach*. Our target audience was potential lay leaders from their early twenties to their mid-forties. Nothing like it had previously been attempted in London, so far as we were aware. We wrote in the first brochure, "No Jewish community in the diaspora today can survive unless it has a lay leadership which is…. conscious of its heritage. Though there are many young men and women today willing and able to become leaders of their people, they have not, perhaps through no fault of their own, been exposed to Jewish learning in its widest sense."

The cover of the brochure for the institute featured an engraving of Haham David Nieto, quill in hand with a globe on his desk and looking every inch the 18th-century man of letters in his wig. He epitomised the great Sephardi tradition, renowned not only for his Jewish knowledge but also for being a Doctor of Medicine as well as a poet, astronomer and mathematician.

We wanted to provide university-level content and we certainly made demands on the students. Entry was selective, participants had to have a degree and pay £40 for the privilege of studying with us, though we offered a few scholarships. The course consisted of two-and-a-half hours of lectures one evening a week for forty weeks, culminating in a three-week session in Israel under the auspices of the Hebrew University. Candidates were expected to present a paper on each of the three areas we covered: Judaism, which included Maimonides's laws of charity, prayer and study along with selected biblical commentators; European Jewish history; and Zionism.

The Israel component was certainly a highlight. It characterised my involvement with the country over the years, which was always more educational than political. While the course was based at Lauderdale Road, it enjoyed the wider support not only of the Hebrew University but also other communal bodies. The Mahamad was happy for the congregation's name to be associated with the venture. By the third year, we had enrolled more than ninety students. We were able to attract some of the top Jewish lecturers, Immanuel Jakobovits, Jonathan Sacks, Chimen Abramsky, Irving Jacobs, as well as taking advantage of Israelis on sabbatical such as Menachem Ben-Sasson, now president of the Hebrew University, or the geographer Yehoshua Ben-Arieh. Many of our graduates went on to take leading positions in Jewish organisations.

I was fortunate, too, to be able to count on the organisational ability of my secretary, Golda Zimmerman. She had been the *Jewish Chronicle*'s first Israel correspondent, a stringer for *The Times* and a speechwriter for Sir Isaac Wolfson. I have never been terribly strong on detail myself. I've been more proficient at coming up with ideas and then finding the right people to help me implement them. Golda was a tower of strength.

Whatever I had done, I knew it was not enough. The Spanish and Portuguese Jews' Congregation perhaps suffered what someone has called an "edifice complex", overly consumed with the preservation of buildings. We have a tendency to be too concerned with structure at the expense of content. It was a theme I often returned to in sermons. While it was right to take pride in our magnificent synagogues in Amsterdam, London or New York, I observed at the centenary service of Lauderdale Road in 1996, we had a choice. "We can be like a hereditary peer who inherits a title and estate," I said. "He usually becomes a caretaker. He tries to preserve the fabric of his castle, he cleans the oil paintings, repairs the Persian rugs and he glories in a past that is no more."

Or we can use the past as a platform to build for the future, innovating by creating educational programmes.

Not long after I had become a rabbi, the synagogue was visited by one of the leading American-Jewish philanthropists, Charlie Bendheim, who had come to the UK to see his daughter Judith (she married Rabbi Harris Guedalia, who was a rabbinic student contemporary of mine and with whom we have remained friendly since). His opinion was blunt: "You are wasting your time

concentrating on a few children here and there. Open a school."
It set me a challenge which, however long it took, I knew I had to
accept. Our son Julian went to Jewish schools, North-West
London Jewish Day School in Willesden and to the Hasmonean
High School in London. But in the 1960s and '70s, middle-class
Jews commonly aspired to send their children to the top English
private schools. Jewish schools simply didn't figure on their radar,
though a few opted for Carmel or, a half-way house, Polack's
House at Clifton.

Traditionally, we ask a blessing for new-born children, that
they should enjoy "Torah, *chuppah*, and good deeds". How many
of those who celebrated their bar or batmitzvah with us actually
made it to the *chuppah* I can't say, but fewer than their parents
hoped. As more and more of our congregants' children married
out, the deficiencies of our education system became all too clear.
I bewailed the situation in a High Holy Day sermon in 1970; "Any
educationalist will admit that two consecutive hours a week with
a whole week to forget what a child has learned is of little value
itself." I would badger Sir Alan Mocatta and other leaders with
the argument that if we simply relied on Sunday mornings, the
children of the community would not be its future members.

One of the first institutions the early Sephardim created not
long after the resettlement was a Jewish school, with the name
Shaare Tikvah, Gates of Hope, which they maintained for more
than 200 years. But I was unable to persuade the Mahamad to
throw its weight behind a modern successor. Even friends such as
Robert Cavalho thought I was pursuing a pipe-dream and told me
to stop worrying about it.

I would have long conversations about my school ambitions
with Conrad Morris, a communal activist and funder who later
became treasurer of Lord Jakobovits's Jewish Educational
Development Trust. We had become friendly through having
children at the North-West London Jewish Day School and,

toying with the idea of sending them to a non-Jewish secondary, had discussed the idea of opening Jewish classes for the numerous Jewish children in such schools. But I realised that if I was ever going to open a school, I would have to gather support within my own congregation.

What turned the tide was the emergence of the new generation from families of Iraqi origin such as David Dangoor, son of Naim, and Jonathan Bekhor, who wanted a Jewish school to send their children to. One or two of the older members such as Alfred Magnus – a descendant of David Levi, who translated the Spanish and Portuguese prayer books into English in the 18th century – were also ready to trust me with their children. They were not going to be cowed by any disapproving noises coming from the Mahamad. Our circle of prospective parents grew.

Early in 1983 we placed an advert in the *Jewish Chronicle* to invite applications for the Jewish Preparatory School for the autumn. I was to be principal but I knew that I did not have the expertise to create a school from scratch, so I recruited Anthony Wulwick, the newly retired head of North-West London Jewish Day, to be our educational consultant. A stroke of luck also came our way. I heard there was someone else who was looking to start their own Jewish school around the same time: Dr Judy Chain, the daughter of the Nobel-Prize winning antibiotics pioneer Sir Ernest Chain. She agreed to join forces and became our first headmistress.

Judy's passion to do the best for children was palpable from the word go and she got us off to a flying start. She cared deeply about every child and no problem would escape her attention. Her mother Lady Beloff-Chain, a biochemist too, came on board as a trustee, proving to be a committed supporter. Golda Zimmerman's practical nous was as invaluable as ever.

If JPS were to enjoy any success, I recognised it would have to offer a good enough secular education to enable its pupils to sit for the best London secondary schools. It would espouse the traditional Sephardi belief in – as one of our later brochures put it – "the natural co-existence of Torah life and secular culture". But as we made it clear from the start, it was open equally to Ashkenazi as well as Sephardi children. In an article in the *Jewish Chronicle*, I expressed the hope that it would plant in its pupils a sufficiently strong sense of Jewishness for them to withstand whatever non- or even anti-Jewish influences they later encountered. Quoting from a governance code produced for Shaare Tikvah some hundred years earlier, I said that we too wanted to raise children "in such virtuous and religious habits as can alone… make them a blessing to themselves and a credit to the community to which they belong."

Against the persistent opposition, I took comfort from the following thought. Every day in our morning prayers (just before the Shema), two of the qualities we ascribe to God are *oseh chadashot* and *ba'al hamilchamot*, "Creator of new things" and "Master of wars". Put the two together and you derive the idea that you can't do anything new without stirring up arguments against it. Some within the lay leadership of the congregation simply did not like the thought that someone they considered an employee had the nerve to do something without their blessing. Some, perhaps, worried that it would distract me from my ministerial duties. But there was also a prevalent fear that I might fall flat on my face, that the school would prove unviable and end up a stain on the congregation's good name.

In September 1983, JPS opened its doors to its first complement of pupils, fifteen girls and thirteen boys in a nursery and reception class. It was an encouraging number. For our motto, I chose a verse from Proverbs, "Start a child on the right road and even in old age he will not leave." For the first two years we were able to use the suite of classrooms at the synagogue in Maida Vale which had been built only a few years earlier. But the Mahamad considered that as we were a fee-paying establishment and that most of the pupils were not children of our members, it was fair for the synagogue to charge us rent for the premises. Not everyone thought it was the most charitable thing to do.

At Carmel, I always took pride in my uniform; we used to buy our purple Carmel blazers from Harrods. JPS pupils were neatly attired in uniforms designed by the Chelsea fashion house Bellville Sassoon, which was jointly owned by David Sassoon, a member of the Sephardi community. The boys were originally kitted out in corduroy knickerbockers, which I thought made them look more the public school part, though I was soon persuaded these were impractical as it was hard to pull socks over the hem in winter. Our children wear blue blazers with maroon trousers for boys and skirts for girls; in summer, the girls switch to light blue and white striped dresses.

But one thing I was adamant about was that an article of Jewish observance such as tzitzit should not be treated as part of any uniform, to be discarded after school. I remember boys at Carmel returning to school after the holidays and saying that this was the first time they had put on the tzitzit and tefillin for weeks. I wanted the boys at JPS to wear tzitzit out of love. So I did not make it compulsory. I would come in and show my tzitzit and say "This is what we have got to wear and if you would like to wear one, I will give you one." And their hands would shoot up to request one. Similarly, I did not force the boys to wear kippot either, except when they ate, were saying prayers or studied Torah. Although it has become standard for Orthodox men to keep their heads covered at all times, there are authoritative rabbis who do not require this. It has also seemed better to me to coax rather than compel.

We use the Sephardi liturgy and, as is the Sephardi custom, recite every word of the prayers aloud. There is no better way to familiarise children with the prayers and by the age of eight, they will know many of them by heart. One former pupil, David Douer, from the year which left in 2009, recalled the £5 reward I offered to children when they mastered *Al Hamichya*, the blessing said on various foods such as biscuits, since it is long and difficult to remember. "From then on I never forgot it because of the importance you placed on it," he told me. I stipulated that the children had to donate at least ten per cent of their prize money to charity.

Our children will also read more clearly than some rabbis who are prone to mumble when they pray. I arranged special lessons for the boys with my colleagues Rabbi Israel Elia and Hazan Halfon Benarroch to learn how to chant the *Zemirot* and the *haftarah*, as we did in the synagogue. We want to make sure that children are equipped with the basics and, however religious or not they choose to be when they are older, they will not find a synagogue service alien to them.

A quarter of the curriculum is devoted to Jewish studies with a strong emphasis on Chumash with Rashi (the medieval Bible commentator) as the basis of knowledge of the Torah. While now we teach Ivrit, we did not do so at the beginning, for which I incurred some criticism. My answer was that I would rather teach the children to speak to God before they speak to an Israeli policeman. In 1988 we held our first Shabbaton at Lauderdale Road for pupils and their families, laying on a hot lunch; as the *Jewish Chronicle* reported, the event swelled attendance at the synagogue's Saturday morning by a half.

I was fortunate in my choice of heads of Jewish studies, who came with a wealth of experience. In 1987, we were joined by Louise Hillman, who had been head teacher of the Independent Jewish Day School. When Louise left, I appointed Fayge Levenburg, who was the daughter of one of the luminaries of Gateshead, Rabbi Moshe Schwab. Despite her background in Charedi schools, she was ready to adapt to a different environment. We respected each other's differences – she would never teach Talmud to girls, whereas I would, so I gave way to her on that – and we never argued. She did wonder, though, about my not making it compulsory for boys to wear tzitzit and kippah, confiding her worries to Rabbi Pacifici, whom I had also enlisted as an educational adviser. Despite his own, more right-wing outlook, he understood our milieu. "Rabbi Levy knows what he is doing," he reassured her.

Fayge often picked Charedi girls of eighteen and nineteen straight out of seminary to teach Jewish studies and they would stay with us for two or three years until they got married. They might not have had formal pedagogical training but what they brought was a passion for Judaism and a deep spirituality which I felt inspired the children.

When famous rabbis from Israel were in town, such as Rabbi Ovadia Yosef and the kabbalist Rabbi Yitzchak Kedourie, I would bring them to see the school and bless the children. One day a venerable yeshivah head from Jerusalem, Rabbi Chaim Pinchas Scheinberg, came to visit. He was famed for wearing dozens of pairs of tzitzit at the same time and he certainly made an impression. Next day, one our pupils, Daniel Hunter, turned up at school, padded with as many pairs of tzitzit as he could muster.

The Maida Vale Synagogue could only be a temporary dwelling-place so I had to begin the search for permanent premises for the school immediately. Almost all of the land in the immediate area, including the synagogue site, was owned by the Church of England. I thought of one possible source of help. The brother of Denzil Sebag-Montefiore had grown up in our synagogue and was a spiritually-minded young man. Unfortunately – at least from our perspective – he went away to boarding school at Rugby, where, beyond the orbit of the Jewish community, he converted to Christianity. But the Right Reverend Hugh Montefiore, then Bishop of Birmingham, never tried to hide his Jewish origins and wrote a book *On Being a Jewish Christian*. "Bishop, you were barmitzvah in my synagogue," I reminded him. He was happy to look for us and found one possible local site, though it turned out not to be suitable. When I got to know him a little better, I told him, "If we had had a Jewish school, you would have been Chief Rabbi, not a bishop." At the funerals I conducted for his brothers, he recited Kaddish more fluently than anyone.

It was another religious organisation which provided us with our home. Bayswater Synagogue in Paddington had been one of the original constituents of the United Synagogue in 1870, the august seat of Hermann Adler before he became Chief Rabbi and Sir Herman Gollancz. Post-war, its fortunes declined and when it was scheduled for demolition to make way for a flyover, the United Synagogue had a windfall in its sights. It thought it would be able to relocate the remnant of the congregation while reaping most of the proceeds from the sale. Bayswater's membership had other ideas and took the United Synagogue to court to force it to build them an alternative. The new Bayswater Synagogue opened in Maida Vale, a splendid marbled affair which could seat 750 – far more than necessary but ensuring that not a penny went to the US.

It had been mooted as the headquarters of Chief Rabbi Jakobovits shortly after he took office but nothing came of the idea. By the time we started JPS, its congregation had dwindled even further, it had fallen into deficit and the US wanted to put it up for sale. The half-acre site had a hall, classrooms, flats and a playground; it had potential for development, at the same time we could use it straight away.

The father of one of our pupils, the writer and music critic Naftali (Norman) Lebrecht, happened to belong to Bayswater. He had first become interested in Lauderdale Road when taking a break from the service at Bayswater one Kippur afternoon, he had strolled past the nearby Sephardi synagogue and was entranced by the melody he heard coming out of it. He helped to persuade his fellow-members that we would be worthy inheritors of the building. So there would be no legal hurdles to cross this time. I will never forget the words of the United Synagogue president Victor Lucas, grateful that at last the white elephant was off its hands. "A building which began as a *Chillul Hashem* [a profanation of God's name] will now be a *Kiddush Hashem* [a sanctification of God's name]," he said.

I needed to find £300,000 but I was lucky to have the money without having to mount a lengthy fundraising campaign. Jonathan Bekhor pledged a third, while the remainder came from another Iraqi family who had made their name in business, Sami and David Shamoon. I had conducted the funeral of their mother and they were looking for a good cause to support in her memory.

Shortly before the conclusion of the sale, I received a phone call from Asher Fishman, treasurer of the United Synagogue. "You are very irresponsible, Rabbi Levy," he rebuked me. "We've barely a month to go before completion and you have not made any mortgage arrangements." The United Synagogue wanted its money. "You need have no worries, Mr Fishman," I assured him, "the Iraqis pay cash."

So a few days later, I headed off one lunchtime into town to collect the contribution from the Shamoons. I made my way down Park Lane, turned past the Hilton Hotel and came to a place where you would not expect to see a rabbi. It was the first time I had entered a casino. The only cards I was used to dealing with were those on which I made notes for my sermon. Sami and David were busy, so I sat patiently and had a plate of smoked salmon. When they were done, they pulled out their chequebooks and I returned to Maida Vale with two-thirds of the money in my pocket.

Two years after its opening, JPS moved to the new site in

September 1985. By 1987, the pupil roll had grown to ninety and Mrs Lever-Chain, as Judy had become after her marriage, had added a computer and science section. In 1988, we launched a major appeal to build additional classrooms and improve facilities to enable us to expand our intake to 150. The Sephardi business community warmed to the school. David Djanogly, who was a regular attender of my *shiurim*, organised fundraising dinners, where guest speakers included my uncle, Sir Joshua Hassan, and the industrialist Lord Alliance, who had arrived in the UK as a boy from Iran. The generosity of many others is commemorated in rooms named after them.

The willingness of our benefactors to invest in education contrasted with the reluctance that had been shown by some of the congregation's leadership. I once calculated that the community owned enough cemetery land to bury people for a hundred years. Yet we had put aside £1 million to buy additional burial space. In a sermon I gave I said, "I had a dream. I woke up in twenty years' time and I went to the cemetery. There were acres and acres of land, but there were no Jews to bury because we failed to educate them." It would have been better to take the money and put it in a school. I was rapped over the knuckles for daring to have even made the suggestion. And then at a meeting where it was discussed, one critic offered the idiosyncratic argument. "Rabbi Levy is wrong," he said. "There could well be an Aids epidemic and then we are going to need all the land we have."

When our first year-six pupils began to leave school, we faced a new challenge: how do they continue their Jewish education at least until bar- or batmitzvah. Some went on to Jewish secondary schools but for those who did not, the part-time Sunday classes at Lauderdale Road and other synagogues were too elementary for them. So we launched a new programme for them on Sunday mornings, Netivot, which offered them a more advanced Jewish curriculum than they would get elsewhere. It was under the direction of Louise Hillman, who was a particularly brilliant Chumash teacher. I could see how she got the children excited. If you can create enthusiasm for Judaism's foundational text, then you have given them a good platform. Netivot, which met on the school premises, attracted not only alumni from our schools but other students such as one of Lord Sacks's daughters, Gila, who lived locally. Later the programme moved with Louise to a different location.

The Bayswater Synagogue building proved a boon in more ways than one. Instead of running overflow services for the High Holy Days in the Montefiore Hall, which was cramped, I suggested transferring them to the more spacious synagogue in the school. For the overflow service, we had also began to use the Iraqi, rather than the traditional Spanish and Portuguese, liturgy, in which most of the worshippers would feel at home. We brought over a hazan from Israel who was familiar with the melodies of the Middle East.

We also introduced the custom common among many Oriental communities to auction the various special mitzvot on High Holy Days. It did not meet universal approval at Lauderdale Road because the donations would be going to the school. Before the first Oriental service, we heard that the banker Edmond Safra was in London to open a new bank and would be spending Kippur with us. The most important mitzvah is to hold the first Sefer Torah which is taken out at the beginning of the Kal Nidre service. Mr Safra indicated that he would like to have it but he did not want to go through an auction. The Shamoons and I agreed that we would make a gift of it to him, which we duly announced on the night. Edmond Safra went on to buy every other honour for the day and sent us a very substantial cheque. He remained a supporter of the school and a block was named after him. At a dinner which the president of Israel, Ezer

Weizmann gave for the Queen during his state visit here in 1997, Edmond's wife Lily promised me, " I am going to tell our friends, the Saatchis, to give to your school too."

Sometimes support arrived from unexpected sources. I received a call one day from Lady Janner, the widow of Lord (Barnett) Janner, who asked if I could help a friend of hers, Lord (Alan) Sainsbury. His mother, Mabel van den Bergh, was Jewish and buried in our Ramsgate cemetery but he had never seen her grave. Lady Janner asked if I would come down with them and show it to him.

They picked me up in a Rolls Royce. Lady Janner had food for the journey in a Sainsbury's bag. The trip down to Kent became a history lesson as Lord Sainsbury recounted stories of some of his acquaintances. "Rabbi, do you remember my friend Chaim?" he asked. "Which Chaim?" I wondered. "Weizmann." I had arranged to have his mother's stone cleaned before the visit. He brought his own kippah with him and, when I said prayers at the grave, he became quite emotional. When I finished, he immediately turned to me and said, "Tell me what you want and I will do it for you." I replied, "I want you to help my school."

His donation helped to endow a scholarship fund and we established the Mabel Sainsbury Scholarships in his mother's name. Whenever he paid a visit to the school, the children would cry "Sainsbury's are here". When Lord Sainsbury died a few years later, we benefited from a substantial gift from his charitable foundation.

The backing we have been able to attract means that, since its opening, the school has never had to borrow a penny. As successive governments seemed only too happy to open their pockets to faith schools, a number of Jewish independent schools opted to go state-aided, which relieved the financial burden. But that was not a path I was prepared to consider. I did not want to yield control of the school. We still have more than enough parents willing to pay for classes of twenty rather than thirty and a number of scholarships to help some families who could otherwise not afford it, although Estelle, I should add, has always had doubts whether private education was the way forward.

Judy Lever-Chain had inspired confidence in the school during her eleven years as head. When she left in 1994, her work was consolidated by her successor, the conscientious Cathy Peters. In 1996, we named JPS after the Shamoons' mother, Naima, and the family continues to take an interest in the school. David Shamoon, who died in 2013, was one of the people I taught to put on tefillin and I used to help him put them on when I visited him towards the end of his life. Every year, we take the year-six children from Naima JPS on a trip to Spain to see Andalucian culture and revisit the Golden Age of religious co-existence, where they are hosted at the Puente Romano, the luxury hotel David owned in Marbella. We hold a little ceremony every year to honour his memory.

The same year that we renamed Naima JPS, we also embarked on a rebuilding scheme overseen by one of our parents, Lisette Keats, who is an architect. We divided the synagogue in two, converting the downstairs into classrooms and putting a floor into the ladies' gallery to leave a 400-seater synagogue that could also be used as an assembly hall. Here was surely a suitable cause for the Saatchis to lend their name to. "Now I can give you and Daisy a synagogue," I was able to tell Nathan. He was delighted. The Saatchi Synagogue, which was consecrated in 1998, however, was not ready in time for Nathan and Daisy's diamond wedding anniversary. I said to their son Charles, the art collector, "You know plenty of artists. Could you ask one to do a painting of what the synagogue will look like?" The picture we presented to them for their anniversary they bequeathed to the school and it now hangs in my study there. (The top hat that Nathan used to wear in synagogue Daisy gave to my son Julian.)

In 1996, we also unveiled our new emblem, which was created by the leading designer Abram Games. Sadly, it was his last commission before his death. The logo blended the cylindrical shape of an Oriental Sefer Torah container with that of a medieval tent. The image of the tent goes back to the very origins of the Spanish and Portuguese Community, alluding to a verse in Job, "And you shall know your tents are at peace". The first community chose it because they believed they had found safety on these shores. Games had used the tent before in his emblem for the 300th anniversary of the resettlement in 1956. There is also a rabbinic interpretation of the verse – but not one which we would tell the children about. From the same verse in Job, the rabbis drew the advice that a man going on a trip should make sure to be intimate with his wife on the eve of his departure so that his home be left in peace.

The demands of the school inevitably left less time for other activities. I increasingly delegated the teaching of barmitzvah boys to my assistant at Lauderdale Road, Rabbi Israel Elia. From Djerba in Tunisia, he had come through the ranks of Montefiore College and then Jews' College and proved a very capable pastor who was good with people. But I did start a Sunday morning programme for parents of children at JPS and at our Hebrew classes in the Montefiore Hall. I found it commendable that parents were coming along to learn about Jewish law, prayer or history when they could have been playing golf or tennis.

Compared with the political battles I had to fight elsewhere, governing the school was an unmitigated pleasure. Naturally, there were times when not everything was working as it should and we had to take action to remedy an area of weakness. The crises which beset us every so often were small rather than big. In my education advisers, I had guardian angels. When one of the Jewish community's leading educationists, Jo Wagerman, the head of JFS, retired, I enlisted her services too.

While I had my run-ins with lay leaders as a rabbi at the Spanish and Portuguese Congregation, I could always count on the loyalty and judgement of my chairmen of governors at JPS; Robert Yentob; Leon Nahon; Judy Dangoor, David's wife, whose unflappability spread calm to all around her; Edward Misrahi, originally from Spain, who is now chairman of Immanuel College; and our current chairman, Sabine Howard. Leon was one of the older guard prepared to back the school early on. His family, from Livorno, in Italy, had the distinction of donating the community's tallest Sefer Torah. To perform the mitzvah of *levantar* – lifting the Torah after it has been read – in our synagogue, it is necessary to pass a test to ensure it is performed correctly and with due ceremony. The scroll must be held straight and with the parchment at the bottom slightly above the holder's eyes. While the usual custom is to display three columns of parchment to the congregation, in our community part of five to seven columns must be shown. But even the most seasoned *levantadores* will tremble at the prospect of lifting the Nahon Sefer.

In 1987, twenty-five years since I was first appointed as youth minister, a friend wrote to me to say that "I know there have been times you have been near to despair and for Estelle it must have been almost worse, feeling for you but powerless to help. Even so, your principal source of satisfaction is the preparatory school you have created which combines so much of what you believe in and want to achieve." Thirteen years later, at a reception the congregation held for me, my friend Lucien Gubbay could say that the struggles over the birth of the school were "long forgotten. All of us now take pride in the school, in its fine buildings, its impressive record of success and its long waiting list".

As principal, I have tried to present a model of Judaism that was warm and inviting rather than forbidding and austere. I wanted the children to find a rabbi approachable. Standing on the *tebah* of Bevis Marks in my full clerical outfit, I represented tradition and authority. But when I sat on the floor with the children during the weekly assembly I did at Naima, that was an equally important aspect of my rabbinate. In particular I would try to impress on the children how privileged they were. "How many children in the world are as lucky as you?" I would ask each year. "Fifty per cent," someone would say. "Nowhere near," I would reply. "Twenty per cent," another would suggest. "You're way off," I said. And so we would go down until I would eventually tell them, "0.0000001 per cent" so they would realise how blessed they were.

In the handsome album which the school produced for me on my seventieth birthday in 2009, one former pupil, Aaron Horn, wrote: "You are by far one of the safest rabbis in the world". It was a compliment that made me feel we were on the right track. Another ex-pupil, Nelly Morgan, wrote that JPS had enabled her and her peers to start secondary school "in touch with our Judaism, prepared academically, socially confident" and feeling capable of anything. "I wish nothing more than to allow my children to one day belong to your synagogue and attend your school," she said.

David Douer, who has been studying over the past year in yeshivah before university, told me he was most grateful for friends he made at Naima – "such a genuine, caring and truthful group of friends. Friends like these stay with you for life and with this it is vital to ensure a happy teenage-hood. Powerful bonds were forged during Naima and to this day we all remain close. This is, I now appreciate, the most valuable gift Naima gave me."

I hope we have made some impact on parents too. One set of parents, as the last of their children left JPS, wrote to me to say that "we all are enriched by the families we met there and the way these relationships have been reinforced by the sharing of Shabbat and festivals which made our home Jewish life richer... We were a family who were not firmly embedded in Jewish tradition, we too were learning and during our time in the school this knowledge grew and deepened." You cannot be a community rabbi without brooking some criticism in the job, but sometimes you need buoying up too.

5

The Squeezed Middle

I HAVE A special reason to remember the marriage of Prince Charles to Lady Diana Spencer in 1981; it led to my first meeting with the Queen. I was part of a delegation of some fifteen or so Jewish representatives who went to Buckingham Palace a few months before the wedding to offer our congratulations to the parents of the groom. The Board of Deputies, jointly with the Anglo-Jewish Association, is one of twenty-seven Privileged Bodies invited for a royal audience on such occasions, along with the Church of England, the Catholic Church and Oxford and Cambridge Universities.

The once-powerful AJA, the mainstay of anti-Zionist opposition at the time of the Balfour Declaration, was now a shadow of the organisation it had been. I owed my attendance to history too, to the fact that the Haham was one of the Board's two ecclesiastical authorities, the other being the Chief Rabbi. Although I did not carry the title of Haham, according to the arrangement that followed Dr Gaon's retirement, as communal rabbi I took over many of the official assignments that went with his office.

Each delegation went in to a private room to deliver their Loyal Address. Chief Rabbi Jakobovits recited the traditional blessing on seeing a monarch, in praise of He "who has given of His glory to human beings". But before we did so, we were ushered into a great hall with the members of other delegations, where we were prepared for our audience: how we should walk in, how to curtsy or bow, how to walk out. We were used to bowing at Lauderdale Road so I didn't need too much practice with my etiquette. As we awaited our turn to go in, I was talking with the emeritus head of the Federation of Synagogues, Dayan Michael Fisher, and the Duke of Norfolk, who was in charge of such ceremonial duties. "My name is Michael Fisher," Dayan Fisher informed the Duke. "You have had two archbishops of Canterbury, Michael Ramsey and Geoffrey Fisher. Which only goes to show, two archbishops are worth one rabbi!" What the duke made of this I don't know beyond his courteous response, "Frightfully interesting."

The photo of us all smiling in front of the palace gates which appeared in the *Jewish Chronicle* presented a spectacle of unity. Our delegation included not only the Chief Rabbi and Dayan Fisher but also one of the leading Reform rabbis, Hugo Gryn. Much as the leadership of British Jewry liked to show a common front to the outside world, the photograph masked the reality that, internally, religious divisions were growing wider.

When he took office in 1967, Immanuel Jakobovits wanted to calm the atmosphere within the community, following the ructions unleashed by the Jacobs Affair. At the same time, he sought to preserve Orthodoxy as the normative voice of Judaism in the outside world, unchallenged by any Progressive movement. Heir to Samson Raphael Hirsch's German tradition of *Torah im derech eretz*, which combined Orthodox piety with appreciation of the best of secular culture, he was confident enough in his philosophy not to feel threatened by the Charedi right. But the right was still gaining ground, as one earlier episode had shown me only too well.

From 1973 to 1975, I was president of a group called the Anglo-Jewish Preachers' Association, whose rather old-fashioned name had perhaps by this time doomed it. It was an interdenominational body where rabbis from across the community met monthly to deliver papers or hold discussions. For many years it had been run by the Reverend Isaac Livingstone, he of the habitual dog collar. Already I was beginning to feel the influence of Gateshead on the United Synagogue rabbinate. A number of Orthodox ministers were refusing to join because of the presence of the Reform and Liberals. Then when I invited Rabbi Nahum Rabinovitch to speak to us, he came under tremendous pressure from other Orthodox rabbis to pull out. He was strong enough to withstand it but it was symptomatic of a different climate. The growing reluctance of the Orthodox to support the organisation made it redundant and it fizzled out.

Harold Levy, the former warden of Jews' College, once remarked to me, "We are becoming a dumb-bell religion." By which he meant, thin in the middle and heavy on the extremes. The Anglo-Jewry of old had more resembled one of those big cigars, thick in the middle and much narrower at the end. But Harold could see the trends that became more pronounced over the next forty years.

The shifting religious ground made me more aware of the need to hold on to our Sephardi way of doing things. The Spanish and Portuguese Community may have been few in numbers, compared to the other Orthodox groupings, but I was convinced that we still had a significant role to play in preserving a worldlier traditionalism than the sectarian East European model.

As I was quoted as saying in *The Club*, Stephen Brook's portrait of Anglo-Jewry published in 1989, "I'm trying desperately hard to stand in the middle." I did my best to keep open channels to different parts of the Jewish community and build bridges where I could. I might have my differences with the Charedim but I never criticised them in public. I had friendly relations with Progressive leaders; on one occasion, travelling between functions with Hugo, I stopped off at his house for a kosher sandwich. I would not give a sermon at a Reform or Liberal synagogue service but, unlike many other Orthodox rabbis, I never had a problem with going to give a lecture in their synagogue hall. The Spanish and Portuguese Community and the Reform had maintained practical co-operation for the better part of a century in one area: jointly managing the cemetery – with separate sections – at Hoop Lane in Golders Green. If we could collaborate over the dead, then at least we could demonstrate some degree of civility while we were living.

I also sat in on meetings Lord Jakobovits regularly held with Reform and Liberal rabbinic leaders in his home. Ostensibly, the purpose was to consult over interfaith relations. The Chief Rabbi was genuine in his wish to work with other movements on matters, such as Israel or defence against anti-Semitism, which did not encroach on our religious differences. But the joint forum was essentially a sop to the Progressives to whom he would not concede any public role in representing Judaism. It was not much more than a vehicle for exchanging pleasantries. Still, it gave us the opportunity for us all to get to know one another.

As for my formal position at the Board of Deputies, I was content to play second fiddle to the Chief Rabbi. Not that he was likely to consider me an equal or the Spanish and Portuguese Congregation as other than a junior partner. Our dealings were always cordial and our families occasionally had Shabbat lunch together. But our relationship was that of a teacher to a pupil, he being the rabbi who had awarded me *semichah*.

The Haham had generally been a supportive associate of the

Chief Rabbi on the wider Anglo-Jewish stage, so much so that a senior Reform rabbi, Dow Marmur, later told me that he felt the Haham had been too accommodating. In truth, there was little in the business of the Board of Deputies to engage my attention. The most serious event involving its ecclesiastical authorities had come a few years earlier during the Haham's time. Rabbi Jakobovits agreed to update the Board's constitution so that it might consult the religious leaders of the non-Orthodox on matters where they took a different line from the Orthodox. His concession immediately prompted the Charedi Union of Orthodox Hebrew Congregations to walk out of the Board, never to return. It was a sign of his strength and self-assurance that he felt able to take such a decision. The Board continued to uphold the monopoly of its two Orthodox ecclesiastical authorities and a few years later produced a code of practice spelling out that it remained duty-bound to follow their religious guidance. I indicated I was happy if the Chief Rabbi was. The Progressives were not, but whispers of withdrawal from the Board soon petered out. Only in one subsequent incident, which I shall recount later, did I find myself at odds with Lord Jakobovits.

Even if I had sought a more prominent role in Anglo-Jewish affairs, there were two constraints. The first is that it took considerable time and energy to launch the school. While I was relieved at the level of support it attracted once it opened, it was not always plain sailing; in the early years, the need to secure the financial underpinning gave me one or two sleepless nights.

The second was the internal situation within the Spanish and Portuguese Congregation. The détente which the powers-that-be had hoped to achieve between Dayan Toledano and myself through the device of the joint ecclesiastial authority proved easier said than done. Any hope that we might co-exist in a kind of creative tension had been too optimistic. It was like asking two chefs to share a kitchen. My friend, Professor Kedourie, put it alternatively, "They want to put you in the same bed together and neither of you want that."

Finally, a group of lay leaders decided that the congregation was not big enough for the both of us. One of us had to go. In the summer of 1983, a front page story in the *Jewish Chronicle*, over pictures of Dayan Toledano and myself in top hats, blazed the news: the dayan "must resign". The Mahamad at the time was led by a sympathiser of mine, Cesare Sacerdoti. In a circular informing congregants of the failure of the joint ecclesiastical authority, he wrote, "Neither we nor our predecessors have found any way of making it work." But the dayan's backers were not going to accept the decision as a fait accompli and mobilised to save their man.

Over the next few months, our community's feuding was laid bare in the *Jewish Chronicle* for all to see. While I had a strong base of support at Lauderdale Road, Dayan Toledano commanded allegiance in Wembley and among a vocal group in Bevis Marks. Events were scheduled to come to a head at a special meeting of members in September but both of us felt it unseemly before Rosh Hashanah and asked for a postponement. At one point both of us offered to retire. It was particularly unfortunate that all this exploded just as the school was about to open but, on the other hand, I was more than glad to have that project to occupy me amid the contention.

In the event, the members' meeting did not happen. By the end of the year, the lay leadership, all too aware of the depth of dissension within the congregation, had pulled back from the brink. They decided to give the dual-headed structure another try. I was awarded the new title of "spiritual head", while Dayan Toledano was authorised to establish a Sephardi Beth Din with himself as head. It drew the demarcation lines between us a little

26 Haham Gaster outside his house in Maida Vale (where the first meeting on the Balfour Declaration was held) with the High Priest of the Samaritans and an assistant.

27 With my colleague of fifty years, the Rev Halfon Benarroch.

28 With Rabbi Dr Isidore Epstein and his wife on his retirement.

29 With Lucien Gubbay, Rev E Abinun, and Sir Alan Mocatta putting up a mezuzah at Lauderdale Road.

30 With Chief Rabbis Lord Jacobovits and Ovadia Yosef at our house.

31 Opening of YJLI with Abe Harman and Sir Alan Mocatta, 1978.

32 With Kabbalist Rabbi Kedourie, at Naima
Jewish Preparatory School.

33 Preaching on the hundredth anniversary
of Lauderdale Road Synagogue, 1996.

34 Lighting the *Ner Tamid* (eternal flame) at the Saatchi Synagogue with Daisy and Nathan, 1999.

35 With Dayan Amor and Dayan Basri at Lauderdale Road.

36 With Chief Rabbi (later Lord) Sacks, VE Day, 8 May 1995.

37 Chief Rabbi Ovadia Yosef with JPS pupils.
38 With Dayan Berger and Rishon le Zion Bakshi-Doron.

39 Lauderdale Road centenary party at the Mocattas' house, 1997.

40 Affixing a mezuzah on the door of Israel Bureau de Liaison Rabat, 1995.

41 Carmel College, with Naim (later Sir) and David Dangoor, 1998.

42 Speaking at the Memorial for my uncle, Chief Minister Sir Joshua Hassan, Gibraltar Synagogue, 1998.

43 With Rabbi Josef Dweck at his inauguration, 2014.

44 With Rabbi Israel Elia completing a Torah scroll.

45 With, from L to R: Sydney Assor, Freddie Salem, André Azoulay, and David (later Lord) Alliance in our succah, 2000.

46 Receiving honorary fellowship Queen Mary University.

47 With David Shamoon, who named the school after his mother Naima.

48 With Rowan Williams, the Archbishop of Canterbury, cooking with schoolboys of the City of London.

more clearly. For the sake of the community, both of us had no option but to try and make a fresh go of it. A key peace-broker was Nathan Saatchi, who actually leaned more towards Dayan Toledano. But I could count on the aid of another Iraqi, Abraham Fattal, a particularly kindly man, who would go to Nathan and endeavour to persuade him to take a more balanced view. He would challenge my opponents, "If you don't like Abraham Levy, then find someone better."

If the Mahamad had got their way, would I have eventually have become Haham? That I could not say. But Lord Jakobovits, who would not, of course, have intervened in the internal affairs of the Spanish and Portuguese Congregation, did confide to me that he felt that in one respect it was a pity the office had remained dormant. He believed it helped to consolidate the status of Orthodoxy within wider society. In this he was prescient. When Prince William came to be married many years later, it was not the Chief Rabbi and the Haham who were invited to attend the ceremony but the Chief Rabbi and the head of the Reform movement.

Establishing a Sephardi Beth Din was no simple task – it had been the ambition of Dr Gaon to do just that after his retirement but he had to concede defeat. I was to sit on it beside Dr Toledano and be allowed a say in the choice of its third member. It was not easy to agree on a suitable candidate. Eventually, we settled on Rabbi Abraham David, the Rangoon-born head of the Od Yosef Hai community in Hendon. But there was one area where I stood firm. I told the Mahamad that we should not allow conversions to be performed here. They are a particularly sensitive area and it is important that they are done in such a way that no one may dispute their validity. I had already had dealings with the head of the Jerusalem Beth Din, Dayan Ezra Basri, whose halachic authority was beyond question. We came to an arrangement whereby we would interview future converts and when we felt they were ready we would send them to him to convert. It actually worked well in practice.

In the aftermath of the 1983 conflict, the congregation moved to elect a Mahamad which appeared more impartial. Until then, the leadership had tended to see-saw between those more favourable to me and those to Dayan Toledano. When it came to lay leaders, I always made a basic distinction: there were those who brought honour to the office and those who sought honour from the office. I always told young rabbis who asked me for guidance that I prayed for honorary officers who were successful in their careers and happy at home because if they were frustrated or unfulfilled, they tended to make the rabbi's job more difficult.

The readers of the *Jewish Chronicle* in the early 1980s might have been forgiven for thinking that the main activity of the Spanish and Portuguese Congregation was staging a religious Punch and Judy Show. Beyond the wrangling, however, during this period we were making progress in other areas of community life, particularly in support of Israel. The Joint Israel Appeal, the JIA, was not only the premier fund-raising organisation in British Jewry but those in its driving seat were regarded as the key decision-makers within the community as a whole. If you wanted to get along in Anglo-Jewish society, fundraising for Israel was one way to do it. I encouraged our members to get involved.

I was introduced to the JIA by Conrad Morris. The Morrises lived close to us and the children of Sabbath-observant families in the area would play in their large garden on long summer afternoons. In the wake of the Yom Kippur War in 1973, Estelle and I went with a group on a two-week mission to Israel. Our ostensible purpose was to help with the citrus harvest as the army was still on alert and there weren't enough workers to pick the fruit. We weren't expected to lead the life of agricultural labourers; the Jewish Agency put us up in four-star hotels. As an exercise in solidarity, the trip was a resounding success. As a contribution to the orange industry, it was an economic disaster. If you had factored in the cost of our flight and accommodation, what we picked would have worked out as the most expensive oranges in history.

Before we went out, a colleague forewarned me that the first day in the orchards would be the best, after that we would have to endure the monotony. That was why, he argued, the Bible said, in respect of the Succot harvest, "You shall gather... the first day". But there was a spiritual bonus to our work outdoors. One felt closer to God, I reflected in a sermon on our return. "It is easy to understand why the early Chasidim preferred praying to God in a field rather than a man-made synagogue," I said. It also made us more appreciative of our metropolitan comforts and what others had to do to earn a living.

It was a moving experience to visit some of the soldiers who had been wounded in the recent war, though I was anxious that we should not come across as do-gooding outsiders whose presence was an intrusion. As we offered them cigarettes and talked, most of the time we felt that they were pleased to see us. "He who visits a sick person takes away from him one sixtieth of his illness," counsels the Talmud. On Shabbat we shared a morning service in the Yochanan ben Zakkai Synagogue in Jerusalem with some young Sephardim who were studying in Israel. The site has been a place of Jewish worship for 2,000 years. It was here that more than fifty Rishonim-le-Zion, the religious leaders of the Sephardi community in Israel, were inducted. Until 1948 a shofar and a jug of oil stood in the synagogue as an invitation to the Messiah. It was as if to say to the Messiah, "If all you need is a shofar and a little oil, here it is waiting for you, don't tarry any longer." The oil would be used to rekindle the menorah in the restored Temple a stone's throw away. None of us could fail to be touched by the deep sense of historical connection. As I emphasised in my sermon, "the Sephardim were always spiritual Zionists rather than political ones and it is only the Sephardim who can claim an uninterrupted presence in the Old City of Jerusalem since the 12th century."

I would often mention in talks that our community's support of Israel went all the way back to the resettlement. One of the first acts of the English Sephardim in 1657 was to create an office to collect funds to send to Torah scholars in Israel, the Parnas de Terra Santa. In the 19th century, long before the JIA, Sir Moses Montefiore blazed a philanthropic trail, visiting the Land of Israel no fewer than seven times and investing in projects to regenerate Jewish communities there. He included a reference to Jerusalem, in Hebrew, in his coat of arms. Such was his love of Zion that before he died, Sir Moses brought back enough earth and stones from the Holy Land to make sure that there would be a layer to cover him when he was buried since he did not know whether he would be buried in the Land of Israel. In the late 19th and early 20th century, the nascent Zionist movement had no firmer friend than Haham Gaster, when much of the Anglo-Jewish leadership was opposed to Jewish statehood. The first meeting to plan the Balfour Declaration was actually held in his home, close by what is now the Naima Jewish Preparatory School.

Besides Davide Sala, there were others who helped to raise the Sephardi profile within the JIA such as Uri David, who came here from Israel and was a strong supporter of its Labour party, Violet Masri and Mat Haruni. At the JIA Sephardi committee's annual dinner of 1985, Mat Haruni made a point of mentioning that the Sephardi fundraising contribution had been pitifully small. I disagreed, saying that Sephardim took a different approach to charity and preferred to be associated with a particular project, as my school had proved. At any rate, the dinner gleaned a more than respectable figure. Mat Haruni's own Zionism went beyond philanthropy. After making aliyah, he founded the Dalton vineyard in the Upper Galilee, one of the new breed of producers that has helped to transform the Israeli wine industry and the image of kosher wine from the sweet concoction dutifully sipped at Kiddush to something that is pleasant to drink with a meal. A Dalton Cabernet Sauvignon or Chardonnay will often grace a kosher table.

The JIA was still in its heyday when Estelle and I participated with 700 mainly UK Jews in a solidarity mission to Israel in 1988. Whereas once Israel was hailed for the derring-do which brought the rescue of the Entebbe hostages in 1976, it was increasingly facing international criticism following the bombing of Beirut in the Lebanon War of 1982 and the outbreak of the First Intifada five years later. The almost universal support among diaspora Jewry could no longer be taken for granted. Our delegation included my uncle, Sir Joshua Hassan, the former Chief Minister of Gibraltar, and other dignitaries. But we were all treated like VIPs and when we disembarked, we were waved through the normal passport controls.

When Davide Sala was named the JIA's Man of the Year in 1989, it marked the modern Sephardi community's coming of age in terms of Israel philanthropy. The same year we paid tribute to another great Sephardi benefactor to Israel, Dorothy de Rothschild, at a memorial service for her at Bevis Marks. Born Dorothy Pinto, she had married the Liberal MP, James de Rothschild, who was the son of the head of the French branch of the family, Baron Edmond. She used her social connections to set up contacts for Chaim Weizmann pre-War as the Zionist movement sought to win political support for its plan for a

Jewish homeland. The projects she funded in Israel as head of Yad Hanadiv, the Rothschild foundation, included the Knesset building and the Supreme Court building. She went about her charitable work quietly with no thought of recognition. On her death, Israel's president Chaim Herzog wrote to her cousin Jacob, the present Lord Rothschild, "Those of us who had the great fortune to be her friends will never forget her kind smile, the beauty of her soul and majesty of her purpose."

We had to work out the seating-plan for the memorial service with the same care as if it were a wedding, arranging which Rothschild should sit next to which. But while prominent members of the community attended in honour of her memory, what most illustrated the affection in which she was held was the turnout from the village of Waddesdon where she had lived. Two or three coachloads of residents came and sat upstairs in the women's gallery, which would otherwise have remained empty, looking out over the candles in the brass chandeliers.

New Israeli Ambassadors considered the Spanish and Portuguese Community of sufficient importance to pay me a courtesy call after their arrival in the UK. The Ambassador I got to know best was Yehuda Avner during the 1980s, whom I first met at lunch at Conrad Morris's. He was religiously observant and since the Ambassador's residence was within walking distance of Lauderdale Road, he would often come to pray with us on a Shabbat morning.

Other Ambassadors would visit on special occasions. When Avner's predecessor, Shlomo Argov, came to Lauderdale Road one Shabbat, I quoted in my address a verse from Ezekiel to express the hope that we would establish an "everlasting bond" – a "*brit olam*" according to the prophet – with Israel. There was a far-fetched hypothesis, I noted, that the British were descended from the ten lost tribes of Israel. *Brit-ish,* means in Hebrew "person of the Covenant". "We in our country are not lost Jews," I said, "but

rather yearning Jews keen to create closer bonds with Israel."
Little did I foresee that in 1982 I would be reciting prayers for his
recovery at a special service after a Palestinian squad gunned him
down in the street – an outrage which sparked the Lebanon War.

With the periodic eruptions of violence in the Middle East,
our anxieties about Israel had become a sad fact of Jewish life.
Even before the outbreak of the Lebanon War, for many years we
had had to take precautions against any backlash. The security
posted outside our buildings made the open doors of synagogues
of my childhood in Gibraltar or my student days in London seem
a distant era. The reality of the terrorism threat was brought home
by the attack on the Neve Shalom Synagogue in Istanbul in 1986
in which twenty-two people were killed. At the memorial service
we held a month later at Holland Park Synagogue, because of its
Turkish connections, I noted the particular sense of violation we
felt at the target. "There was a time when a place of worship was
considered as a refuge from those fleeing from terror," I said.
"Today terror enters into places of worship and there is nowhere
to escape." The victims had only just finished reciting a prayer in
Ladino used at Holland Park too.

What lent additional poignancy to the occasion was the
presence at our service of a young Iranian Jew who had been in
Istanbul and had been intending to go to Neve Shalom that very
day. Instead, he suddenly changed route and decided to go to
another synagogue. The imam of the Regent's Park Mosque,
although unable to attend, sent a message to convey his
abhorrence at the killings. "How sad we feel that this occurred in
Istanbul, for Jew and Muslim lived in what was the Ottoman
Empire in peace and tranquillity," I observed in my address. The
following year, when I visited Turkey with the Jewish Identity
Group from the UK, I recited Kaddish for the victims of the
terrorist attack at the reopening of the synagogue.

However bad the situation was in the Middle East, I always

tried to recall the historic periods of co-existence and express the hope that the past might serve as a signpost to the future. But I kept clear of the nitty-gritty of politics. Lord Jakobovits, on the other hand, was prepared to go out on a limb with his outspoken dovishness. His advocacy of territorial compromise earned him the wrath of many of his Orthodox peers, prompting the Ashkenazi Chief Rabbi of Israel, Shlomo Goren, to call on British Jews to "spew this dangerous man from our midst". I believe Lord Jakobovits was even advised to avoid going to Jerusalem at one point. But his warnings that the retention of the West Bank could prove a thorn in the side for Israel were prophetic. Even if privately I agreed, I was not inclined to echo them from the pulpit. My community was prone to division enough as it was without me risking further argument by openly taking up positions on the peace process.

Nor was I tempted to become involved in support of the Sephardi political enterprise, Shas, which emerged as a force in Israel in the 1980s. Given the depressed, downtrodden state of the Sephardim in Israel which I had described in my pamphlet a decade earlier, a new-found assertiveness and pride was to be welcomed. But I wish it had taken a different form than a religious political party, even if it was headed by no less a figure than Israel's former Sephardi Chief Rabbi, Rav Ovadia Yosef.

While I retained the greatest respect for his religious authority, I regarded it as a mistake for him to lend his name to Shas. When I first met him, he did not seem cut out for politics. At the time of his visit to London, he had clashed with his Ashkenazi counterpart, Chief Rabbi Goren, over the latter's decision to remove the status of *mamzerut*, illegitimacy, from a brother and sister in Israel. Rabbi Goren's reasoning had proved highly controversial among halachists and Rav Yosef asked me to help him meet other British rabbis so that he could explain his differences with Rabbi Goren, who he felt was more practised in getting his view across. *"Ani lo ish televisia,"* he told me – "I am not a TV man". Who would predict that Shas would propel him into becoming the most powerful political rabbi in Israel?

I never thought the cause of religion was best served by getting mixed up in party politics, especially in Israel, where secular Jews already resented the influence of religious parties in the legislature. My attitude to them was summed up in an address I gave to the Board of Deputies in 1993: religious parties may have helped to raise religious standards among the few but "they have not helped in improving the religious dimension of the country and the people as a whole... In our preoccupation to save the few spiritually, we are estranging the masses." What was particularly unfortunate was that Shas did not embody the more accommodating tradition of Rav Uzziel, Israel's first Sephardi Chief Rabbi, who died in 1954. Instead, it tried to mirror the "Torah" parties of the Charedi right even if it appealed to a broader constituency.

This was perhaps inevitable given what had happened in Israel in the years before. With the lack of any Sephardi educational infrastructure, thousands of boys from North Africa were taken into right-wing Ashkenazi yeshivot: they adopted Ashkenazi styles of dress, donning wide-brimmed black hats, and even Ashkenazi pronunciation. Some were so embarrassed by their roots they changed their names. The Ashkenazi world certainly performed a mitzvah in educating these youngsters, but had it been more altruistic, it would have schooled them in the traditions of their ancestors. Instead, these ashkenazified yeshivah graduates became the vanguard of Shas.

Rav Yosef always remained an honoured guest in London. I remember him once having a meal at our house when there was a knock on the door. A pair of Jehovah's Witnesses wished to be let in to pitch their religious wares. "I have the Chief Rabbi of Israel with me, I don't think you are going to be very successful," I told them. When later I saw Rav Yosef's son, David, I pleaded with him to "keep your father in cotton wool – he is too precious" in order to protect him from the political fray. The intemperate outbursts against Arabs and others for which, sadly, Rav Yosef became notorious in his latter years may never have occurred, I believe, had he not become involved in politics. But they should not obscure his reputation as a revered Torah scholar. The huge turnout of 800,000 people at his funeral in 2013 showed how unique he was.

Although a British Friends of Shas was established, it made little headway and I had nothing to do with it. To me, it would only have been a distraction from more immediate local concerns. The success of our school led me to dream of expansion. When the Shamoon brothers snapped up a big piece of land next to it, that became a distinct possibility. I thought it also might be used as a centre for wider cultural activities, which could help put the Sephardi community more firmly on the map. But the Shamoons decided to sell the land to developers and the project faded away.

Others were also talking about the idea of a Sephardi community centre, which could have had a unifying role as a focal-point for the different Sephardi groups as well as a place to showcase our heritage more widely. Elias Dangoor, a cousin of Naim Dangoor, looked at acquiring a site at the Sternberg Centre, home of the Reform movement, which had plenty of room for a building in its spacious green grounds. In one way, it would have been a good location in the heartlands of north-west London Jewry. But I was worried that it would look as if we were joining forces with the Reform and that this would cause us problems with the other Orthodox. I would have had difficulty supporting the scheme if it had gone ahead but it never got beyond the drawing-board.

I was largely happy to stay out of the religious politics that bedevilled the community. But there was one major dispute during the tenure of Lord Jakobovits in which I was called on to play a role behind the scenes. It was not, as you might expect, between Orthodox and Reform but between Orthodox and Orthodox, specifically between the Chief Rabbi and the Charedim. It was triggered by a report in 1985 from a quango called the Farm Animal Welfare Council (FAWC) which threatened the future of kosher meat in this country.

The time-hallowed method of kosher slaughter, *shechita*, is with a swift cut to the animal's neck administered by a *shochet*, who must be rigorously trained for the task. We believe it to be a humane method but *shechita* has periodically been challenged. The FAWC wanted to introduce stunning before *shechita* – for example, by captive bolt through the brain – but that would have damaged the animal, and therefore rendered it unfit for kosher consumption according to Jewish law.

While the government, fortunately, rejected the recommendation to outlaw the non-stunning of animals before slaughter, the Ministry of Agriculture was keen to press ahead with other changes to *shechita* practice. It wanted to replace the rotating pen in which the animal was slaughtered on its back with an upright model. The *shochetim*, however, preferred to have the animal lying flat because this made it easier to avoid putting pressure on the knife.

Lord Jakobovits, who took it on himself to represent the community, had initially signalled to the government that we were willing to make concessions. One evening I received a phone call at home from the senior vice-president of the Board of Deputies, Israel Finestein, who told me that the Board had approved the Chief Rabbi's position and asked me to go along with it. I remember sitting on the hall stairs with the receiver in my hand. "What is the point of telling me when it is already a fait accompli," I said. "But Abraham, you have to authorise it," he said. "I'm very sorry," I said, "I'm an ecclesiastical authority of the Board and I don't agree to this." But my opposition was mild to that of the Charedim, who were incandescent at what they believed a dangerous compromise.

The Chief Rabbi must have felt entitled to take the lead in responding to the community's proposals since he chaired the Rabbinical Commission responsible for licensing all of the country's *shochetim*. His influence with government, moreover, was at its zenith. His championship of traditional virtues such as personal responsibility was particularly admired by Prime Minister Margaret Thatcher, who regarded him as more in tune with her thinking than the leaders of the Church of England and elevated him to the peerage in 1988.

One of the strictly Orthodox rabbis called my brother James in Gibraltar, who was close to the Charedi world, and asked him to persuade me to intervene. So one day I set off to Stamford Hill to visit the home of the head of the Union of Orthodox Hebrew Congregations, Rabbi Chanoch Padwa. I was accompanied by Rabbi Chaim Feldman, the rabbi of Munk's, in Golders Green. Rabbi Feldman was a respected figure in his own right, a man of great integrity, but I was struck by his reverential attitude towards the elderly sage. As we discussed what was to be done, he would turn to Rabbi Padwa and inquire, "What would the Rav think?"

Rabbi Padwa knew I was no halachist but he seemed to like me. At any rate, it was agreed that I should take a message to Lord Jakobovits; the Charedim were adamant that the conditions the government wanted to impose on the kosher trade were unacceptable and they were ready to fight their cause. A bust-up between the Chief Rabbi and the Charedi establishment at such a sensitive time was the last thing anyone wanted.

Shortly afterwards, I was invited to another, larger meeting attended by the leading Charedi rabbis from Manchester and Gateshead as well as London. In this bearded company, I was the only one who was clean shaven. We were about to begin when the phone rang for Rabbi Padwa. When he was told the nature of the call, he stopped to take it. A woman had a query about family purity and wanted to know whether she ought to go to the mikveh or not. It was evidence of the care he took to give the right guidance to a member of his community that he was prepared to delay an important meeting of rabbis. When he had dealt with her question, he placed a letter in my hand to take to Rabbi Jakobovits. The Chief Rabbi was, in effect, being given an ultimatum: either he withdrew his approval of the objectionable measures or they would inform the Ministry of Agriculture that they refused to accept his authority in representing the community on this issue.

When I went to see him, Lord Jakobovits was at home and convalescing from a heart attack. I summarised the Charedi position: "We need a retraction from the government. If you get it, we'll keep quiet. But if not, then all hell will break loose." At first he was very agitated, but he calmed down and agreed to sign the letter conveying disquiet about details of the proposed changes. Later that night, I received calls from the Gateshead Rav, Rabbi Bezalel Rakow, and others with whom I did not have occasion to speak very often, to express their gratitude.

Eventually, a compromise was reached which everyone could live with. An upright pen was introduced but with modifications that enabled the *shochetim* to do their work. Although the Charedim had never looked to the Chief Rabbi for halachic direction, they had respected the office. A public show of independence would have damaged its standing and brought disunity when the protection of *shechita* was better served by maintaining consensus. The same day that I visited Lord Jakobovits, his wife Amelie wrote to thank me for my help in getting her husband out of a tight corner.

Amelie had by this time established a unique position for

herself as the unofficial First Lady of the community. Her outgoing nature, easy way with people and boundless good sense made Lady J, as she was affectionately known, an invaluable asset to her husband's chief rabbinate. In 1986, she jointly led a groundbreaking tour of some forty British Jews, among them Estelle, to China. I have to say I did not share my wife's sense of adventure or curiosity about far-flung places. China was not as it is now, transformed after its rapid economic evolution. Estelle felt that in some places she had been transported back to a pre-industrial society. There was not a car to be seen in the streets, only bicycles. The trip caught the imagination of the community in signalling that there was nowhere on the map that an observant Jew could not go without a little preparation: the world was open for exploration. They took their kosher food with them, packed in dry ice.

When it came to travel, I was content with the self-catering holidays we spent in Albufeira, in the Algarve in Portugal. It was a simple village then, not at all built up, offering a peaceful setting and a plentiful supply of beautiful fresh fish. One year, we decided to go further afield, to the Caribbean, which happened because our house was burgled. Among the items taken by the thieves were the silver jewellery Estelle had painstakingly made at evening classes. We decided to use the insurance money for a holiday rather than replacing our losses and took a flat in Barbados.

The Spanish and Portuguese Community have a long association with the island and are responsible for the cemetery in its capital in Bridgetown. In the 18th century, members from our community went there to do business and during their time, some of them sired second families. One afternoon when I had nothing else to do, I leafed through the local telephone directory, looking for names that I reckoned must be the descendants of those Sephardi merchants. When the Bridgetown synagogue was sold in 1929, London inherited some splendid pieces of silver. When the synagogue was reopened in the 1980s, they wanted the silver back; we declined on the grounds that they now represented a different community – they were Ashkenazi – but we allowed them to make replicas.

During our stay in Barbados, we took a "Jolly Roger" cruise, which turned out to be not so jolly for me. They were serving an orange and rum punch on board. It was hot and I downed several glasses, convinced the cocktail consisted of ninety per cent orange juice with a little rum. But the proportions were more like half and half. As the boat bobbed around the bay, my head began to reel – and continued throbbing for a good day after. I don't think I have ever felt worse in my life.

Needless to say, I have not touched a drop of rum since. But I am no puritan. I like a whisky and keep a selection of malts in our cabinet. Lauderdale Road, however, is not one of those synagogues renowned for its whisky at Kiddush on a Saturday morning. For one thing, many of the Jews from the Middle East, because they grew up in Muslim lands, rarely drink. But everyone used wine, at least for making Kiddush on Shabbat and festivals. A senior Italian rabbi told me he attributed the growth in local kosher wine-making there to the influx of Jews from Libya after the Six Day War. The Libyans were particularly strict and would no more have drunk non-kosher wine than they would have eaten non-kosher meat.

The Sephardim generally have been strict in using only wine manufactured under rabbinic supervision, wine having a special status that makes it different, say, from whisky. It used to be the case at some kosher Anglo-Jewish functions, you could order an unsupervised fine wine from the bar. Our Sephardi Kashrut Authority always insisted on rabbinically-approved wine. The London Beth Din finally stopped unsupervised wines being available from the bar in the 1980s. But with French vintages and an ever-increasing range of labels from Israel and elsewhere produced under rabbinic supervision, no wine-drinker need feel deprived.

While we were strict on wine, it remained the policy of our kashrut authority to make keeping kosher as convenient as possible. But I can say there is probably no area of communal life that frustrated me as much as the administration of kashrut in the UK. It is ludicrous that in a small community, certainly compared with the United States, London's three mainstream Orthodox bodies, the United Synagogue, the Federation and ourselves, maintain separate kashrut authorities (besides Kedassia for the Charedim) with little appetite for co-operation.

To underline the absurdity, when it came to kosher meat, the three of us worked hand-in-hand in jointly managing the consortium which licensed butchers in the capital, the London Board for Shechita. It is true that this alliance was sorely tested in the late 1980s when first some butchers briefly defected to the Federation, then the United Synagogue tried to go it alone, but the unity of the Board was eventually restored. It might not have always been easy to keep the peace with *shechita*, but we were worlds apart on kashrut.

Our own Sephardi Kashrut Authority was established in the 1960s by Dr Gaon, who did not want our community to be left behind. The Spanish and Portuguese Community had been only sporadically involved in licensing till then. When British Jewry celebrated its tricentennial in 1956, a grand banquet was held in the Mansion House in London, which was prepared by the royal caterers Ring & Brymer under Sephardi supervision. Ring & Brymer were also the in-house caterers at the Royal Festival Hall, the chosen venue for the wedding of the Haham's daughter, also prepared the food on that occasion. The caterers used to tell me that if they did a non-Jewish function, they would make the money on the drinks and almost give the food free, but if they had done the same for a kosher function, they'd have been out of pocket.

The Jakobovitses wanted to use the same venue for the marriage of their eldest daughter but the use of Ring & Brymer meant that they would have had to hold the function under our supervision. The Chief Rabbi felt that he could not do so without putting the nose of the United Synagogue out of joint so he asked if we would allow joint supervision. Eric Nabarro, who headed our kashrut authority, was in no rush to agree to something we thought superfluous but eventually we did the gentlemanly thing and acceded to the Chief Rabbi's request.

I remember inspecting a kosher function myself which was under both Ashkenazi and Sephardi supervision where the *mashgiach*, supervisor, we provided happened to be an Ashkenazi and theirs a Sephardi, which only goes to show what nonsense it is for different authorities not to respect each other's standards. Since the synagogue bodies earn income from their licensing enterprises, they have little incentive to collaborate even though the kosher consumer would benefit if they did.

Kashrut rivalry reached its nadir in 1987 in what the *Jewish Chronicle* sarcastically labelled the "great kosher bunfight". A United Synagogue caterer had wanted to serve a brand of cake at a function which was made under the supervision of the Federation of Synagogues but the London Beth Din would not allow it. The United Synagogue went on to reinforce an old regulation that only caterers under its own authority would be permitted to operate on its premises. The Federation threatened to retaliate tit for tat unless the US backed down. For the majority of the kosher-eating public, it mattered not a jot which rabbinic logo their food was under. I was not going to abandon our open-door policy and drag the Sephardim into any turf war. I made it clear that "we will allow any caterer in any of our establishments who is under a recognised supervising authority".

The antics over kashrut partly reflected longstanding competition between the Federation and the United Synagogue. The smaller Federation was founded in the late 19th century to serve the Yiddish-speaking immigrants of the East End of London who felt the United Synagogue too anglicised. By the time of Lord Jakobovits, some thought the Federation an anachronism. But the Federation certainly didn't see itself as such and its appointment of an energetic young American rabbi, Dayan Yisroel Lichtenstein, as the head of its Beth Din in 1988 demonstrated its independence. I got on well with Dayan Lichtenstein and found him a friendly ear when I needed to talk to him. American Charedim always seemed more outgoing than their English counterparts. His religious outlook was to the right of mine but he always showed understanding of my position.

In general, my view was that if it was permissible to do something in Jewish law, then we should find a way to do it, rather than look for reasons to say no. For example, I conducted a wedding at Lauderdale Road on a Saturday night, which, while common in Israel, was a novelty here within the mainstream Orthodox community. The London Beth Din didn't like the idea on the grounds that there was a risk of people profaning Shabbat because there might not be enough time after nightfall to get ready for the *simchah* – for caterers to set up or women to do their hair. Since other places in the Jewish world managed to negotiate Saturday night weddings, however, I didn't see why London had to be the exception. The first I did was for Michael and Danielle Gross. He was an Ashkenazi and was a United Synagogue officer at one time, and Danielle was Sephardi. "To marry you, Michael," I told him, "I would do anything."

Although achieving co-operation over kashrut was an almost hopeless cause, we remained partners in other joint enterprises such as Jews' College. While Lord Jakobovits was its president, I became deputy president as the representative of the Spanish and Portuguese Community. The institution was never to recover the stature it had enjoyed before the Jacobs Affair. In the wake of that episode, the Chief Rabbi tried to ensure that no student of the college was tempted to follow Rabbi Jacobs by introducing a clause in the *semichah* which would allow him to revoke it if any of us went off the rails.

The college suffered from an increasing preference for British students to go to Israeli yeshivot in order to study for the rabbinate. While some students from Gateshead and other yeshivot found it useful to take degrees with us, they did not look to the college for their religious ethos. People like me were not their role models; their mentors remained in Gateshead and elsewhere.

When the college had to sell its attractive central London premises in Montagu Place and repair to temporary premises in Finchley Synagogue, it was in dire straits. Had it not been for Stanley Kalms, head of the Dixons' retail chain, whom the Chief Rabbi drafted in to restore the institution's fortunes, Jews' College would have been doomed.

Stanley Kalms took the college by the scruff of the neck and gave it a new lease of life. But he was not content simply to write cheques or make sure the books balanced. He had strong views on the direction which the United Synagogue and mainstream Orthodoxy should be going and he championed the middle-ground above the perceived drift to the right. When the college moved into its new, purpose-built headquarters in Hendon, he placed high hopes in its new principal, Jonathan Sacks.

Relieved of the pastoral duties of a congregational minister, Rabbi Sacks now had more time to devote to his intellectual interests. As his reputation as a speaker grew both inside and outside the Jewish community, so did Stanley Kalms's belief that he had found the next Chief Rabbi. The businessman was mesmerised by his protégé. One time I took Estelle for a break at Champney's, the health club in Tring, which she had always wanted to try. When we got to the spa, we ran into Lord Kalms. "Whatever Jonathan Sacks wants," he told me, "I am here to help."

Kalms took us all off one weekend for a retreat in a country hotel near Basingstoke – senior United Synagogue rabbis, Jews' College Council members – where we deliberated over the future of British Orthodoxy. The presentations were very business-like with lots of flip charts. It felt as if the Jakobovits era was coming to an end, and a new one beckoned under the leadership of Jonathan Sacks. In 1988, hundreds of people attended a one-day conference in London staged by Lord Kalms entitled "Traditional Alternatives", featuring some of the leading Orthodox rabbis from the United States and Israel (from the rightward-leaning halachic scholar David Bleich to the radical David Hartman). It was a chance for Jonathan to shine on a grand stage and he did. The event was widely seen as the launch of Kalms's campaign to make him Chief Rabbi.

I got on pretty well with Lord Kalms but he wasn't always a man whose reactions you could predict. Jonathan and I wanted to recognise his support for the college so we came up with the idea to award him an honorary doctorate. But when informed of the honour, he could not see the point and brusquely declined it. I tried to pacify him, "Stanley, you have been very generous to this place and this is the most valuable thing we could give back to you." He wrote to apologise that he had been too hasty – and as his son told me, you did not get an apology out of him that often – but he did not seem inclined to change his mind. Sometime later, Jonathan was able to bring him round and Stanley Kalms became D.Litt.

Despite the patronage of Lord Kalms, it was not a foregone conclusion that Jonathan Sacks would succeed Lord Jakobovits. Cyril Harris was a credible candidate and he would certainly have made a worthy Chief Rabbi. I remained good friends with Cyril. Our houses backed on to each other and my son Julian and his son Michael – who later became a rabbi – used to jump over the fence and play cricket together. When Cyril pulled out of the

Chief Rabbi race, I told him, "You have to find a project to occupy yourself. When I was frustrated by what was happening in my community, I started a school." I didn't know then that he was already negotiating to become Chief Rabbi of South Africa. It was a role he was to perform magnificently as he led its Jewish community through a time of transition into a post-apartheid world. All his Jews' College contemporaries must have felt a surge of pride when they saw the video of him saying a prayer at the induction of President Nelson Mandela.

When Jonathan Sacks duly took office in September 1991, he did so against a backdrop of great expectations. A month after he had announced his Decade of Renewal for British Jewry at his installation address, my own community was again attracting the attentions of the Jewish press for a rather less lofty reason. Since the retirement of Dr Gaon, the Haham's chair had remained vacant at the side of the ark in Lauderdale Road. I would sit on the *tebah* in the place that was reserved for the hazan. But some in the congregation thought that was too lowly a position for the rabbi and that I should be elevated to the front. I, of course, could not occupy the Haham's chair so a compromise was struck whereby I would sit on the other side of the ark. I remember when Lord Jakobovits came to preach, I had to squash a second chair alongside mine as our visitor puzzled over the empty chair opposite.

That was not the last of the matter. It was felt that if Dayan Toledano were to visit Maida Vale, he should be accorded equal status and therefore sit alongside the ark, too. The Haham's chair was put into storage and two reproduction Windsor chairs were bought. The issue was still being discussed at the annual meeting the following year, which happened to be on the evening of a general election. When one of my supporters dismissed the new furniture as "kitchen chairs", the purchaser sturdily defended their quality. While most of the country was waiting to see if Neil

Kinnock had ousted John Major, the Spanish and Portuguese Jews' Community was debating the merits of the rabbi's seat. The saving grace of this pantomime was that it provided ample sport for Chaim Bermant's comic pen. Not for nothing did the *Jewish Chronicle's* columnist write, "Blessed are the Sephardim".

6

Crisis and Continuity

IN 1992, THE week before Pesach, Zachary Citron, the administrator of Bevis Marks, and his wife Emma were entertaining some Friday night guests in their flat next to the historic synagogue. Their ten-month-old son Joseph had not gone to sleep so they brought him downstairs and sat him in his highchair. Suddenly there was an almighty bang. The windows blew in and showered the Shabbat diners with glass. A large bomb had exploded at the nearby Baltic Exchange in the heart of the City of London. Fortunately, the Citrons and their guests, who were taken to hospital, escaped with only minor cuts. For baby Joseph, it might have been a close thing. Upstairs, where he would usually have been sleeping at that hour, his travel-cot had been speared with shards of glass.

Bevis Marks itself, which had survived the Second World War unlike its Ashkenazi neighbour, the Great Synagogue in Duke Place, was caught in the blast. Some of the original leaded windows had shattered, there was structural damage to the roof and a wall, and the tablets on top of the great oak ark needed repair. Although the Jewish community had for some years been on guard against terrorism, this outrage had nothing to do with the Middle East and the synagogue was not the target; the perpetrators were the IRA.

Services did not resume in the main sanctuary until some months later and renovation was not complete when, a year after the first attack, Bevis Marks was again hit by another IRA bombing in Bishopsgate. The Shabbat morning worshippers were evacuated to the basement following a police warning but the choirmaster, Sam Dias, went upstairs to bring down a Sefer Torah. He was lucky; when he came back down, a piece of glass was lodged in his top hat.

The damage sustained in the second attack was minor compared to the first. But the overall repair bill ran into hundreds of thousands of pounds and we were grateful to receive some help from the Corporation of the City of London, which recognised the historic importance of the building. At a service entitled "Relighting the Candle" to mark the restoration of Bevis Marks, some of our younger members sat in the same seats at the service as their ancestors had occupied when Bevis Marks had opened. It was, I noted, "a bastion in Anglo-Jewry symbolic of excellent relations which have always existed between Christians and Jews since our resettlement". The City of London had welcomed Jews into high office even before they were able to take seats in Parliament.

I noted too that it was particularly fitting to have with us the country's most senior legal figure, the Lord Chief Justice, Peter Taylor, who opened the *hechal*, the ark. Magnificent as the ark was, carved in the style of a Renaissance reredos, an altarpiece, it was, I pointed out, "in reality nothing but a bookcase". What mattered was its contents, the scrolls of the Torah. While other religions may have specialised in theology, what defined Judaism more than anything was its preoccupation with law. So much so that in the Jerusalem Talmud God is quoted as saying, "Forget Me if you must, but always keep My law." For it is through keeping the law, I said, that we sense God's presence.

That special service was one of a number I was privileged to conduct at Bevis Marks. They helped to cement its place as the community's "cathedral synagogue", equivalent to Westminster Abbey or St Paul's for celebrating landmark occasions. Its antiquity was proof that Judaism had been part of the life of this country for several centuries. According to legend, at the time of its construction in the 18th century, Princess Anne, the future Queen, had donated an oak beam from a Royal Navy ship to be used in its roof. I valued Bevis Marks too as a place of unity where, from time to time, the various factions of Anglo-Jewry could set aside their differences and gather as one. Those occasions were all the more welcome for the cohesion of the community was to be tested in the ensuing years.

No other synagogue in Britain possessed the atmosphere of Bevis Marks, as many couples knew when they began their married life there under the *chuppah* at night, illuminated only by candlelight. Naturally, it was the place where my son Julian and his bride, Sian Okrent, from Southport, chose for their wedding in 1998. Jonathan Sacks officiated with me. After the ceremony, it is the Sephardi custom for the fathers of the couple to open the ark and for the newly marrieds to receive a blessing. I asked Lord Jakobovits to deliver it. I wanted to show honour to the Emeritus Chief Rabbi, who was ailing and seen in public less often than he used to be.

Yet, while Bevis Marks was a prized asset and recognised as a building of "outstanding value" by the Royal Commission for Ancient and Historical Monuments as far back as 1929, the cost of maintaining it had long been a burden on the Spanish and Portuguese Congregation. As Jews began to move west out of the East End of London, there had even been a proposal in the 1880s to demolish it. When I was a young rabbi, Dr Gaon had asked me to help with a study to consider its future. I recommended that while we should do all we could to revive it, if that proved impossible, then we ought to sell it and build a school. Somebody at the time prophetically corrected me: "You will not close it," he said, "but you will build a Jewish school." I was naïve to think we could ever have sold it.

Some years later, I came up with another scheme. There is a loft in Bevis Marks with quite a sizeable space. Why not allocate it to the Jewish Museum, which was looking for alternative premises? It would have been an ideal location in the centre of the city and in the birthplace of modern British Jewry. But the idea was too audacious for some of the loyalists among the congregation who would brook no tampering with their beloved building. Although the number of Jews who actually lived in the vicinity remained small, we did our best to attract those who came into the City to work. Our hazan, Halfon Benarroch, who devoted his life to Bevis Marks, led daily services during the week; the year after the bombing, he started a weekday lunch club, supplemented with activities such as a music circle and lectures.

The early 1990s were a period of optimism within British Jewry, for two main reasons. The Oslo Accords of September 1993 held out the promise of peace between Israel and the Palestinians after decades of conflict. On the domestic front, the accession of Jonathan Sacks as Chief Rabbi brought hope of change inside the Jewish community.

I happened to be in the United States when the historic handshake took place between the Israeli Prime Minister Yitzhak Rabin and the PLO leader Yasser Arafat on the White House lawn. It was a sight most of us would have scarcely thought possible. Only a couple of years before, the image on television of Benjamin Netanyahu in a gas mask as Saddam Hussein launched missile attacks on Israel during the Gulf War seemed a more likely representation of the state of affairs in the Middle East. While in New York, I had begun working on my sermon for Rosh Hashanah, which was only a few days away, but in the wake of Oslo I had to tear it up and start afresh.

Although some parts of the Orthodox world were opposed to the accord, notably the influential Lubavitch movement, I was ready to welcome it. In my sermon, I said that we had all watched the White House signing ceremony "with delight, if tempered with caution". I endorsed Rabin's willingness to give back captured land by drawing on Rabban Gamliel's famous saying that the world rests on three pillars – truth, justice, peace; the last of these, I explained, entails "flexibility and compromise". I also recalled the peaceful relations between Muslims and Jews that had once prevailed in the Ottoman Empire, citing the early 19th-century Rabbi Eliezer Pappo, from Bulgaria, who encouraged his students to live in Muslim lands "where Jews can raise their eyes to heaven and devote their hearts to God". I mentioned that members of our own synagogue who had lived in Muslim countries often spoke to me of the trust that had existed between their neighbours and them. "Jewish bankers tell me how their Muslim clients would leave money in their banks without even counting it," I said. The optimism I felt at the time, of course, turned out to be misplaced.

Lord Jakobovits had elevated the chief rabbinate as a national institution, as his peerage proved, and given his successor a platform to build on, but he appeared still to be a rabbi of the old school. His biographer, Chaim Bermant, called him a defender of Victorian values. Jonathan was very much viewed as a man for the times ahead. His brilliance in analysing the challenges facing contemporary Jewry encouraged confidence in his ability to tackle them. When he called for a Decade of Renewal in his installation address, it was greeted with a high level of expectation.

A few years before he took office, I advised Jonathan to set up his own charitable trust in order to give himself independence to initiate projects, as I have done myself. He accepted the suggestion and appointed me one of his trustees. (When he became Chief Rabbi, he closed it on advice that it would no longer be appropriate to keep it.) We had known each other since he taught for the Young Jewish Leadership Institute, when his talents as a speaker were quickly apparent, and I always felt we had an understanding. We met a month after his installation in September 1991, after which he wrote to say that he felt, "There are great things we can do together and we must be seen, on occasions, to be working together to break through the mirage of communal divisions."

I happily took part in one of Jonathan's first ventures, donning a baseball cap for a mass charity walk in Hyde Park one summer afternoon. Organisations across the community, including from the Progressive wing, had been invited to come along to an event whose primary aim was to promote unity. But as even this most seemingly innocuous of activities was to demonstrate, unity was an elusive ideal that lay beyond the best of intentions. No one had foreseen that an application to join the walk would come from the Jewish Lesbian and Gay Helpline. When it was rejected, there was an outcry from the Progressive rabbinate. The event, at any rate, passed off peacefully and thousands enjoyed their outing in the sunshine. But the controversy over the exclusion of the helpline was a harbinger of things to come.

We were nevertheless able to maintain a semblance of unity at the annual commemoration of Yom Hashoah, which took place around the monument in Hyde Park. More than once I joined Jonathan and Hugo Gryn as we remembered the six million. It was not a formal religious service in the sense of following a prescribed liturgy nor did it take place in a synagogue. It was the only occasion in the communal calendar when an Orthodox and a Reform rabbi would jointly participate.

While I admired Jonathan's efforts to revitalise the community, I was not actively involved in any of his projects. Like any Chief Rabbi, he had to devote a fair portion of his time to cultivating good relations outside the Jewish community. Visiting his house, I was struck by one particular item, Grace after Meals booklets with transliteration of the Hebrew into English, which enabled non-Jewish guests or the more assimilated of our brethren to follow. It seemed evidence of the wide circle he and Elaine were entertaining at home.

I was more preoccupied with the pursuit of renewal closer to home. As I never tired of reminding my congregation, since the early days of resettlement our synagogue was more than a place of worship but a centre of community which provided welfare, educational and other services. If something is missing, a rabbi has to be a catalyst and persuade his congregants of the need to act. At times he has to be prepared to reinvent the wheel, especially when it comes to young people. When one generation of youngsters grows up and moves on, they leave a gap; activities fall into abeyance and we have to start anew. What worked for teenagers in the 1970s was not going to work for teenagers in the 1990s. We could never muster the numbers to sustain a peer-led youth movement such as Bnei Akiva of our own. Thanks to the commitment of a team of parents led by Peter Fraiman and Dalia Sehayek, we were able to launch a new youth group in 1993 called Launchpad, which we supported with a part-time worker. It enjoyed a period of success for a time and was recognised by being named runner-up in the category for youth in the Chief Rabbi's new Awards for Excellence.

I had hopes that the new Shasha-funded Sephardi Centre, which I mentioned before, would be a magnet for young adults. I was especially keen to attract the growing number of children of immigrants from the Middle East who may not necessarily have been associated with the congregation. I thought its message would resonate beyond the immediate Sephardi community. As I stressed at the opening in 1994, "we can present a religious interpretation of Judaism which does not have an ideological adjective such as Orthodox or Reform attached to it.... We Sephardim, with a little give and take, have always managed to have only one Jewish community."

I was sufficiently well established within the Spanish and Portuguese Jews' Congregation to press ahead with initiatives such as the centre but I could not pretend that I always got my way and that every member of the lay leadership was my ally. One incident where I ran into criticism involved the death of Davide Sala, the leading Sephardi philanthropist, in 1992. His wife Irene had been killed in a plane accident in South America on the way to an archaeological dig in Chile and he survived her only by a year. The Salas, particularly Irene, were liberally minded and, unusually for someone from the Iraqi Jewish community, Davide was cremated.

Although cremation was strictly forbidden by Jewish law, both the United Synagogue and ourselves retained a provision to bury the ashes of the deceased in a coffin in our cemeteries. According to our regulations, a hazan was restricted from officiating beyond reciting the *hashcabah*, the memorial prayer, in the prayer hall. When it got out that I had accompanied the coffin to the grave, one of the elders believed I had overstepped the mark and called for my reprimand. The rules allowed a little discretion depending on circumstances. One of the members of the Mahamad, Bernard Mocatta, publicly defended my conduct and said he was sure his colleagues were satisfied I had acted properly. I remarked that it was sad that the death of a man who had done such good in the community should be the cause of dissension.

On another occasion a couple I was due to marry at Bevis Marks asked if Louis Jacobs could say a few words at the ceremony since he was a longstanding friend of the family. I had no problem and agreed to the request. But there were some within our hierarchy who felt that this would be breaking Orthodox ranks. I did not feel it was a battle worth fighting so in the end Louis did not speak. The episode, at any rate, did not sully our friendship.

As Jonathan embarked on his programme of renewal, I wondered how far he was going to be able to go. The conservative instincts of his Beth Din, I felt, were always liable to act as a brake on his ambitions. In 1993, he launched Jewish Continuity, which was intended to be the third pillar of community fundraising to support youth and education, as the JIA did Israel and Jewish Care, welfare. The following year, he instigated his review of Women in the Jewish Community.

With Continuity, he was forced to confront the reality of religious politics. If it wanted to be a community-wide organisation, it would have to contribute to Progressive educational causes. But how could an Orthodox Chief Rabbi be party to support for non-Orthodox education – at least without incurring displeasure from the right? In fact, there was a precedent with the Jewish Educational Development Trust started by his predecessor. I remember Moshe Davis, Lord Jakobovits's aide, explaining to me, "We've got to work with the Reform. If they have a Jewish school, the way out is that we'll give them money for their kitchen, but not for Jewish studies." But Continuity could never surmount the politics. The Reform movement was more assertive than in the days of Lord Jakobovits and not minded to be treated as second-class citizens. A review by Professor Leslie Wagner, who had been a member of the selection panel which had chosen Jonathan as Chief Rabbi, described the organisation as a "proxy battleground" between Orthodox and Progressives and recommended Jonathan take a back seat: in 1996, it merged with the JIA to become the UJIA.

Those who anticipated that radical change would come out

of the women's review were always destined to be disappointed because Jonathan did not have a great deal of room for manoeuvre. It was only in 1993, under his chief rabbinate, that the United Synagogue had agreed that women could sit as full members of its governing council. It was decades behind the Spanish and Portuguese Community in this respect; the first female representative on our Board of Elders was Lady Mocatta, who, in 1950, was elected with the highest number of votes that year.

I should add that our prayer book had long contained prayers for *zeved habat*, the celebration of a birth of a girl. We have a ceremony either in the synagogue or at home where the baby is brought in and we bless the child in the presence of her parents. In Ashkenazi communities, the name might be announced in synagogue without the baby being there. I always felt strongly that a child who has to live with the name should at least be present when it is given to her. Jonathan Sacks liked it so much that he later introduced an adapted version of it into his edition of the Singer's Siddur for the United Synagogue.

The women's review kindled hopes of a solution to the predicament of the *agunah*, a woman chained to a broken marriage because her husband refused her a *get*, a religious divorce. There was some movement on this in 1996 with an amendment to family law which gave judges in the secular courts the discretion to withhold a civil divorce if there was any impediment to religious remarriage; it was designed to deter husbands who held their wives to ransom by demanding unfavourable financial terms in exchange for a *get*.

But it always struck me as a pity we have had to rely on the laws of the country to do our work for us. I believe there are solutions to the *agunah* problem available within *halachah* if only rabbis had the courage to adopt them. Upstairs in my study is a little booklet written in Hebrew by rabbis in the early 20th century

– and republished by the-then Rishon le Zion, Rabbi Bakshi-Doron – which suggests various options on the way forward. Some rabbis, for example, believe it would be possible for the husband to sign a clause at the time of the marriage which would subsequently enable a rabbinic court to dissolve it in certain circumstances. It is a weakness of our times that not everyone is ready to consider the potential for halachic development.

When rabbis are confronted with an issue like the discovery of electricity, for example, you find some who say it can be used on Shabbat, some who say it cannot and others who say it can be used on Yom Tov but not on Shabbat. The last option may be unfamiliar to many but you will find observant people who regard it as perfectly acceptable to switch on lights on Yom Tov. It takes time for the law to crystallise but legitimate differences may remain.

In no way could blame be attached to Jonathan for not coming up with his own answer to the *agunah*. The English rabbinate is small fry when it comes to halachic decision-making in the Orthodox world and no rabbi here is going to take a stand on his own. On such an issue as this, there is great pressure for consensus. It would take the clout of a leading rabbi in Israel to institute change. And the prospect of that is receding because the Israeli rabbinic establishment is becoming more intransigent by the day. I found one amusing example of the trend to greater stringency in a Charedi book in Israel; it reprinted the famous engraving of Manasseh ben Israel from the 17th century, except his beard had been lengthened from the original representation, which to some Charedi eyes failed to conform to what a proper rabbi should look like.

The forces that the Chief Rabbi was up against were plain for all to see when controversy over the annual Limmud conference in the UK burst into the open in 1995. Limmud had begun as a retreat for Jewish educators in the Christmas holidays in 1980 but it had grown into a family education conference attended by hundreds at the time (now by thousands). One of its founders had been Clive Lawton, whose mother was from Gibraltar. The London Beth Din disapproved of the idea that Progressive rabbis could teach Torah on an equal footing with the Orthodox and did its best to discourage United Synagogue rabbis from going. Jonathan intervened in order to make it clear that in his view rabbis should be free to decide for themselves whether they wanted to take part or not. He maintained a diplomatic distance by staying away from the conference himself in order to avoid a public show of difference with his Beth Din.

I was under no such constraints and never had an issue with visiting Limmud. I actually went to speak at the conference the year after the controversy in the United Synagogue, the meagre participation of whose rabbis in the event illustrated how much sway the Beth Din had. If people were spending time and money on Jewish education, then boycotting the event seemed to me a case of cutting off your nose to spite your face and I always encouraged younger rabbis to go.

It was no easy task trying to keep the different parts of the community happy. After Jonathan came back with his wife Elaine from their first visit to Gibraltar, he remarked on the challenges its Chief Minister, Joe Bossano, was having in dealing with his critical constituents. "I know exactly how he feels," he told me.

The Chief Rabbi knew at least when he came to Bevis Marks he was among friends. I welcomed his presence at a service marking the 50th anniversary of the Allied Victory in Europe in 1995 as a sign of strengthening relations between our communities. He was in good company; other guests included the Home Secretary Michael Howard, the Opposition Leader Tony Blair, the Archbishop of Canterbury George Carey and the Archbishop of Westminster, Cardinal Basil Hume. The event was in the long tradition of services of thanksgiving that had been held at the synagogue in years past. Our forebears had gathered to offer their gratitude for victory over Napoleon at Trafalgar in 1805 and then at Waterloo ten years later. They had even rejoiced in the "restoration of peace and religious liberty" to Bulgaria, Serbia and Romania in 1878.

I noted that our custom of singing the National Anthem in Hebrew on such occasions had been started by a rabbi in Gibraltar, Moses Benaim, in the 19th century, who had translated it and incorporated it into the festival liturgy there. I also mentioned that shortly before the service, I had shown Cardinal Hume a picture of the Ten Commandments in Hebrew and Spanish in the foyer, whereupon he began to read the Hebrew aloud. His Hebrew, I thought, was "slightly better than my Latin."

But this remembrance event was eclipsed by another later in the year, whose tone was anything but thanksgiving. The Albert Hall was full as Anglo-Jewry came to mourn Israeli Prime Minister Yitzhak Rabin. The shock of his assassination at the hand of a fellow-Jew, particularly one who claimed religious motivation for his action, was still sinking in. I lit one of the candles, as did Hugo Gryn. At another memorial meeting a few weeks later, I reiterated my long-held view with greater urgency, "Religion and politics do not mix and the sooner they are separated, the better."

While Rabin's death cast a pall over the Jewish world, at least our congregation could look forward the following year to a cause for local celebration: the centenary of Lauderdale Road Synagogue. The synagogue had followed the path of many Sephardim who had gone west to live out of the vicinity of Bevis Marks. But more than that, its founding constituted an act of regeneration. For, as I quoted the *Jewish Chronicle* from 1896 in a pamphlet for our 75th anniversary, the Sephardi community had appeared at the time "in a state of irremediable decay". The fortunes of a congregation may ebb and flow but after a hundred years, Lauderdale Road was in a healthy state: Shabbat morning services in Maida Vale were well attended and our all-round activity was high. While architecturally it has the appearance of a cathedral synagogue from outside, it seats only around 400 people, so with 150 to 200 people, it looks pretty full. There are larger synagogues in London which seem almost deserted by comparison. Our Sephardi Centre, which stood on what had once been the community's orphanage, had become an attractive educational setting.

For the centenary, Estelle co-edited an anthology of recipes with Judith Sacerdoti collected from members of the congregation, called *A Sephardi Feast*, which included some from her own Turkish and Salonikan community of Holland Park; such as choumleck, baked vegetables in klema, a tomato sauce, and spinach or leek sfungato, a flan. It was more than simply a cookbook; it contained profiles of the different communities from North Africa and the Middle East from which our members originated, using the text of an exhibition mounted a couple of years earlier by the Jewish Museum, *A Tapestry of Many Threads*. It showed how far we had evolved from our Spanish and Portuguese beginnings to our present multi-cultural make-up.

She also contributed one of a new set of synagogue vestments produced for the anniversary by some of our women. Estelle had become accomplished in embroidery, having taken it up many years earlier through the encouragement of Esther Carvalho and had been lucky enough to be taught by Beryl Dean, the Church's most famous embroideress. She reckoned embroidery must be "in her blood"; in Salonika, when a girl was born, her elders immediately began embroidering her trousseau. Estelle once helped to make a new cope for the Bishop of London for the Queen's Silver Jubilee, depicting the churches of his diocese. While each of her class stitched a different building, Estelle, as a rabbi's wife, was tactfully given not a church but the house in which all the embroidery was done.

The first item she made for the synagogue was one of a pair of new white Torah covers for the High Holy Days in 1975, which displayed the tablets of the Ten Commandments swathed in flames symbolic of the revelation at Sinai. But the motif also alluded to one of the most tragic incidents which happened during our time in the community. The design had been created by the artist Edward Toledano. He and his wife had waited many years for a child and eventually they had a daughter; but when she was a little girl, tragically, she died in a fire.

Another Torah cloak, as we like to call them, which Estelle embroidered for the synagogue had a special provenance. The material for it was acquired by Clemens Nathan who ran a textile business and was one of the community's leading human-rights campaigners: the fabric actually came from one of the last pieces of the same bright red velvet that had been used for the Queen's Coronation.

Estelle would embroider our initials on the corner of our talletot, as is the Sephardi custom. Sometimes she would use symbols; one of mine bears the emblem of the synagogue, while Julian's has a shofar. For her centenary piece for Lauderdale Road, she made a purple mantle to hang over the pulpit, embroidering an image of the rose window above the *hechal* and inserting in the middle the letter *kof*, standing for 100.

In my sermon at the centenary service in October 1996, I said it was a "festive and emotional" occasion for all of us – especially for one *Yehida* (female congregant), who was actually born before the synagogue was built. It was not our role to sit back and polish the family silver, I stressed, but to add to the "great and noble inheritance" we had been handed for the future. We should strive to be like Abraham, who was compared in the Midrash to perfume – whose fragrance was not something to be bottled up but spread afar. "At a time when Anglo-Jewry is tearing itself asunder," I said, "we stand for a type of religion which is welcoming to all who appreciate our methods and approach."

I hardly needed to elaborate on my reference to the rift within British Jewry because everyone in the community knew that the tensions between Orthodox and Progressive had been growing worse. The catalyst was the death that August of Hugo Gryn. Hugo died at the relatively young age of sixty-six but he had been ill with cancer for a while. At a wedding he had conducted a few weeks earlier I was told he had looked painfully frail. Hugo had long been one of the country's leading interfaith advocates whose message of reconciliation carried the authority of an Auschwitz survivor who knew all too well the terrible effect of hatred. In the days before Holocaust Memorial Day, no one had done more to keep the memory of the Shoah alive in Britain. In his latter years, he had come to be more widely known as a voice of wisdom through the BBC Radio 4 programme, *The Moral Maze*.

Estelle and I went to the funeral in Golders Green, collecting Elaine Sacks from the Chief Rabbi's residence in Hamilton Terrace to come with us. Although I did not enter the prayer hall at Hoop Lane, I went to the graveside and with the other mourners put earth into the grave. I had not been before to the funeral of a Reform rabbi because I had never had occasion to, but I did not see anything controversial in it. I was doing my duty as a Jew to bury a fellow-Jew.

Jonathan Sacks, as well as Lord and Lady Jakobovits, visited the Gryn family at their shivah. But I was, as far as I was aware, the only Orthodox rabbi to go to the funeral itself. The absence of any rabbi or senior lay leader from the United Synagogue immediately caused controversy. Sir Sigmund Sternberg, a senior figure in the Reform movement who was certainly no hothead, wrote in a letter to the *Jewish Chronicle* that, while gratified Elaine, Estelle and I along with a member of Jonathan's staff had gone, he was astounded the United Synagogue had sent no formal representative. Chaim Bermant found the conduct of the US unforgivable. Through the rest of the summer, resentment simmered.

A few weeks later Professor Leslie Wagner, in a letter to the *Jewish Chronicle*, suggested that the Board of Deputies hold a memorial meeting for Hugo on behalf of the whole community. The Board liked the idea and a meeting was arranged for February where Jonathan would lead the tributes. The Council of Christians and Jews, of which Jonathan was the sole Jewish president, would jointly host it. It seemed a good way to dispel the acrimony of the past months and honour one of the community's favourite personalities.

For some, however, the Chief Rabbi was going too far in being willing to pay respect publicly to a Reform rabbi. Shortly before the memorial event, the Union of Orthodox Hebrew Congregations stirred the pot by saying Jonathan's attendance would amount to a *Chillul Hashem*. What was worse for Jonathan was that his own United Synagogue rabbinate could not bring themselves to come to his defence; hopelessly divided, they could agree only on a limp, neutral statement that they "understood" his position. It was an indication of how much pressure he was under from the right.

At the meeting Jonathan alluded to private efforts he had made to head off dissent at his attendance, though these had failed. I wasn't party to any diplomatic manoeuvres. I simply had a walk-on role, sitting with Louis Jacobs on the platform at the front. Jonathan spoke with characteristic eloquence of Hugo as a "living symbol of hope". It ought to have been a fitting conclusion and I was unaware that more trouble was brewing.

All appeared well the following week when both Jonathan and I spoke at a unique occasion at Bevis Marks, a service to mark the first state visit to Britain by an Israeli president. After all the prayers for Zion which had been uttered within the walls of this old synagogue, few services here could be "as moving and momentous as this service of welcome", I told President Ezer Weizman and his wife Reuma. I imagined the spirits of the two great historic supporters of the Jewish return to Israel who worshipped at Bevis Marks, Sir Moses Montefiore and Haham Gaster, smiling over us and saying, "I told you so, I told you so."

For more than a hundred years, until 1780, it had been our custom to present visiting Lord Mayors from the City of London with a silver platter (I later revived the custom). Our annals record that the first gift, to Sir Richard Ford in 1671, was actually a pipe of wine for which the synagogue paid £48; it must have been some vintage. When I learned that one of the trays, presented in 1737, was now in the Israel Museum, I ordered a similar piece and had it inscribed with the coat of arms of the synagogue to give to President Weizman. I was hoping the president in turn would present it to the museum to sit alongside the original although I was to be disappointed in that.

It was indeed a moving occasion but it did not go quite as smoothly as planned. The president, a former fighter pilot and a typical no-nonsense Israeli, took umbrage that we had not recited a prayer for the Israeli Defence Forces and left the service early. Luckily, few people were aware of the reason for his departure. (Now we do mention the IDF in our prayers on Shabbat morning – my son Julian having been among the most vociferous campaigners for it – as well as Her Majesty's Armed Forces.)

We had little time to bask in the celebration of the President of Israel's visit because, a fortnight later, the community was catapulted into its worst crisis since the Jacobs Affair. In his attempts to disarm criticism of his participation in the memorial event for Hugo, Jonathan had appealed for understanding in a letter to the head of the Union of Orthodox Hebrew Congregations, Dayan Chanoch Padwa. It was drafted in formal rabbinic Hebrew and couched in terms that he hoped would weigh with the elderly rabbi. Jonathan made out that he had no option but to speak at the event otherwise he would risk the Reform setting up a rival to the chief rabbinate.

Of course, the letter was never intended for public consumption but a copy fell into the hands of the *Jewish Chronicle*, which published a translation, along with an explanation by Jonathan of why he had written it. The explosion was predictable. Whatever upset had occurred at the time of the funeral paled into insignificance with the widespread outrage that followed the letter's revelation. The Sunday after its publication on Friday I was called to an emergency meeting at the house of the Chief Rabbi.

The small group of us there included Lira, Lady Winston (wife of Lord Winston), who had been involved in Jewish Continuity and the solicitor Charles Corman. It was obvious the Chief Rabbi was in a deep hole and under considerable strain. I felt sorry that his ill-fated peace initiative was now blasted all over the press.

For all the furore, I did not believe that the chief rabbinate was in jeopardy nor that Jonathan would have to resign. The days might have gone when King Edward VII could refer to Nathan Adler as "my Chief Rabbi," but the office was still too useful as a port-of-call for government and others for anyone acting in the best interests of the community to want to scupper it. Jonathan was unmatched not only as a spokesman for Judaism to the world but for religion more generally. As many said, he was the Archbishop of Canterbury the country never had.

I felt confident the dispute would eventually blow over. My advice was for the Chief Rabbi to lie low for a while. I didn't see the need for any more visible campaign on his behalf. The day after the meeting Jonathan wrote to thank me for "your personal support during these painful and difficult days – it has meant a great deal to Elaine and myself at a time when friendship is most needed and appreciated." There could be no doubt, he said, "it will take time to heal the wounds. But the preliminary indications are that responsible figures within the community want a process of healing now to take place. At such times, we learn who our true friends are; I will always cherish the support you gave when it mattered most."

It took a while but at the end of the following year, the United Synagogue reached agreement with the Reform, Liberals and Masorti to set up a joint consultative committee. The Stanmore Accords, as they became known, were a set of protocols designed to govern inter-denominational dealings and prevent the recurrence of recent events. We were asked to take part but I saw no point. We had no quarrel with anyone and I did not need to sit on a committee to maintain amicable relations with other sections of the community.

As a rabbi, you naturally like to open schools rather than to close them. But I was one of the governors of Carmel College who decided in 1997 that my old school had no future. I had been asked to join the governing body by my Jews' College contemporary Stefan Reif after Kopul Rosen's son Rabbi Jeremy – we knew him as Rooky after his Hebrew name of Yerucham – resigned as headmaster; we appointed Philip Skelker as his successor, who kept it going for a number of years but the educational tide was against him. The college was losing money and had become over-reliant on the children of affluent families from abroad. Without the support of its chairman, Cyril Stein, it would have shut earlier. Parents were less inclined to send their children away from home and Carmel faced greater competition with the opening in 1990 of a new Jewish day school in London, Immanuel College, which was named after Lord Jakobovits.

I was concerned, however, that with the planned sale of the land to a developer, we had set the price too low. Most of the board sided with Cyril over the disposal but I felt we should hold out for more, especially as it was a charitable enterprise and any money we could recoup from the sale could go towards Jewish education. When I sought advice from Sir Gavin Lightman – a High Court judge, who had been a regular attender of one of my study groups at home – he encouraged me to continue my resistance. Crucially, I had the support of Conrad Morris, who was a very good friend of Cyril's. My persistence paid off and instead we sold the site to Sir Naim Dangoor's Exilarch Foundation, fetching at least a £1 million more than first envisaged, which could be donated to Immanuel and other schools.

Naim's son David, who himself had been a pupil at Carmel, asked me, "Why didn't you come to us earlier? We could have bought the site and then let the school go on without paying rent." But it was too late. Some Carmel pupils transferred to the Jewish boarding house at Clifton College in Bristol, Polack's, which itself was only to survive for another eight years.

I had one emotional duty to discharge: to oversee the transfer of the remains of Rabbi Rosen, who had died young aged only forty-nine, from his burial-place in the grounds of the school to the Mount of Olives in Jerusalem. That sensitive task I assigned to the registrar of our Beth Din, Rabbi Isaac Abraham, an upright man whom I could trust to take the greatest care. It is a mitzvah to rebury someone in Israel and there is a particular halachic process to follow; the family, for instance, has briefly to sit shivah again, for an hour or two.

Even though the college may have closed, I had dreams for the campus to continue as a Jewish education centre. I envisioned it as a countryside retreat running short residential courses primarily for young Jews as well as summer programmes for Israeli university students, who would be taught by top-quality visiting scholars. Academics from abroad, I believed, would be attracted by being able to use the Bodleian Library in nearby Oxford, which has one of the world's most important holdings of medieval

Judaica. There was nothing quite like the centre in Anglo-Jewry, which would have a strong Sephardi flavour. Lucien Gubbay and I wanted to bring in the Montefiore Endowment, the charity responsible for Sir Moses's educational legacy. The scheme would have required substantial investment because the buildings needed a lot more than a lick of paint. But I couldn't find other donors. The Dangoors, however, did enable the site to be used for camps and seminars for a number of years until it was eventually sold for development.

I enjoyed better luck with another project I became involved in. The Saatchi Synagogue we had inaugurated at Naima JPS was used daily by the school and by our congregation for the High Holy Days but lay empty most weekends. One day I was approached by Dr Michael Sinclair, the youthful-looking philanthropist who had emerged on the leadership scene after he was picked by the Chief Rabbi to head Jewish Continuity. "You know, Abraham, the Saatchis have given you much more with their name than their money," he told me. His idea was for a new synagogue which would try to appeal to young Jews who would otherwise seldom show their face inside one.

The name "Saatchi" had instant magnetism. Michael was ready to pour money into the venture and he could not have been more generous. The choice of a rabbi to lead it was inspired. Pini Dunner, still in his twenties, had a strictly Orthodox pedigree – his grandfather Joseph was one of the most eminent rabbis on the Union of Orthodox Hebrew Congregations and his uncle was a dayan there. But Pini, who had presented the Jewish show on Spectrum Radio, was charismatic and cosmopolitan and understood his generation. The new Saatchi Synagogue would offer Friday night dinners with informal services in the singalong, neo-Chasidic style of Shlomo Carlebach and entertaining after-dinner speakers.

It launched in autumn in 1998 with a flamboyant advertising campaign, which featured one poster with the picture of a large fried fishball and the promise that at the new synagogue this was "the only thing that gets rammed down your throat". The promotional tactics were meant to convey something different from the stuffy image of conventional communities that many of our youth held, fairly or not, and naturally they got one or two people's backs up. All I can say to the critics is that they should have seen some of the poster ideas I vetoed.

Gabriela Pomeroy, who reviewed the new enterprise for the *Jewish Chronicle*, said it "tickles the curiosity of hundreds of people who would not normally dream of showing their faces in a synagogue on Friday night". While some guests sang and others talked after dinner in the "warm and buzzy" atmosphere, she reported, "the approachable Rabbi Dunner mingled, chatting to us about politics and religion. He listened intently and seemed prepared to acknowledge the existence of greyness in many issues."

Pini proved a rabbi able to reach parts other rabbis could not. The Saatchi experiment flourished under his dynamism. He maintained an impressive guest list of speakers including Benjamin Netanyahu, who had taken a break from politics after his first term of office as Prime Minister; I don't think the Community Security Trust was overly pleased with the invitation because of the security headache. Pini, who liked to be his own boss, was not the easiest person to get along with. Since I felt religiously responsible for the site, I expected him to defer to my authority and on occasions we clashed over what I felt was a lack of consultation. But the Saatchi Synagogue brought many young people to Shabbat dinner who might otherwise have spent Friday night out at a non-kosher restaurant. The historian Todd Endelman, in his book *The Jews of Britain 1656-2000,* contrasted Saatchi with the slowness of Anglo-Jewry's older institutions to grapple with change. When I had dinner with Professor Endelman, I reminded him it was the rabbi of the community's oldest congregation that had given the new venture a home.

Around the launch of the Saatchi Synagogue I was preparing for another event at Bevis Marks. Following his election as Lord Mayor of London, Lord Levene asked me to be his chaplain. Lord Levene was the eighth Jewish incumbent, the first being Sir David Salomons in 1855. As he was to be sworn in at the Guildhall on Friday afternoon and afterwards would have a dinner in the Mansion House, he thought it would be nice to have a Friday night service in between. I was happy to oblige. As an alderman, he had attended services at the synagogue and he had great affection for it.

The Bishop of London, the Right Reverend Richard Chartres, attended. Indeed most of the guests were non-Jewish. "My wife asked me the other day what were my precise duties as one of the chaplains to the Lord Mayor in addition to dressing up and eating," I said in my address at the service. In truth, beyond such attendance at such ceremonies, not a great deal. Lord Levene sat in the chair next to Sir Moses Montefiore's, whose seat has two armrests. "He could not sit there today," I explained, "not because he is too fat but because his mayoral gown is far too bulky."

When I had been asked by the Master of Ceremonies at the Manor House what I was going to wear, I was at first at a loss because I didn't know. I pulled out of the wardrobe my old doctorate gown from the University of London which I hadn't worn in ages. It was red and I matched it with a maroon kippah from Naima JPS. When he saw me, the Bishop of London joked: "I thought you must be the Cardinal Archbishop of Westminster, dressed in red." (Perhaps the colour suited me – my friend John Martin chose to paint me in my academic, rather than rabbinic, gown for a portrait which now hangs at home.)

After the service, we walked to the Mansion House where butlers were waiting with trays of kosher wine. "As it's Friday night, we ought to say Kiddush," I said to the new mayor. "Abraham, you say it," he replied. But I told him "you are the *ba'al habayit*, the master of the house, the honour must be yours." So he went upstairs, fetched his well-used siddur and recited Kiddush. The Chief Rabbi, unable to make the service because of a prior engagement (he'd been summoned to a royal reception for Prince Charles's fiftieth birthday party that evening), walked from Buckingham Palace to the Mansion House and joined us for dinner.

We were put up for the night in style, in the magnificent State Bedroom Number One. It was "like a small palace", Estelle said. In the morning, we were able to catch part of the Lord Mayor's parade before Julian and Sian joined the hundreds of other guests for lunch. Later in the year, our children's choir was invited to sing at the Lord Mayor's banquet. From one of the galleries in Guildhall, they launched into *"Bendigamos"*, the Ladino hymn said before Grace after Meals, led by our choirmaster Maurice Martin. Whether it was the first time Ladino was sung within Guildhall, I do not know but it was wonderful to hear it.

When the new mayor was sworn in before the country's two most senior judges, the Lord Chief Justice and the Master of the Rolls (who happened then to be Lord Woolf) he was presented to them by Michael Hyam, the Recorder of London – the head of the Old Bailey – another ancient office which dates back to 1298. His parents had been married in Bevis Marks but he was non-practising. While I met people who did their best to conceal they were Jewish, Michael happily acknowledged his background and, as we got to know one another better, he would open up to me sometimes about his Jewish connections. After he died suddenly while giving a lecture, Lord Levene contacted me and said that although Michael's wife and children were not Jewish, they wanted a Jewish funeral for him. The prayer hall at the cemetery was packed with law lords, appeal judges and other members of the judiciary. When the time came for Kaddish, as the children did not know Hebrew, I invited the congregation to say it with me. The words of the prayer resounded around the hall as the vast majority of those present fervently joined in.

The heritage of Bevis Marks had become so treasured that the Corporation of London hosted a dinner in the Mansion House to mark the synagogue's tercentenary in 2001. It wasn't the first banquet given by the Lord Mayor for our congregation. That occurred in 1675 before the construction of Bevis Marks. Our accounts recorded an outlay of £6 and 4 shillings on the meal and £4 15 shillings on wine for the Lord Mayor's sword-bearer. "Either we ate very little," I observed, "or the sword-bearer drunk a lot." But we most certainly did not hold back on the celebrations three centuries later, enjoying duck confit and champagne as the Band of the Life Guards played *Fiddler on the Roof* and *Summertime*.

The anniversary culminated in a service at Bevis Marks at the end of the year graced by the presence of Prince Charles and Camilla Parker-Bowles. While the Jews had been readmitted by Oliver Cromwell, there had been no document to enact this. It was King Charles II in 1664, I recalled, who had confirmed the legal status of Jews in the City, "so long as they demean themselves peaceably and quietly with due obedience to His Majesty's laws and without scandal to his government." Our choir sang part of an ode composed specially in Hebrew by Professor Raphael Loewe, who translated it in the printed order of service: "But God respite designed for wanderers' despair/In Holland, and to find welcome in London, where/His worship is enshrined in this fane's holy air." Bevis Marks, I said, was probably the only synagogue in Europe that had remained open uninterrupted for 300 years.

But there was a surprise in store for one guest, Camilla Parker-Bowles. Evidently, she must have complimented Renée Dangoor, Naim's wife, on her outfit at the service. A few days later, a similar gown arrived at St James's Palace as a present for Camilla from Sir Naim. "I have a feeling the coat will be worn on many occasions," the prince wrote back, "and whenever I see it, it will remind me of your most unexpected generosity."

7

An English Citizen, Too

THE SAME MONTH we were toasting Bevis Marks on its tercentenary at the Mansion House, archaeologists made an extraordinary discovery not far away. Workmen on a new office development who had been digging under the former gold bullion vault of the State Bank of India came across a curved bath made of green sandstone, four feet across and over four feet deep, with seven steps leading down to it.

I received a call from Lord Levene, the former Lord Mayor of London, "We think we have found a medieval mikveh," he said, "I'd like you and Dayan Ehrentreu (head of the London Beth Din) to come and take a look." It was no surprise that one of the oldest relics of Jewish life in Europe should have been a mikveh, a ritual immersion pool. For however vital a synagogue is, there is one institution that takes priority over it; before a community opens a synagogue, it should have a mikveh, such is the importance attached by rabbis to the laws of family purity, which underlie the traditional Jewish approach to sexual morality. The ancient bath was found near a house that dated back to the Jewish community before its expulsion in 1290. Perhaps it was even around when Ibn Ezra, the great commentator on the Bible, visited London in the middle of the 12ᵗʰ century, when its inclement weather led him to characterise England as a "land of darkness and gloom". There was a suggestion of rehousing it in Bevis Marks but a home was found for it in the Jewish Museum in Camden.

When Bevis Marks opened 300 years ago, it of course had a mikveh attached. But that had long gone. I was conscious that the congregation had since lacked a mikveh of its own. Not only that, but there was no mikveh at all in the vicinity of Maida Vale and those who wanted to use one had to go further afield to north-west London. It was like a missing limb from the community. So I set about trying to build one.

Although I knew that many women in centrist Orthodox communities may not be the most frequent mikveh-goers – perhaps visiting just once in their lives before the day of their wedding – *taharat hamishpachah*, family purity, remains a fundamental observance. To have a mikveh would be making a statement of its importance. Although one elder of the community cast doubt, arguing that he "could find better use for the money", I was encouraged by the fact that young more observant families were moving into the area who would benefit from a mikveh nearby.

Something else was happening locally. A number of Oriental families who belonged to our congregation had grown more religious over the years. Some had started out taking classes in Jewish history and Jewish film with Robin and Nitza Spiro, the adult education entrepreneurs who now run the Spiro Ark, but found themselves wanting more than secular Jewish subjects. Rabbi Elia and I gave them private lessons. In such instances, I would use *Sefer Hachinuch*, the 13ᵗʰ-century educational guide by Rabbi Aaron Halevi of Barcelona, which gives a lucid explanation of each commandment. Or I would take a chapter from Maimonides's own law code, *Mishneh Torah*. But I don't think it matters what text you choose. It's more about how you teach than what you teach and your willingness to depart from the text and answer any question your students throw at you. These families were with us on the mikveh all the way.

Our first projected site for the mikveh was next to what is now the Marriott Hotel in Maida Vale, which was being built by one of our members, Maurice Shasha; his son Ilan was one of the new religious enthusiasts (they were no relation, incidentally, of the Shashas who funded the Sephardi Centre). But then I realised it would be possible to house a mikveh in part of an upper floor above the Naima JPS School, which was just as well because the Shashas later sold the hotel. Dayan Ivan and Rachel Binstock, from the neighbouring St John's Wood Synagogue, were a great help and I also persuaded the elders of the Spanish and Portuguese Congregation to contribute: some time back, some land next to Bevis Marks containing the "bath-house" where the original mikveh had stood had been sold, so they agreed to make a donation to the new one. The bulk of the money needed came from our major benefactor, Beno Salem, who wanted to do something to honour his brother Raymond, who had been in a coma for many years. Sony Douer, the father of my Naima pupil David, took charge of the project.

Appropriately, the mikveh opened during the tercentenary celebrations for Bevis Marks and round about the time of the announcement of the discovery of the medieval mikveh. I felt as if we had restored the circle. The presence at its dedication of the Sassover Rebbe, Rabbi Simcha Rubin, head of one of Golders Green's oldest *steibls* (small synagogues, usually a converted house), showed that our efforts were blessed by the Charedim. More than a hundred women now use the mikveh monthly and we are already embarking on its renovation.

There is still one facility, however, our area is without – an eruv, which would make life easier in particular for young observant families. The Sabbath laws do not allow carrying in public, an activity which includes pushing a wheelchair or a buggy. An eruv is a notional boundary which converts otherwise public space into "private" space where carrying is permitted. Major thoroughfares or natural features like a canal can serve to demarcate the boundary, but where there is a gap, symbolic gateways can be erected at a number of points, which consist of a set of lamppost-like poles linked by a thin, and virtually invisible, wire.

The London Beth Din opened the first metropolitan eruv in the UK in 2003, covering Finchley, Hendon and Golders Green. It was certainly a coup for Dayan Ehrentreu, since he braved considerable opposition from the Union of Orthodox Hebrew Congregations, which contended the bounded area was too large for an eruv zone. Although I did not always see eye to eye with the Beth Din, I had tremendous respect for the dayan, who was close to my brother James in Gibraltar (he licensed James's brand of Tio Pepe, which remains, as far as I know, the world's only kosher sherry).

The sight of young men in kippot or women in hats pushing prams on the street on Shabbat became normal, inspiring other eruvin elsewhere in various areas of London and Manchester. But an eruv in our part of town I had to leave to our Ashkenazi neighbours. The eruv is one aspect of *halachah* in which the Sephardim, unusually, are stricter than the Ashkenazim and I could not see any Sephardi authority approving the construction of one locally. What I told my congregation was "I respect people who use the eruv, I respect people who do not use it. But what I do not respect are those who do not use the eruv but criticise those who do." I asked one of my then students, Rabbi Jeff Berger, who is Ashkenazi, to act as our liaison with the local United

Synagogue, St John's Wood. Early in 2017, Dayan Binstock won approval from Westminster Council for an eruv, which will include within its coverage Lauderdale Road and Naima JPS.

While we managed to raise the funds for the mikveh easily enough, another institution gave me a lot more trouble. Jews' College was still turning out the odd rabbi or hazan but it had lost its primary role as a provider of congregational ministers since they generally preferred to study for *semichah* abroad. Its relaunch in 1998 under the new name of the London School of Jewish Studies was an attempt to give it more academic gravitas, like London University's School of Oriental and African Studies. It entered into partnership with SOAS, which offered degrees in Hebrew. I loathed the new name and still call it by its old (I always remember Neville Laski insisting on referring to the *Manchester Guardian* long after the paper dropped "Manchester" from its title).

By 2002, the rebranded college was going through one of its periodic financial crises and a flurry of talks was taking place to save it. Jonathan was president and I was deputy president. One day Jonathan called me to his house, "Abraham, the United Synagogue wants to buy the college for £1." I told him there was no possibility the Spanish and Portuguese Community would go along with that. The rescue plans left us, for the only time, on the opposite side of the fence.

The United Synagogue wanted to split the college in two. It would take over the college's campus in Hendon in order to launch a new venture specialising in adult education and teacher training. The academic rump, the degrees and library, would continue as LSJS but be based elsewhere.

Carving up the college, I warned, would jeopardise years of Sephardi-Ashkenazi co-operation. Nor should the US imagine it was simply going to be handed a building worth close to £1 million on a plate. Sir Moses Montefiore had co-founded the college. A century ago, a prominent member of the Spanish and Portuguese Community, Joshua Levy (a great-great uncle of Professor Daniel Jackson) had devoted much of his life to keeping it afloat. Sir Alan Mocatta had been its chairman and Sephardi donors such as Davide Sala had helped to maintain it more recently. Putting my foot down, I said that if the US pursued its ambition, we would have to go to the Charity Commission.

As rival plans were tossed back and forth, the college took steps to claw back its deficit, selling rare books from its library. I had few regrets about that, for our priority was to preserve the institution. It took a year, and with Jews' College on the brink, before the various parties finally agreed a rescue package in spring 2003. The college would henceforth focus on adult education and run an evening MA course, but the *semichah* programme and the BAs would go. The college's main financial backer, the Ashdown Trust – whose chairman Clive Marks, a supporter of Naima, is one of the unsung heroes of British Jewry – generously agreed to write off a large debt.

The clash over the college was the only instance when I openly differed with Jonathan but there were no ill feelings. At the end of the day, Peter Sheldon, the president of the United Synagogue, said to me, "I wish we had you in the United Synagogue."

While the fate of the college still hung in the balance, a new problem beset the Orthodox community. Shortly before Rosh Hashanah in 2002, to coincide with the first anniversary of the 9/11 terrorist attack on New York, the Chief Rabbi published a book called *The Dignity of Difference*, an appeal for religious tolerance and respect for diversity at a time of growing militant fundamentalism. It was widely acclaimed – in the *Guardian*, the Bishop of Edinburgh, Richard Holloway called it a "wise book" by a "large-hearted man" – except in his own backyard. A number of rabbis under his aegis, especially in Manchester, took exception to certain passages about other religions, suggesting that what he had written deviated from belief in the absolute truth of Judaism. Attacks on the book spread like wildfire, until he was even being accused of heresy in some quarters. To silence the objections, Jonathan agreed to make amendments and bring out a revised edition.

I could see what had roused his critics but they seemed determined to make a meal of it. In essence, the Chief Rabbi's views about other religions drew on precedents in the works of Maimonides and other spiritual giants. We have to learn the truth from whatever its source and other religions may have something to teach. That hardly compromises belief in the uniqueness of the Torah.

At the height of the campaign against the book, I telephoned the former principal of Jews' College, Nahum Rabinovitch, in Israel, who had given Jonathan his rabbinic ordination. "Jonathan is in trouble, is there anything you think you could do for him?" I asked. He replied that he could, although I don't know if anything came out of it. Although some within the community would have preferred the Chief Rabbi to stand his ground and defend the first edition, that was a lot to ask unless he could count on significant support among his rabbis. Pragmatism prevailed. The bruising episode convinced him to make sure to keep out of controversy's way and avoid battles that he was unlikely to win. "Abraham," he told me, "I have now learned to ride a bicycle."

The *Dignity* affair was an example par excellence of the Orthodox community's drift to the right. It was not enough simply to have a debate about the book, the book had to be altered before the condemnation would die down. The trends towards narrowness were soon to have a direct impact on our own congregation.

Lauderdale Road gained from the group of congregants I mentioned earlier who had become more religious. They increased the enthusiasm for Jewish learning and proved a mainstay of our daily services but they reached a stage where they felt that the congregation was not religious enough for them. When they decided to go and hold their own services, I was heartbroken. Rabbi Elia and I had encouraged their religious quest but they were abandoning us.

The sermon in which I addressed these events later that year, 2003, was among the most important I ever gave. We had had our internal rows and quarrels over the years, but never such a split. I was speaking on *Parashat Korach*, the Torah portion on the rebellion against Moses. I chose my words carefully because I wanted to convey my feelings but not to exacerbate tensions.

The rabbis drew a critical distinction between personal arguments motivated by ego or lust for power and those *le'shem shamayim*, "for the sake of heaven". "When the argument is for the sake of heaven," I said, "everyone wins, especially God! If a controversy is not for the sake of heaven, everyone loses and the Kahal [congregation] suffers."

Quoting the maxim from Ethics of the Fathers, "do not separate yourself from the community", I noted that the *Hebrew* word for "community", *tzibbur*, had a root of three letters *tz, b* and *r*, which stood for three types of people, *tzaddikim*, righteous, *binonim*, average, and *resha'im*, disinterested. Our community was inclusive, welcoming Jews of all types. It was the traditional Sephardi way, which had "kept us free from the painful divisions which have so plagued the Ashkenazi community".

I stressed that "I always wanted us to be one community as I believe that this is the way for the more observant to encourage the less observant – to work from within and not separately…

"What is not negotiable is division. There has to be one Kahal united in purpose, albeit at different religious levels, and there has to be one organisation, one leadership, lay and spiritual. Otherwise the result is confusion."

Nevertheless, I concluded, "If a group is unable to live with the principles of an inclusive community and has, for the time being, moved so far away from us that they can no longer share a Kahal with us, then let us abide by our principle of tolerance and be ready to welcome them as visitors, as members and as friends whenever they wish."

The loss of these religiously committed members made it more difficult to muster a minyan for some of our daily services but we managed. Anshei Shalom, as the breakaway group called themselves, eventually settled in St John's Wood Synagogue and grew with the influx of French Jews, who came to the UK because of better economic opportunities or fear of growing anti-Semitism in France.

While I regretted the departure of the founders of Anshei Shalom, I nevertheless could still draw some satisfaction that we had helped them to become more religious. Our school, too, enabled many pupils to discover a more spiritual path but, over the years, I witnessed the phenomenon whereby children, who had grown up in families which kept little, by the time they reached the *chuppah*, had fallen into the arms of the strictly Orthodox. It was as if they felt secure in their Judaism only in the more protective environment of the Charedim or that they equated greater stringency with authenticity. Some would continue to show respect for their former teacher but others considered me as a lesser religious being than their new mentors.

I could understand the attraction of a Charedi lifestyle. As I mentioned before, I often employed seminary girls as teachers in Naima because their zest for Judaism proved infectious. When I addressed the Board of Deputies for the 350th anniversary of the resettlement in 2006, I said that while many Jews had contributed to British life in many fields over that time, "sadly many of them had a passion for only one culture – British culture – and quickly ignored their Jewish roots. On the basis of this experience, many others believe that to attempt a synthesis of cultures is dangerous, hence they try a different approach. For them only the Torah matters and there is defiance at any attempt to water this down."

Yet from experience, I knew that scrupulousness over ritual does not always come with an equal emphasis on ethics. Sometimes I'd get a phone call from a member of a strictly Orthodox synagogue whose child was going to marry someone from a family I was acquainted with. The conversation would go like this. "Do they boy's parents use the eruv?" they'd asked me. "Yes," I said – which would be a minus for them. "Does the mother wear a *sheitel* [a wig]?" And I would tell them yes or no. And we'd continue in the same vein until they'd thank me for the information and be about to ring off. "But wait," I'd say, "you haven't asked me if they are people of integrity or who tell the truth." Sometimes the business of finding a *shidduch*, a match, places too little importance on basic values and is reduced to whether or not you use the eruv.

Our Sephardi Centre continued to promote a broader Orthodox ethos which combined cultural as well as religious activities. We were unable to go ahead with plans to run an MA in Sephardi Studies in conjunction with SOAS. But the centre maintained a strong programme under the capable direction of Rabbi Saul Djanogly. Saul came from a highly successful business family and I saw he had leadership potential. But he did not see the rabbinate ultimately as his vocation and opted instead to become a stockbroker.

Our Sephardi Kashrut Authority, the SKA, meanwhile was growing from strength to strength, even though I had not given up hope of greater co-operation between the different kashrut authorities and continued to call publicly for it. We were always on the lookout for ways to improve life for the kosher consumer. Shoppers perennially grumble about the price of kosher chickens compared with their supermarket equivalent. Some years back, I had been talking to Lord Sainsbury, a supporter of our school, and I said, "Wouldn't it be wonderful if you could do a range of kosher chickens in your stores?" "I'd be delighted to help," he replied and gave me the contacts to pursue the idea.

Supermarket mass production meant that Sainsbury's would have slaughtered an entire month's supply of kosher chickens for the mainstream London market in a day. How naïve I was – the logistics were impossible. I would have needed to assemble thirty to forty *shochetim* in one place on one day. It couldn't be done.

I happened to be at a wedding in the country near Cirencester in 1991 when I met a son of the Littmans, the founders of the Littman Library for Jewish Civilisation, which publishes serious books of Jewish thought and history. He mentioned that he had a farm in Devon which makes cheese. The thought of a top-quality kosher Cheddar swam into my mind, so I put the idea to him. Dayan Abraham David of our Beth Din worked hard on the project and out came our first supervised kosher cheese, Ashley Chase Cheddar, fresh from the farm. If you walk into a kosher grocer's today, the fridges will be stocked with rows and rows of supervised cheeses from all over the world. But, at a time when there was not such choice, Ashley Chase helped show the way. My ultimate ambition was to produce a brand of kosher Stilton, for which I could see a healthy export market to Israel and the USA, but there is a world of difference between the kosher manufacture of Cheddar and Stilton and the latter, in the end, was too difficult.

The SKA's biggest coup, however, came in 2005 when we secured an agreement with Allied Bakeries to supervise a range of Kingsmill and Sunblest breads. No authority had reached such an agreement with a general bread manufacturer in Britain before, though it was long the norm in the United States. According to *halachah*, a Jew should eat only bread baked by a fellow-Jew, and not by a Gentile but the rabbis made an exception for bread that was commercially (as opposed to privately) baked by non-Jews, called in the Talmud *pat palter*, providing of course its ingredients were kosher. Our director David Steinhof carried out a lot of research on this and the Beth Din consulted Dayan Basri of Jerusalem before we were ready to give the bread our SKA stamp.

The deal was a breakthrough. It meant that people living in small communities without a kosher bakery, families on holiday and students on campus could buy a range of certified kosher bread from the supermarket and at a reasonable price. It was regaraded as a communal service rather than a profitable enterprise. Of course, the availability of mass-produced loaves would result in more competition for kosher bakeries in Jewish areas which was why some people were not so willing to laud our initiative. Shortly after we announced it, I heard that a talk had been given by one Orthodox rabbi of a large London congregation, who was asked, "So now we can eat Sunblest?" The rabbi responded, disparaging the suggestion, "My dear, you should eat God-blessed." As if he was part of some elite few who had a hotline to Heaven.

The arrogance of this attitude still rankles, as does the refusal of the United Synagogue to list our bread in its kosher food guide. Lo and behold, more than a decade later, the United Synagogue concluded a similar arrangement with Hovis under its own kosher label. It is always nice to see others come round, even belatedly, to your way of thinking.

At one stage, the SKA was prepared to do something even more daring than supervising bread and that was to allow hindquarter meat into one of our restaurants. Cuts like rump or fillet steak had long been unavailable in the UK after the London Beth Din felt that removing the forbidden fats and veins from the rear parts of the animal was too difficult to be done properly; as a result, the hindquarters of animals in the kosher trade were sold to the general market.

Whereas kosher butcher shops were under licence from the London Board for Shechita, which we jointly supervised with the United Synagogue and Federation, our restaurants were under our own control. We had a restaurant at the time called El Gaucho, an Argentinian-style steakhouse in Golders Green. Dayan Toledano planned to import hindquarter meat from Argentina, which was prepared under the label of the Chief Rabbinate of Israel. I fully supported the idea but our new steaks were never to reach the table. We received a letter from the Israeli Chief Rabbinate suggesting we ought to be wary of the kosher standards of Argentinian hindquarters. That was odd, given that they had put their name to the meat but it was enough to throw a spanner in the works.

If there was one incident to illustrate my exasperation about kashrut, it was a fundraising dinner at the Savoy Hotel for the Saatchi Synagogue. The Savoy had a kosher kitchen under our own supervision which was used for weddings and other functions. The kitchen was short of dishes so we phoned up the London Beth Din and asked if we could borrow some from one of their caterers for the Saatchi dinner. The Beth Din said no. Who should be at the dinner? None other than Dayan Ehrentreu, the head of the London Beth Din. Pini Dunner was close to Dayan Ehrentreu and the dayan supported him. I waited until the end of the meal before approaching Dayan Ehrentreu. "Did you enjoy the food?" I asked him. "Did you know that your Beth Din would not allow any of your *kelim* [vessels] into our hall?"

As for the Saatchi Synagogue, it prospered under Pini but as his young family grew, it became more uncomfortable for them to spend Shabbat in Maida Vale. His wife preferred to be in Hendon and eventually he left. The congregation found a new home down the road in 2006, setting up as an independent minyan, just as Anshei Shalom later did, inside St John's Wood Synagogue. Now known as the Saatchi Shul, its current rabbi, Mendel Cohen, a young Lubavitcher from Leeds, has made it his own. From time to time I speak there – though its name still strikes me as rather incongruous, Saatchi being Arabic, and shul Yiddish. The original Saatchi Synagogue remains in use by the pupils of Naima.

The year 2006 was especially memorable as it marked the 350th anniversary of the readmission of the Jews to England, which naturally we wanted to celebrate. A civic service was planned to take place in Bevis Marks for 13 June where the guest of honour was to be Prime Minister Tony Blair. I was determined that the event would be one where British Jewry stood united, particularly after some of the altercations in recent years. In my address to the Board of Deputies earlier in the year, I warned that if our young people see "an Anglo-Jewish leadership which is torn apart by conflict, politics and disagreement, they will want nothing to do with us and will run away from us." The past years had seen "too much discord and hatred between different forms of Judaism, different religions and different peoples".

To get the various sections of the community on board required delicate diplomacy. I worked hand-in-hand with Henry Grunwald, the respected president of the Board of Deputies and chairman of the recently formed Jewish Leadership Council and Sigi – Sir Sigmund Sternberg, who as the community's premier interfaith activist knew how to bring people together. We were able to arrange that before the recitation of the Prayer for the Queen, the ark would be opened by representatives of different sections of the community including Sigi, who was president of the Reform movement, and Joe Lobenstein, the former Mayor of Hackney and spokesman of Stamford Hill's strictly Orthodox community. To have leaders from the Progressive and Charedi wings of the community share a mitzvah showed that, despite the undeniable religious divisions, we could sometimes act in unison. We joked about this afterwards – when the doors of the *hechal* were opened, Joe stood on the left and Sigi on the right.

The main challenge lay over the role of the Chief Rabbi. In days gone by, he would have expected to speak with me on such a big occasion and I would have been happy for him to have done so. He had spoken the previous year at Bevis Marks at the service we held to commemorate the 60th anniversary of VE Day. However, the 350th was much bigger. The Reform movement took a tougher stand than it once would have done and insisted, "If the Chief Rabbi is going to speak, then we want to have a speaker too." I was given an alternative: "Since it is your synagogue, then if you were the only rabbi to speak, we would have no objection." Jonathan consented. We ensured that he had pride of place with a seat next to the Prime Minister.

The negotiations safely concluded, there was no religious factionalism to rain on our parade. It was a glorious day – so hot that glasses of water had to be handed out to prevent some of our visitors wilting. Our choir was at its most angelic.

Welcoming Mr Blair, I said we believed it was the first time in the synagogue's history that "a Prime Minister has attended one of our services, unless of course we give credence to the apocryphal story that Benjamin Disraeli, who was born a member of our synagogue and who described himself as the blank page between the Old and New Testament, would quietly come to the courtyard outside to listen to our prayers on the Eve of the Day of Atonement".

In his address, Mr Blair said that it was "impossible to imagine the modern United Kingdom without the Jewish community. Yet for almost four centuries Jews were forbidden to worship, even in private, in this country. Since that was changed in 1656, arts, sciences, commerce, politics, the worlds of learning and thought, philanthropy and many more areas – all of these have been illuminated by the names of distinguished Jews who have made their mark, added to the store of knowledge, and helped to make our country a better place."

It was instructive, he said, to note that the appeal to Cromwell to readmit the Jews to England had come from someone who was "not just a rabbi – Rabbi Manasseh Ben Israel – but also an author, printer, publisher, bookseller and scholar."

The Prime Minister went on, "Throughout the years since then, the community has shown how it is possible to retain a clear faith and a clear identity and at the same time be thoroughly British. As the oldest minority faith community in this country, you show how identity through faith can be combined with a deep loyalty for our nation."

The values the Jewish community stood for – "the family, help for the needy, care for the sick, compassion and aspiration in equal measure" – were also the best of what Britain stood for. He referred warmly to Israel, saying that relations with Britain had never been better.

"For someone like myself," he said, "it is moving to be in this historic and beautiful synagogue, so evocative and so expressive of such a deep faith tradition." He registered too that "today, here, every section of the Jewish community is gathered."

But the words that moved me the most came from four of the children of the Naima JPS School, Daniella Loftus, Jonah Summerfield, Eliana Ostro and Daniel Amir. It was fitting that those who carried our hopes for the future should be accorded a prominent place in the service too. Reading her poem, nine-year-old Eliana declared:

"In other countries we were tortured.
We were slaves all through the land.
No food was given,
Our religion was forbidden.
We could not now pray
Or even manage to say
That I am a Jew, but now an English citizen, too."

49 The Queen with Chief Minister Hassan Gibraltar, 1952.

50 With Estelle and Princess Anne.

51 With Ariel Sharon.

52 With Sidney Cuby and Yitzhak Navon, 1977.

53 With Queen Sofia, 1992.

54 With King Juan Carlos and Queen Sofia.

55 Speaking in front of the King and Queen of Spain, Shimon Peres and others, 1994.

56 With King Mohammed VI of Morocco, 2000.

57 With the Lord Mayor of London, Sir Michael Bear, and his wife, 2010.

58 With Lady Thatcher and my brothers, October 2002.

59 With previous Lord Mayor, Lord Levene, and his wife Wendy.

60 My brother Solomon, first civil Mayor of Gibraltar, and heads of other religions in Gibraltar united in handshake.

61 With Prime Minister López Aznar of Spain, 2004.

62 With Prince Moulay Rachid, brother of King Mohammed VI of Morocco, at the opening of *Sacred,* an exhibition held at the British Library, 2007.

63 With Sarah and Prime Minister Gordon Brown, 2007.

64 With Rabbi Holtzberg lighting Chanukah candles in Mumbai, 2008, shortly before he was murdered.

65 Receiving the OBE, March 2004.

66 With Sir Sigmund Sternberg and Tony Blair, VE Day, 2005.

67 Speaking at a rally for Israel in Trafalgar Square, 2008.

68 The Queen, with Estelle and others, 16 January 2007.

Michael Brandon, whose family have been generous donors to Bevis Marks, said afterwards the children were "child priests providing pragmatic spiritual leadership to the congregation of all Britain's ethnic minority children". One leading Progressive rabbi, Baroness Neuberger, congratulated us on a "completely wonderful" event – "everyone felt so included and so welcome and it was done with such style and grace." Rabbi Avrohom Pinter, from Stamford Hill's strictly Othodox community, commented, "It was a great *Kiddush Hashem* and I appreciate the tremendous efforts that I know you invested in order to enable all sections of the Jewish community to attend." I believe only the Sephardi community could have pulled the different strands of Anglo-Jewry together, as we did that day.

The attendance of the Prime Minister had been facilitated by a close ally of his, Lord Levy. Michael Levy was a consummate fundraiser who had built Jewish Care into the community's premier welfare organisation and was nationally recognised as treasurer of the Labour party and Mr Blair's Middle East envoy. In 2007 he found himself under police investigation over allegations of promising honours in return for political donations (which turned out to be unfounded). He was in the harsh glare of the media spotlight and, I felt, being unfairly treated. He had helped us and now he needed moral support. So when he was made president of the Jewish Lads and Girls Brigade, I hosted a reception for him in the Montefiore Hall.

For the Sephardi community, the most important development at this time was the arrival of Dayan Saadia Amor as the head of our Beth Din in 2007. Dayan Toledano had retired and went on to be rabbi, and then Haham, of the Spanish and Portuguese Community in Amsterdam.

I had had my eyes on Dayan Amor for many years. He came to England from Morocco in the 1950s to study in yeshivah and then studied in Israel. He was an *illui*, a prodigy, and grew up to be the model of a *talmid haham*, a saintly man whose humility belied his erudition. Dayan Amor commuted to us from Manchester. He had a modest job as a rabbinical supervisor in Rakusen's, the Leeds-based matzah-makers, for the London Beth Din, a job far below his talents. He always made himself available to advise people on matters of Torah, responding to requests from all over the world. He never politicised religion and was known for his desire always to try to find a lenient answer if he could. I had immense respect for him. His wife said after his death in 2015 that the years he spent with us were professionally his happiest.

His new role undoubtedly enhanced the standing of the Sephardi community. The year after his arrival he addressed a conference of Sephardi rabbis from across the community, the first of its kind for many years. His presence made it easier for me to convene such a gathering. It was a first step towards bringing the different Sephardi groups closer together and, while I was not so naïve as to imagine that this could happen overnight, I hoped to lay the groundwork for my successor. I was, of course, aware that the prime interest for some congregations was what help they might be able to get out of the Spanish and Portuguese Community.

Our 350th anniversary service at Bevis Marks took place within a calmer atmosphere inside the community. While religious divisions remained, they did not manifest the kind of vitriol that they had a decade earlier. Perhaps it helped that the chief executive of the Reform movement, Rabbi Tony Bayfield, was a Cambridge University contemporary of Jonathan's. Perhaps the Stanmore Accords committee kept the lid on potential blow-ups. Whatever the reason, relations between the different groups seemed better.

I attended one meeting at the Chief Rabbi's house where Tony Bayfield was present too. Representatives of the children's charity Norwood wanted to know how to respond to a new law strengthening the rights of gay couples to adopt. At first, we were unsure what to advise since Norwood is a cross-communal charity and attitudes might vary between Orthodox and Reform on an issue like this. I turned to the Norwood people and said, "Do you ask us questions on how to keep Shabbat in Norwood homes?" "No, we don't." "Do you ask us questions about keeping kashrut?" "No." "So, why do you ask us questions about this?" I said. "Sometimes the answer is not to give an answer, you should do what you think fit." Which everyone seemed happy to go along with.

If publicly we appeared less disputatious as a community, that did not mean there were no issues of disagreement. More than kashrut, one festering sore, as far as I was concerned, remained the unyielding attitude of the London Beth Din towards Jewish status. There were children whom I accepted as Jewish into Naima JPS but when they wanted to go on to a Jewish secondary school, the London Beth Din refused to accept them.

When I opened the school, I had a long conversation about the children of converts with Rabbi Rabinovitch who advised me not to ask the family too many questions. You might have a woman who had been converted in Israel but the family was subsequently not leading a particularly observant lifestyle here. If they wanted their child to have a Jewish primary education, that was a mark in their favour and if they wanted the child to go on to a Jewish secondary school, so much the better: it was sensible to take them in.

The London Beth Din, however, prided itself on the strictness of its conversion standards. If one of my children was turned down, I would complain, "What are you doing? I've given them eight years of Jewish education. The proof of their commitment is they want to continue." Sometimes I won, sometimes I lost.

On my 70th birthday in 2009, the Chief Rabbi rang up to offer me his best wishes. "Are you enjoying the day?" he asked. "No,"

I replied, "it's awful. The Beth Din has rejected one of my pupils because they don't like his mother's conversion." "Leave it with me, Abraham," Jonathan said. He phoned me back later and told me he had good news, "The child is in."

The obduracy of the Beth Din, however, was about to backfire. I would say to myself "this can't go on, sooner or later something is going to happen". And it did. Stories had appeared in the press about a couple of children who were turned down by JFS because the validity of their mother's Orthodox conversion was disputed and so they were not considered Jewish. Out of the blue a third case emerged, that of a child who had been rejected because his mother had converted under Progressive auspices. The infuriated father took his fight to court, supported by one of the other families.

The first round at the High Court in 2008 went to the school but the following year the Appeal Court reversed the decision and ruled in favour of the boy. The United Synagogue in turn appealed to the Supreme Court in order to protect the right to choose children according to *halachah*, but it lost. According to the judgment, Jews are legally recognised as a racial as well as a religious group; to admit a child to school on the basis of parental descent is to use a racial criterion; and while schools can choose children on the basis of religion, they cannot do so on the basis of race. So JFS was found to be acting in a discriminatory way.

There was an outcry against the verdict from the Orthodox community. As a result, the whole system used by most Jewish schools had to be scrapped. Instead, schools now have to apply a religious practice test for entry, using, for example synagogue attendance. You don't even have to be Jewish to go to synagogue a few times a year and collect attendance points. If only the London Beth Din had shown greater flexibility, we might have been spared the whole fiasco.

Talks went on for a while inside the community about how to

go about changing the law in order to restore the status quo. The Board of Deputies would only support this if there were consensus. As one of the Board's ecclesiastical authorities, I tried to see if we could reach agreement between the different religious camps. The Reform movement felt questions of Jewish status should be sorted out within the Jewish community rather than the secular courts but wanted the children of its converts to be accepted into schools such as JFS. At the end of the day the Board could find no common ground and the matter was quietly dropped.

That same year I was made a joint president of the Council of Christians and Jews, an appointment which I mention only because it signalled a shift in religious representation of the Jewish community. While there were five Christian presidents of the CCJ, Lord Jakobovits had insisted on remaining its sole Jewish president. In an act of conciliation to the Progressives after all the bitterness over Hugo Gryn's funeral, Jonathan eventually agreed to a second president from the religious left of the community. The first Progressive holder of the office was Rabbi Albert Friedlander, from the independent Westminster Synagogue. But when he was succeeded by Rabbi Bayfield from the Reform, the Liberals felt they merited their own presidency, too. So in addition to the Chief Rabbi and Reform president, we ended up with a Liberal president and a Masorti president, and to rebalance the Jewish representation which now had a non-Orthodox majority, I was invited to be the second Orthodox president. Here we were: five Christian presidents, representing millions of adherents, and five Jewish ones, representing a little over a quarter of a million.

The Progressives had become more demonstrative in their demands for equal treatment, which complicated arrangements to celebrate the Board of Deputies' 250th anniversary in 2010. I wanted to hold a commemorative service in Bevis Marks similar to the community's 350th but I had to concede defeat this time because we could not find a format that would please everyone. I settled for second best, a special "meeting" of the Board – rather than a service – at Bevis Marks, with participation from across the community, including Councillor Lobenstein from Stamford Hill. Addressing the *"Senhores Deputados"*, I recalled that the Board had been conceived in the vestry of Bevis Marks in 1760 and was an idea that "instantly united Sephardim and Ashkenazim in England". Today, I said, we needed unity more than ever, which "requires mutual respect, even if we do not accept each other's religious views".

Initially, however, despite our historical role in the Board, we were not represented in the delegation to visit the Queen for the 250th anniversary. (It was precisely to pay respects on behalf of the Jewish community to the monarch, George III, that the first *deputados* had been organised by the Spanish and Portuguese.) After I remonstrated, the president of our Board of Elders, Alfred Magnus, joined the party to go to Windsor Castle.

In these years, the biggest religious confrontation I had was with a Charedi group from Stamford Hill and it sprung out of a long-running tussle over the fate of an old cemetery in the East End of London. In the early 1970s, our community sold most of the Novo Cemetery (it was "new" when it opened in the 18th century) land to London University's Queen Mary College. The Spanish and Portuguese Congregation said it had no choice because the college would have otherwise applied for a compulsory purchase order. But the Charedim felt we ought to have put up more resistance. I was excluded from the decision to the sell the land and, in retrospect, am glad I was. Most of the remains, including those of the boxer Daniel Mendoza, were reinterred in a grassy plot in Brentwood, Essex. Angry at the transfer, the Charedim mounted a demonstration at the Novo.

Some 2,000 graves remained in the Novo, which was now within the precincts of Queen Mary. Around twenty years later, workmen on the site disturbed some of the graves, exposing the bones. An alert student called us and I got in touch with Rabbi Elyakim Schlesinger of the Committee for the Preservation of Cemeteries in Europe. Volunteers worked through the night to collect the remains and we held a ceremony to reinter them.

Rabbi Schlesinger seemed happy with the way we had handled the incident but the concord was not to last. There was a path near the Novo which the Committee wanted us to declare forbidden territory although I did not see the necessity for this. I actually consulted a senior figure in Stamford Hill, Rabbi Joseph Dunner, who said I did not have to do so. I therefore had air cover when I defied the Committee which was increasingly agitating to take control of the site. I had built up a good relationship with Queen Mary and I was not going to sacrifice it for what I felt were unreasonable demands.

When, in 2011, the college revealed it wanted to widen the path, our opponents went into overdrive. In the *Jewish Chronicle*, one Charedi rabbi called the plan "disgraceful" and threatened protests. Pamphlets circulated attacking us in no uncertain terms. The college showed great sensitivity, promising to do no digging without one of our rabbis being present. Dayan Amor wrote a *teshuvah*, a halachic response, permitting the works to proceed. "This is *nishten halochoh*" [not Jewish law]," cried the opposition but they had nothing in their locker to make Dayan Amor backtrack.

Queen Mary, at their own expense, not only widened the path but improved the site, erecting a border and a viewing platform with information about the cemetery, which has since been listed by English Heritage. Visitors are now more aware of its historic importance and of the rootedness of the Jewish community in England more generally. When the college made me an honorary fellow, I noted "until the middle of the 17th century, this country was torn apart by religious hatred, by feuds and by open warfare.

The Jews were perhaps the first faith minority that gained tacit acceptance in England." I said it was "fitting therefore that this college which has so many students from so many different faiths and traditions should have a permanent reminder of the way this country has behaved towards its minority groups." As a young man, Sir Naim Dangoor had studied engineering at Queen Mary before returning to Iraq and had later endowed scholarships there in gratitude. When I showed Princess Anne round in 2012, I told her that an ancestor of her husband Sir Tim Lawrence, one Zaccaria Levy, was buried in the Novo.

I had one particular reason to be grateful that the presidency of the Council of Christian and Jews came my way; my position was responsible for one of the more pleasant occasions of my rabbinate: lunch with the Queen and the Duke of Edinburgh at Buckingham Palace on a Thursday in December 2011. The small party of nine other guests included the Regius Professor of Botany at Cambridge, David Baulcombe, and the tennis player turned TV presenter, Sue Barker. We were joined too by the Queen's corgis which enjoyed titbits fed them by their mistress under the table.

Great efforts went into the kosher arrangements on my behalf. A couple of days before the lunch, a *shomer,* or religious supervisor, went to the palace to *kasher* some silver cutlery. The wife of the kosher caterer, Arieh Wagner, shopped around to find some plates for my food that would resemble as closely as possible the palace dinner service. While the other guests enjoyed a mousse of game to start, mine was identical in appearance but made of duck. For dessert, I could use the same splendid antique server set as everyone else, as the dish was cold.

I told the story of the key that Sir Moses Montefiore had given to the Queen's ancestor, Queen Victoria. Before she came to the throne, Victoria, daughter of the Duchess of Kent, used to stay next to Sir Moses's country estate in Ramsgate in a house less splendid than the Montefiores'. He had a golden key made for the princess so she could enjoy his gardens. "We must look for the key," said the Queen. I am told that an attempt has been made to find it but such is the state of the archives that it would be like searching in a giant haystack.

Writing to the Master of the Household, Air Marshal Sir David Walker, to thank my hosts, I said that "I felt so relaxed and at ease in their company" and offered my good wishes to the Queen on the eve of her Diamond Jubilee. I mentioned, too, that as spiritual head of the oldest Jewish congregation in the country, I often observed from the pulpit that "England has been good to the Jews and the Jews have been good to England".

8

Outward Bound

THERE MUST HAVE been space for twenty guests around the table but lunch this time was reserved for just two. At one end sat Dr Alberto Aza, Spanish Ambassador to the UK, and opposite him at the other end, me. A plain dish of smoked salmon had been prepared because my hosts knew I would only eat a cold meal there. I had always considered the embassy's white stucco building in Belgravia one of the most beautiful in London and my visits had been more frequent as a result of the Sepharad 92 commemorations. However, I was not on religious business now: I had been asked to undertake a delicate diplomatic assignment by my uncle Sir Joshua Hassan.

Sir Joshua, my mother's brother, was Gibraltar's most famous politician who, after the Second World War, had steered it from a military-run colony to civilian self-government and served four times as its Chief Minister. At the reception at St James's Palace to mark the 350th anniversary of British Jewry, I had the pleasure of introducing the Queen to some of the communal notables. I mentioned to her that when I was at boarding school, in my dormitory I had a picture of Sir Joshua showing her and the Duke of Edinburgh around Gibraltar when they visited early in her reign. "Your uncle," she said to me, "was a great man." British stamps were printed in his memory. When I spoke at his memorial service in a synagogue in Gibraltar in 1997 – as he had requested at a Shabbat lunch at my home two years earlier – I remarked he had been trusted not only by his fellow Gibraltarians but also by the British government and the Spanish people. That was "a pretty rare quality in today's political scene," I added. It was his religion which had given him "the principles of decency, honesty and integrity".

Towards the end of his life Sir Joshua had wondered if there might be a longer-term solution to easing relations between Gibraltar and Spain. Knowing that I had established good links with the embassy, he had asked me informally to sound out whether the Spanish might be interested in a particular proposal he had in mind. I met Dr Aza a number of times and he was perfectly affable but all I can say is the Spanish idea of compromise was not the same as Sir Joshua's. My brief foray into diplomacy ended with us no further forward.

Even before Sepharad 92, and indeed before the restoration of democracy to Spain following the death of General Franco in 1975, our congregation had contacts with the Spanish embassy here. I have a book which claims the dictator himself was actually of crypto-Jewish descent. Such ties as there were testified to the affection for Spanish culture and language which had endured among Jews despite the trauma of the expulsion of 1492; they had been fostered particularly by Dr Gaon in his efforts to build up the World Sephardi Federation.

But there is no doubt that Sepharad 92 marked a turning point. In a symposium in Jerusalem two years earlier which looked at the expulsion, the Chief Rabbi Lord Jakobovits commented that it was "seen by Jews at the time as the supreme disaster since

Roman times by putting an end to what had been the most flourishing Jewish community in the Middle Ages". I certainly did not want to gloss over the pain and persecution but I wanted to focus also on what that community had achieved and the legacy it laid for the future. As I told the *Jewish Chronicle* early in 1992, "There are those who feel we should not make so many contacts with Spain. But I believe Sepharad 92 is the ideal opportunity to show the Jewish world about the Sephardim's great contribution to Judaism and to remember the thousands who gave their lives in the name of God."

The Spanish regarded Sepharad 92 as a vehicle for reconciliation with the Jewish world by acknowledging the place of Judaism in their history but the whole exercise could have been derailed before the year of commemoration even began by an outlandish proposal from some Catholic bishops to canonise Queen Isabella, the co-author of the expulsion decree. I joined the protests by writing to *The Times* in 1991. In response to my letter, a woman wrote to me about her experience of a recent tour of Granada. Her group had included two charming Catholic women, she wrote. "I shuddered involuntarily when the guide spoke not only of the edict of expulsion but of the Pope's praise of Isabella for 'turning Spain into a country of one religion'. The two women turned to each other, their faces lit with joy and said, 'Imagine that – one country, one religion.' I would have minded less had these women been ignorant or ill-educated." Fortunately, the canonisation idea was shelved, thanks to the intervention of organisations such as the International Council of Christians and Jews and its most prominent advocate, Sir Sigmund Sternberg.

It was Sigi who did most to convince me of the value of Sepharad 92. I admired his approach to interfaith work, which was built on the bedrock of good personal relations rather than academic theology. His particularly strong links with the Vatican were evident from his award, rare for a Jew, of a papal knighthood in 1988. For his investiture, he had to acquire a special outfit which had to be made by tailors in the Vatican. I am told that when he learned how much it would cost, he inquired whether it would be possible to find a second-hand one. No, he was informed; since papal knights were supposed to be buried in their uniform, there would be none available.

Sepharad 92 was marked by a global programme of events which included the *Tapestry of Many Threads* exhibition on Sephardi communities at the Jewish Museum in London. We could not, of course, escape controversy. When we began the year with a commemorative service at Lauderdale Road, one or two people boycotted it in protest at the presence of the Spanish Ambassador, Dr Aza's predecessor. In a message to my community about the event, I observed that among other things Sepharad 92 was "the occasion on which the Spanish King and his government have chosen to express regret for the action of their ancestors and to extend a hand of friendship to the Jewish people and to Israel. We should welcome this offer of reconciliation with dignity."

When I echoed these sentiments in an article for *The Times*, it elicited an unexpected response – a letter from Helmut Schmidt, my economics teacher at Carmel many years before. A good historian, he told me, "remains aware of the ever-changing wheel of fortune". There was "never a last act in history. Look at Japan and Germany now and at Tito's Yugoslavia and Stalin's Soviet Union or Churchill's Empire. In 1944/5 I remember Jewish soldiers inspecting Titus's triumphal Arch in Rome. Some even wanted to blow it up!" You are never too old to receive the encouragement of a teacher. If Sepharad 92 was part of the move towards a new concord between Jews and Christians, I felt, it was worth supporting.

In April, I went to Spain for a special synagogue service in Madrid attended by King Juan Carlos, which earned me a photograph in *¡Hola!*, the Spanish version of *Hello!* magazine. Be that as it may, the single most important event that year was the declaration made by Spain's most senior Catholic churchman, Cardinal Ramon Torrella, the Archbishop of Toledo, to acknowledge the historic wrong. The fate that had befallen Jews and Muslims in 1492 was "the opposite of what should be done according to the principles of our faith", he said.

In London, we also held a special service of thanksgiving at Holland Park, the synagogue founded by Turkish Jews, to remember Turkey's benevolence in welcoming the refugees from Spain. In front of the Turkish Ambassador, Candemir Onhon, I recalled what Sultan Bejazid II was said to have exclaimed: "Can you call King Ferdinand and Queen Isabella of Spain wise by expelling the Jews of Spain, they have impoverished their country and enriched my kingdom." Within two years of their arrival in Turkey, Spanish Jews had set up the first printing press in Istanbul.

My most lasting contribution – I hope – to the anniversary was the publication of an illustrated history, *The Sephardim*, which was jointly written with Lucien Gubbay. I say "jointly" but – while I supplied information, it was Lucien who did pretty much all the writing, a skill at which he was far more accomplished than me. Lucien and I have collaborated for more than fifty years and I could not ask for a stauncher ally.

The son of a Syrian-born father who was expelled by the Turks after the First World War to Cairo, Lucien grew up in Manchester. While he was a civil engineer by day, in the evenings and at weekends he devoted himself unstintingly to the Sephardi and wider Jewish community. He was in charge of building the Wembley Sephardi Synagogue, our home for the elderly, Edinburgh House, and later the Sephardi Centre. After he edited my early pamphlet *A Problem of Survival?*, we wrote a book together, *The Ages of Man*, which was a plain guide to Jewish practice. Lucien felt there was little suitable around, particularly one which included Sephardi custom. Its American version, *The Whys and Whats of Judaism*, ran into three editions. He is the author himself of an elegant short history of Sephardim in Muslim lands, *Sunlight and Shadow*, and he has recently edited the English translation for our new daily prayer book.

In another, unpublished, article, I reflected on the experience of Jews in the Ottoman Empire after the expulsion from Spain. While life under the Sultan was "glorious" compared to the lot of their brethren in many other lands, I noted, by the end of the 17th century Jewish communities in Turkey were in decline as their levels of education fell. In response, rabbis began writing books for the people in Ladino, foremost the *Me'am Lo'ez*, a multi-volumed rabbinic commentary on the Bible which first appeared in 1732. "If a single theme can be detected in all these works," I wrote, "it is one which encouraged ethical Jewish living by addressing the heart as well as the mind. It advocated a good, decent, upright but passive lifestyle, with little desire to expand or experiment." (There was no parallel to the revolutionary spiritual ideas of Chasidim in 18th-century Eastern Europe, for example.) In a word, these Ladino writers developed the quality known as *bondad*.

Bondad remains an important word to me. Judaism is not Judaism without it. As I would often say to students of Jews' College at their graduation, their purity of heart would ultimately count more than their erudition. But *bondad* was not enough. The Ashkenazim invested more in intellectual sophistication than the Sephardim through the system of yeshivot they established in Eastern Europe. Even today we lag behind. There is still no Sephardi yeshivah in Israel which regards a university education desirable and where I can feel comfortable sending students from the diaspora.

For my work on Sepharad, I was rewarded the following year

with an honour from the Spanish government, the Encomienda (Knight Commander) de la Orden del Mérito Civil, along with Sigi and the third member of the community responsible for organising its commemoration in Britain, Hayim Pinner, the former secretary-general of the Board of Deputies. We were presented with the Order by Dr Aza in a ceremony at the Spanish Embassy. I smiled not only at the fact that here I was, a Gibraltarian, being decorated by the Spanish but also that this was a similar honour to the one bestowed on my ancestor Jacob Cansino by King Charles V. There were sixteen generations between Jacob and me and seventeen generations between King Juan Carlos and King Charles. Sending his congratulations, Rabbi Hugo Gryn wrote "it must have given you and your family particular pleasure that history, as it were, be set right and that the King of Spain should now make this a formality as well."

The process of reconciliation went further more recently when both Spain and Portugal made the offer of citizenship to the descendants of the medieval expulsions. Since the Brexit referendum in 2016, I have signed an increasing number of letters to confirm the ancestry of those applying for passports, because British people want to preserve their freedom of movement within the European Union.

My participation in Sepharad 92 gave me a wider entrée into interfaith relations. While I had long been a member of the Council of Christians and Jews in the UK, I had not travelled overseas in the cause of interfaith fellowship but now I found myself receiving regular invitations to conferences and events overseas.

One of the most moving events was the centenary of the Shaare Tikvah Synagogue in Lisbon in 2002. It was not only because of a deep family connection to Lisbon: my ancestors had helped to re-establish the Jewish community in the early 19th century after the medieval purge of Jews and my great-great uncle,

Abraham Levy, had helped to found Shaare Tikvah. The president of the congregation during the centenary, Samuel Levy, was a descendant of his too. What was notable about the synagogue was that it was the first to be built in the country after the end of the Inquisition in 1821 – a fact which showed how long much of Europe had been plagued by religious hatred. By contrast, Gibraltar had long been a haven of tolerance. Lisbon, too, had been the birthplace of Manasseh ben Israel, whose intercession with Oliver Cromwell had led to the re-establishment of English Jewry.

The occasion was thought significant enough for the President of Portugal, Jorge Sampaio, to attend, who, as it happens, is halachically Jewish. I opened my address by managing a few sentences in Portuguese, which I spoke as a child during our evacuation in Madeira. I concluded by saying the Jewish people were proud to welcome guests from other faiths, Christians, Muslims, Hindus, Bahais. "You demonstrate a religious tolerance and unity which is the envy of the rest of Europe during these troubled times," I said. "May we always remember that what unites us is more important than what separates us."

In my address I recalled the heroism of Aristides de Sousa Mendes, the consul of Portugal in France who had saved thousands of Jewish lives during the Second World War by issuing them Portuguese passports. De Sousa Mendes's selflessness stood out, especially when you consider the context of the times, when it was easier for officials to keep their heads down and ignore what was happening around them.

A few years ago information came to light about a prominent member of the Jewish community in wartime Portugal in whom I had more than passing interest; he happened to be a relative of mine by marriage. Professor Moses Amzalak was a devout Jew and also a devout anti-Communist, who was close to the Portuguese dictator António de Oliveira Salazar. According to my cousin David Blackburn, who researched the story, in the 1930s Amzalak was considered a helpful influence in Portugal by the Nazi regime to the extent that he was awarded a German Cross of Honour. During the War, he did pass on a request to Salazar from a Dutch-born American rabbi to "repatriate" Jews in the Netherlands of Portuguese origin, which came to nothing. "There is no record of Amzalak having pressed the matter further," David said.

I have some of Amzalak's prayer books, whose worn pages testify to his personal piety. In one of them is a typed note where he records that he went to Salazar to ask him to let Jews into Portugal and afterwards he said to his wife, "God can now take me because I have helped to save my people." Whether he was referring to the repatriation request or something else, we don't know. David speculates about the reasons why he left the note; it could reflect genuine sentiment, be a "self-serving claim" left for posterity or else be evidence of "an implied regret for past actions of which he hoped and believed that the action he had just taken would provide expiation".

There was another country my interfaith work took me to which I also had a personal link: Morocco. My father had been born in Tangiers and when I was a child, we used to stay with my aunts in the city. The powdery beaches of Tangiers must be some of the finest in the world. Morocco was a moderate voice within the Arab world so it seemed especially important to maintain good contacts.

I first went on a mission to Morocco in 1995 with Greville Janner, the former president of the Board of Deputies, and Sidney Assor, the lay leader of Moroccan Jews in Britain. Greville had been active in setting up one of the first charities to promote Muslim-Jewish dialogue. I had always worked well with Greville and I had known his family for a long time. I recited prayers at his father Barnett's shivah and his mother Elsie asked me to officiate at her funeral. Once when she was ill, she wrote to me to tell me "Rabbi, I nearly needed your services." She ordered an Israeli flag and a British flag to be placed on top of her coffin.

For me, the highlight of that trip was fixing the mezuzah to the Rabat office of the head of Israel's new liaison bureau, David Dadon. It was an historic event following the establishment of diplomatic ties between the two countries the previous year which I was able to celebrate by reciting the *berachah* over the mezuzah. A special concert of Andalucian music was put on for our party where, in a demonstration of interfaith harmony, a rabbi and an imam sang an identical piece, the one with Hebrew words, the other with Arabic. The event stretched into the early hours of the morning. In our programme, Sidney Assor wrote "this is to certify that Mrs Estelle Levy has stoically sustained four hours plus of Andalucian music".

Although we did not meet the King, we were taken to his palace. At the end of the visit, the mother of a young man who had married into the royal family turned to me and asked, "Rabbi, I would like you to give me a blessing." I started to bless her in English but she interrupted me, "No, I want you to say it in Hebrew." That indicated the relationship which, at its best, had existed between Jews and Muslims in this part of the world.

I returned to Rabat three years later for a conference of Muslims, Jews and Christians called by King Hassan II and supported by Unesco. In face of rising fundamentalism and sectarianism, this was a challenge to promote "a culture of peace". The King told us, "Peace-lovers and believers place high hopes in you." The rabbinical delegation included Chief Rabbi Joseph Sitruk of France, the Sephardi Chief Rabbi of Israel, Eliyahu Bakshi-Doron and Rabbi Haym Soloveitchik from the USA. Rabbi Bakshi-Doron mentioned that on Shabbat he had officiated at the induction of the new Chief Rabbi of Morocco. "It is my hope that I should be able in the near future to attend similar ceremonies in Iran, Iraq and elsewhere," he said. That conference now seems a long time ago.

In 2000 Estelle and I returned to Morocco as part of a delegation from the Board of Deputies invited by Hassan's son, King Mohammed VI. There had been a tradition in Morocco of kings having a Jewish adviser and Mohammed had inherited his adviser, André Azoulay, from his father. I got to know André quite well. We were given our own chauffeur-driven car and taken in a cavalcade from the Hilton Rabat to our meeting with the King in Tangiers. He was in his mid-thirties and not at all self-important. "The Palestinians are my friends and the Jews are my friends," he told us, "I will do anything to help."

In the wake of 9/11 and the 7/7 attack in London, not to forget the Madrid bombing in 2004 (for whose victims we held a memorial service in Lauderdale Road) interfaith relations took on a new urgency. I attended the second congress of Imams and Rabbis in Seville in 2006. At home I had grown to admire Dr Zaki Badawi, an Egyptian-born sheikh who had founded the Three Faiths Forum with Sir Sigmund Sternberg and the Reverend Dr Marcus Braybrooke, and whose outlook on Islam resembled mine on Judaism. He had started a college in Ealing to train imams for English-speaking communities rather than import leaders from abroad. Sadly, he had died earlier that year. Estelle happened to mention to one of the British imams at the conference that we had been friendly with Zaki. "I wonder who is going to succeed him," she asked innocently. "Nobody," was the firm reply. I worried that the kind of Islam Zaki represented, traditional but accommodating, was growing out of fashion.

Back home, we remained on good terms with the Moroccan Ambassadors. To this day Mohammed Belmahi, who was posted here from 1999 to 2009, always sends us greetings for Pesach and the New Year. When his successor, the King's cousin, Princess Lalla Joumala Alaoui, visited Lauderdale Road on a Shabbat morning in 2010, Rabbi Elia greeted her in Arabic and we served *adafina* for lunch, spiced with peppery harissa sauce. Rabbi Elia and I made the dish ourselves. (I'll sometimes cook it at home, though it is not one of Estelle's favourites). I recalled in my welcome that the very first rabbi of our congregation, Jacob Sasportas, had sometimes acted as a roving envoy to the King of Morocco. In fact, between 1691 and 1827 no fewer than five Jews were appointed as full ambassadors for Morocco to the Court of St James's, beginning with Haim Toledano. I recalled, too, the service held in Bevis Marks to mark the return of Sir Moses Montefiore from his successful mission to Morocco in 1864. After the killing and imprisonment of a number of Jews in the town of Safi, Sir Moses, who was in his late seventies, had set off to intercede on their behalf. Received with "great pomp and ceremony", he came away with a *Dahir*, an edict, from King Sidi Mohammed IV, which promised protection to the Jews.

But it was the ambassador of another country who turned to me for help when he found himself in a spot of trouble. In 2001, the French Ambassador in London, Daniel Bernard, had been at a dinner party and made a comment about Israel being a "shitty little country". Word soon got out, provoking fury in the Jewish community and in Israel. Anxious to make amends for the damage he had caused with his remarks, he went to Lord Levene, who suggested he come to see me. I remember that week particularly well because it was the week of the birth of my first grandson, Avi.

"What I suggest you do is to host a fully kosher dinner at the French embassy and invite leading members of the Jewish community and of Jewish organisations," I told him. "It will show your regret at what you said." He seemed happy with the idea. I gave him a copy of Lucien's and my book, *The Sephardim*, whereupon he made a sign to his chauffeur outside, who came in and presented me with a gift for my grandson. I believed he was ready to go ahead with the reparation dinner but it never happened. Shortly afterwards, he was posted to Algeria and died a couple of years later.

From time to time, I travelled abroad to one of the meetings of the Conference of European Rabbis, an organisation which Dr Gaon had helped to start. It was a useful place to exchange views, though some of the discussions on kashrut and conversion policy I found tedious and with little achievement to show for them. I can't say I played a particularly active role there. I once proposed a conference on Jewish education where all the Chief Rabbis of Europe would come with their top educators and promised we would finance it but despite our offer, the idea fell on deaf ears.

I have one vivid memory of a trip I made on behalf of this august body from Grunewald in the Swiss Alps, where we had been meeting, to Geneva in order to attend a party marking the retirement of the Chief Rabbi of Romania, Moshe Rosen, in 1994. It was a long coach journey and we stopped for a break in a little village where there was just a single toilet. Imagine the scene: a long line of European Chief Rabbis in their suits all in a row, queuing for relief. It would have made a splendid photo.

My only tangible achievement at the CER was to make sure a senior position was reserved for Jonathan Sacks. The organisation's first two presidents had been the Chief Rabbi of Britain but after the retirement of Lord Jakobovits, it was decided Chief Rabbi Sitruk of France should become its head. Jonathan would simply be one of a number of vice-presidents. "You can't do this to him," I told them, so, instead, they instituted the position of associate president for him – above the vice-presidents; this position is now occupied by his successor, Chief Rabbi Mirvis.

It was for my interfaith work that I received an OBE in 2004. My father would have been delighted that all three of his sons received honours from Britain. My older brother Solomon was made an MBE for his service to Gibraltar, and my younger brother James did even better with his CBE.

When I was chaplain to Lord Levene as Lord Mayor in 1999, he made a luncheon for the great and the good at the Mansion House attended by the Queen. Hundreds of people were there from many different fields, from playwrights Alan Bennett and Sir Tom Stoppard to the founder of the web, Sir Tim Berners-Lee, and the mountaineer Sir Edmund Hillary. For Grace, I recited not just the *berachah* over bread but also those on seeing the monarch and on seeing men of "wisdom". When Lord Levene introduced me as his "chaplain from Gibraltar, Rabbi Levy", the Queen remembered she had met my brother Solomon at a function only a few weeks before, where he had implored her to make another visit to Gibraltar. "I can't," she had replied, "I don't want to upset my cousin, King Juan Carlos." Solomon, however, was not taking no for an answer. "Ma'am, you have to come, it's British."

That same year, I had to say Grace at a Mansion House function for the President of China, Jiang Zemin, who was on a state visit. I wrote to Michael Loewe, Raphael Loewe's brother, who was a sinologist at Cambridge University, and asked him if he could suggest a blessing in Chinese I could recite. It was difficult, he explained, because "there is no concept of a beneficent Creator in Chinese". He offered an alternative, which I learned in transliteration. Translated, it went: "When the winds blow and the rains fall in their due seasons and the five crops of the fields grow in rich abundance, then will peace reign in hearth and home."

My approach to interfaith relations is best characterised by an address I gave at a service at Bevis Marks to commemorate the 50th anniversary of the Council of Christians and Jews in 1991. "Dialogue can be social or theological," I said. "Social dialogue, for example, ensures that we work together on those matters of our lives where a united front can improve the quality of life and the standing of communities guided by Divine Providence."

Theological dialogue, on the other hand, is "a little more

complex", I said. "The Jewish people are still sore from the wounds of Jewish-Christian disputations through our history, which caused so much heartache and persecution to us. For since faith is such a profound personal matter and since we cannot rationalise or be scientific about it, little benefit may be achieved by comparing aspects of different faiths, even if pursued by those with the best of intentions."

My upbringing in Gibraltar, as I mentioned then, had been a lesson in social dialogue. The more I took part in organised interfaith encounters, the more I remain wedded to my view. Comparing the beliefs of different religions only invites the invidious question as to which is better. What was more productive was encouraging co-existence, or as we say in Spanish, *convivencia*.

In my talks I always tried to cite examples of mutual respect between religions. At a civic service in Liverpool, I recalled the time we were renovating our community centre at Lauderdale Road and had asked the local Catholic primary school around the corner if we could hire their premises. "Not only were they prepared to accommodate us," I said, "but they would not even consider making us a charge, saying that we were all united in the service of God, albeit in a different language and ideology." When we used their premises for the first time, "I was very moved... to see that they had taken the trouble to put a blackboard in their hall with the word *Shalom* beautifully written on it." When we left the school, one of our lay leaders Michael Jackson, an eminent computer scientist, wrote on that same board beneath *Shalom*, "*Pax Vobiscum in Nomine Dei*".

The Council of Christians and Jews would take part in Mitzvah Day, the Jewish community's day of social action. On one occasion, my fellow-CCJ president Rowan Williams, then Archbishop of Canterbury, and I joined boys from the City of London School in making cakes for a homeless centre. I started decorating mine with the word *Shalom* in Hebrew, and when the archbishop, who reads the language fluently, saw it, he decided to do likewise. My cake decoration influenced him more than my later attempt at lobbying. I wanted the CCJ to put out a statement denouncing the delegitimisation of Israel but I couldn't get them to agree to the organisation taking a forceful stand. That, I have to say, upset me.

In 2013, I arranged a trip to Gibraltar for the head of the Catholic Church in England, the Archbishop of Westminster, later Cardinal, Vincent Nichols. I wanted him to see a living example of interfaith civility. I invited Ephraim Mirvis, the Chief Rabbi-elect, to come along too. Maurice Ostro, the CCJ's Jewish vice-chairman, designed "Rock Tour" t-shirts for the party, which included the CCJ's chairman, the Bishop of Manchester Nigel McCulloch. Rabbi Mirvis and Archbishop Nichols hit it off the moment they stepped on the plane. We were entertained in Gibraltar by the governor, then we separated while the archbishop went to meet his parishioners and Rabbi Mirvis and I visited the Jewish school. The rapport the two spiritual leaders seem to have enjoyed since personifies the progress made in Catholic-Jewish relations.

How far we have come since medieval days was demonstrated to me not so long ago when I was among 120 rabbis who went to a conference in Israel in 2015 with Catholic religious leaders. The venue was Domus Galilaeae, an attractive modern building of Tuscan limestone overlooking the Sea of Galilee, which had been inaugurated by Pope John Paul II on his historic visit to Israel in 2000. Designed to be a centre to teach Christians about the "living tradition of Israel" and the Jewish roots of Christianity, it enshrined the values of reconciliation to which the Catholic Church had committed itself with the *Nostra Aetate* declaration of 1965.

Inside the main hall, the Ten Commandments were displayed

in both Hebrew and Latin. At the centre of the library was a Torah scroll. Visible on the shelves were volumes of the Talmud, the same book which centuries earlier priests had publicly burned in the squares of Europe. In many old churches, contempt for Judaism is depicted by a pair of statues of two young girls, as I saw myself in Strasbourg Cathedral; a dejected young girl holds a broken stick with the Old Testament, while opposite her a jubilant young girl bears aloft a stick elevating the New Testament. But in this peaceful place in Galilee, two new statues repudiate the supersessionist imagery of the past; a beautiful girl holds the Torah, while beside her a second, beautiful girl looks on it and smiles.

9

The Montefiore Legacy

IN MY STUDY I have a copy of a Victorian illustrated magazine. It contains a reference to the 100th birthday which had just been celebrated by the most famous Jew of the day, Sir Moses Montefiore. Beneath a cartoon of Sir Moses, a puff of tobacco ascending from his contented lips, runs the caption: "All may not reach Sir Moses Montefiore's great age but all may prolong their lives and add to their enjoyments by smoking ALLEN AND GINTER absolutely pure cigarettes!"

Few Anglo-Jewish communal leaders have attained the status where they could be chosen to feature in an advertising campaign (even if one with such dubious medical claims). Sir Moses was the very exemplar of integration, a passionate Jew and a passionate Englishman who remained true to his religion and served his country with distinction. When he was invited to dine at Buckingham Palace, he brought his own kosher beef with him. One of his duties as Sheriff of London was to open the courts of law at the Old Bailey but Sir Moses recorded in his diaries that if official business clashed with Rosh Hashanah, "My duty to my

God and my respect for our holy religion are above all other duties and I must give up my official occupations for these days."

From an early age, Sir Moses was already a man of stature, being over six feet tall. While he had started as a clerk in a tea company, his marriage to Judith Barent Cohen in 1812 opened doors to greater opportunity, since Judith's sister Hannah was married to Nathan Mayer Rothschild, founder of the English branch of the famous financial family. First as a broker to his brother-in-law and then as a partner in the insurance company they established, Sir Moses made his way in the world. The £15 million loan Montefiore and Rothschild raised for the British government in the 1830s helped to finance the abolition of slavery.

Devoting himself increasingly to philanthropy from his forties, Sir Moses took especial interest in the fate of his co-religionists abroad. When he reflected if only there were an Abraham Lincoln for the Jews, he must have been imagining himself in that role. But his humanitarian concern extended beyond his own community; as chairman of the Syrian Relief Fund, he also aided Christians suffering in the Middle East. In his eighties, when he had outlived most of his contemporaries, he was still travelling to help beleaguered Jewish minorities.

But there was no cause closer to his heart than improving the situation of the Jewish community of the Holy Land. He made the last of his seven trips to the Holy Land in 1875 at the age of ninety-one. Although the windmill he erected in Jerusalem in 1857 might not have actually milled much flour, it stands today as a landmark proclaiming the bond between British Jews and the Land of Israel. The settlement of Mishkenot Sha'ananim he built was the first Jewish neighbourhood in Jerusalem outside the walls of the Old City. While not all his charitable investments in Israel succeeded, he never lost faith, writing: "The Jews would return to the land of their ancestors and to a rebirth of their national life. I am quite certain of it, and I hope it will be realised some day, when I shall be no more." He was, according to his biographer Abigail Green, "one of the first truly global celebrities". (I married Abigail, a distant relative of Sir Moses, to her husband Boaz, whose grandmother had lived in Mishkenot Sha'ananim.)

The proceeds of the fortune Sir Moses made during his long lifetime are still financing good causes today. Of how many people can you say that more than 130 years after their death? The Montefiore Endowment, the trust that administers his charitable assets, has enabled us to do many things that we could not have otherwise done. It is thanks to Sir Moses that we are still training modern Orthodox rabbis in Britain.

Sir Moses's connection to the Kent town of Ramsgate goes back to 1812, when he honeymooned there with his wife Judith. Then, in 1831, he bought a country house in the seaside town and, emulating English aristocrats who prayed in private chapels in their mansions, he erected a synagogue close to his estate – his mausoleum and the synagogue he built next to it still stand there. It was an illustration of her own religious sentiments that, as an act of thanksgiving for her happiness, Lady Judith later gave her wedding dress to be made into a Torah cloak for the Ramsgate synagogue; it remains on exhibit today at Bevis Marks.

For the Torah scrolls, Sir Moses went to the best scribe in Vilna, obtaining rabbinical permission for the Sefer to be written in a Sephardi script, even though this was in deepest Lithuania. He was so pleased with the scrolls he received that he arranged for the scribe to work exclusively for him and promised he would not be short of commissions.

According to custom, the donor of a Sefer Torah writes the last three words of the scroll himself, *le'enei kol Yisrael*, "in the eyes of all Israel". Sir Moses, however, would always write four, as the word before was Moshe, his own name: *Moshe le'enei kol Yisrael*. The scrolls, a number of which we have restored, are masterpieces of scribal art.

When Lady Judith died in 1862, he placed her in a domed mausoleum which mirrors the Tomb of Rachel in Bethlehem. It was a poignant choice, for Rachel's tomb is where women traditionally go to pray to have a child. Lady Judith, who was never to be blessed with children, prayed there herself and the original site was in such disrepair that she had it renovated. In Judith's memory, Sir Moses also built a college where he intended that ten students should dedicate themselves to Torah study and he left an endowment for it to continue after his own death.

The college had a chequered history. Some years later, Haham Moses Gaster conceived the ambitious plan to turn it into a rabbinic seminary, at a time when Chief Rabbi Adler would allow graduates of Jews' College only to emerge with the title "Reverend". He selected its students on the basis more of scholarship than spirituality, which proved the venture's undoing. After a student committed suicide, the seminary closed under a cloud.

That it enjoyed its heyday after the Second World War was down to the determination of Haham Solomon Gaon. He arranged with the Jewish Agency to bring over young men mainly from North Africa and prepare them to become religious teachers and rabbis. Its graduates went on to serve Sephardi communities around the world, including our much-loved hazan for many years, the Reverend Halfon Benarroch, the Reverend Yossi Houri of Wembley Sephardi Synagogue and our own Rabbi Elia.

As Ramsgate was dwindling as a Jewish community, Dr Gaon no longer felt it was a congenial environment for young Torah students, especially when it became harder to entice tutors to settle there. So he relocated it to London in 1961 (where it survived until 1985). The building in Ramsgate was sold – in contravention, some have argued, of the bequest of Sir Moses. Yet had he been able to foresee the future, he surely would not have objected to Dr Gaon's move.

The Montefiore Endowment, which was responsible for the estate, was also looking to sell the last of a row of cottages which had originally housed students of the college. But Estelle and I persuaded the trustees not to and instead to use it as a weekend retreat for visiting ministers, who could lead Shabbat services in the synagogue for the remainder of the Jewish community. Estelle, Julian and I went down many times and were made especially welcome by one of the stalwarts of Kent Jewry, George da Costa, a lovely man who would bring us Dover sole and asparagus from local farms. He had a toy company and he took Julian once to his warehouse; when he told Julian he could choose anything he wanted, Julian's eyes almost popped out of his head.

By the time I became a trustee of the Montefiore Endowment, there was little money in the kitty but we were to benefit from the shrewdness of Haham Gaster, who, although his college scheme had failed, proved the salvation of the Endowment. An avid bibliophile, when he heard the collection of Leopold Zunz, father of the Wissenschaft, the academic Jewish study in 19th Germany, was up for sale, he got the trustees of Sir Moses's legacy to acquire it for something in the region of £1,000.

The Zunz collection became worth a small fortune. We could see little point in continuing to keep it at Jews' College, where it lay unused. So we removed it, preserved it for future scholarship on microfiche and instead put part of it up for sale at Sotheby's in New York. The assets would be used for various projects some of us had in mind which we thought would be eminently suitable to fund in Sir Moses's name.

When Lucien Gubbay, Ronnie Musri, another trustee of the Endowment, and I arrived in America, we were taken into a private room by a Sotheby's director. He told us the reserve price was too high and we should drop it by around a quarter. We were adamant, "Under no circumstances". The Zunz sale netted around £4 million. We did not sell all the lots, yet we had still miscalculated by selling too much; we glutted the market when it would have been better to stagger the release of the books. There were Chasidic works, for example, which we didn't think so valuable but were eagerly sought by followers of a particular rabbinical dynasty and would have fetched a much higher price had we waited. The rest of the books we have retained for my successor so that he might have a fund for initiatives, too.

We still had to see to the upkeep of the synagogue and tomb in Ramsgate which had grown more challenging. The land around it had become derelict and a haunt of drug addicts, and in addition we were worried about the risk of vandalism to the premises. In 1999, we arranged for a coachload of people to come from London to Ramsgate to mark the *anos* (*yahrzeit*) of Sir Moses so they could see the state of the site themselves.

The local council which had bought the land where the college stood had originally intended to build a primary school there but never did. However, when many years later they considered plans for a housing development, they met stiff opposition on two fronts, from a local heritage committee and from Charedim. Increasingly, the synagogue was becoming a place of pilgrimage for Stamford Hill on the anniversary of Sir Moses's death, with hundreds flocking to the synagogue for the annual event to say prayers for the man they embraced as a pillar of Orthodoxy.

Forced to abandon its initial scheme, the council was more successful a few years afterwards when it sold the land for a medical centre, but not without a planning battle into which we were inevitably sucked. The endowment wanted to sell a small strip of land, which had remained in our possession, to the developers of the surgery. The Spanish and Portuguese Community was accused of betrayal by some of our religious detractors. Finally, however, the Charity Commission, rejecting a challenge to the Endowment's actions, approved the sale in 2006.

The Ramsgate synagogue is open now on special occasions and for visitors by appointment. I took a group of rabbinical students down there a few years ago with Dayan Amor when we stayed in the house of Augustus Pugin, the architect who designed the Palace of Westminster. We were right to be protective of the synagogue. In 2001, some silver Torah bells were stolen. What the thieves had not reckoned on was that we had had the silver valued by Sotheby's. They took their booty to Israel, where they tried to sell it through Sotheby's, who checked its provenance. The Tel Aviv police were alerted and the silver was delivered safely back into our hands.

Controversy over the site continued to fester, however, and at times became singularly unpleasant. I'd even get letters from Charedi girls in New York saying they couldn't sleep at night because of what we were supposedly doing to poor Sir Moses.

In fact, we remained mindful of the legacy of Sir Moses. After one visitor had indicated his predilection to sit in the seat of Sir Moses in the synagogue, we took no chances and had a glass case installed around the seat. When one strictly Orthodox VIP, the head of the Gateshead Yeshivah, Rabbi Abraham Gurwitz, came for the *yahrzeit* one year, I made sure he had a place of honour by sitting him in the former seat of Rabbi Shemtov Gaguine, the college's principal and head of our Beth Din.

In another respect, Sir Moses and Lady Judith's resting place was a source of disagreement. Israel was keen on removing their remains to the land they had visited so often and done so much to promote as a place of Jewish settlement. When the office of the then President, Zalman Shazar, suggested a plot on the Mount of Olives, Haham Gaon supported the idea, as did some members of the Montefiore family. Writing to Dr Gaon in 1969, Denzil Sebag-Montefiore contemplated something similar to the Ramsgate mausoleum although in a different location – between the Windmill and Yemin Moshe, the Jerusalem neighbourhood built after Sir Moses's death by his estate. He suggested the

Haham make an announcement shortly about "the wisdom of maintaining the mausoleum at Ramsgate and the danger of vandalism" but while Denzil was in favour of reburial, he warned "I think there will be quite a lot of opposition from several members of the family and particularly my brother Oliver... it would be tragic if it caused a row."

Opposition came not only from within the family. When Israel's government made a fresh attempt to move Sir Moses, this time to Mount Herzl, local people in Ramsgate lobbied the council to stop it. More recently, the historian Simon Sebag Montefiore suggested that Jerusalem was the most appropriate place for his illustrious ancestor but Lucien Gubbay argued the proposal was outside the Endowment's remit.

At an earlier stage leading rabbis had differed over whether Sir Moses should be reinterred or not. The Sephardi Chief Rabbi Ovadia Yosef had confirmed to Dayan Toledano that not only could we move him, but we should. America's greatest 20th-century halachist, Rav Moshe Feinstein, however, believed the great man should lie where he was. Shortly before Rav Ovadia's death, I wrote to his son David, through the good offices of Miguel Abadi, to ask if his father's view remained the same. The response came back: "Although it has been delayed a long time, it is a mitzvah to bring his bones to the Land", particularly as the tomb was in a place where barely any Jews remained. While Rav Ovadia's words must carry weight, I doubt whether the people of Ramsgate will be any more amenable to the transfer than they were before, so I do not see it happening. Mind you, they could simply remove the bones and leave the mausoleum and the synagogue intact as a tourist attraction.

I was fortunate to possess one heirloom of Sir Moses myself, his personal Bible which had accompanied him on his travels. On his deathbed, Sir Moses had given it to his nephew and heir Joseph Sebag (who added "Montefiore" to his surname); it passed down to Joseph's daughter-in-law, Sarah Floretta Sebag-Montefiore; to her daughter Harriet, to Harriet's daughter Margaret, and finally to Margaret's daughter, Esther Carvalho. Esther presented it to me as a gift to mark my twenty-five years of service to the synagogue. The Bible was in English but Sir Moses had asked his secretary Louis Loewe to insert in Hebrew not only the name of every *parashah* but each of the seven stops when a person is called up to the reading of the Torah: *rishon* (first), *sheni* (second) etc. In the frontispiece of the Bible, Sir Moses recorded his arrival in Jerusalem on one visit and added in Hebrew, *Lamaron Shevach*, "May the All-High Be Praised", a phrase which appears more than once in the book as a note of thanksgiving.

I had long wanted to do something special to honour his name. The Endowment's first practical efforts were more modest. We ran a Montefiore *kollel* jointly with Jewish Care on the theme of "Living and Giving" where a number of rabbis, including some of those who had graduated from our own congregation such as Rabbi Jonathan Cohen and Rabbi Michael Kedourie, undertook an in-depth study of the laws of charity for a term.

However, it was the sale of the books and manuscripts that gave us the means to think more boldly. Since Jews' College had dropped s*emichah*, Lucien and I felt there was a gap in Anglo-Jewry. It might be laudable that so many young men were going off to learn in yeshivot in Israel for years but the yeshivah syllabus did not necessarily prepare them to be good congregational rabbis or teachers in Britain. In an article in the *Jewish Chronicle* in 2004 entitled "Gifted Amateurs", I suggested we ought to offer an alternative model of rabbinic recruitment. I recalled Maimonides's opposition to a paid rabbinate, citing a Mishnaic saying: "Do not fashion [the Torah] into a crown with which to magnify yourself nor into a spade with which to dig."

On this theme, I can cite an example from my own congregation, from a family descended from the great spiritual leader of Baghdad in the 19th and early 20th century, Rabbi Yosef Chaim, known as the Ben Ish Chai. The family did a great deal for our community. I shall never forget the time when one of them, Rabbi Alan David, was sent a cheque for lecturing on one of the Montefiore programmes. He arrived at the office, holding it at arm's length as if it were some hideous reptile. "Take it away, take it away," he cried.

In my article, I quoted the story of an Italian rabbi who used to walk a long distance every Shabbat to serve a small community but refused to accept payment for his troubles. "The moment you feel that you have paid me for the Torah, it will become yours to do with as you please," he explained to them. "Keep it, therefore, as my present to you." It was accepted that rabbis needed financial security but we were not necessarily better off with a salaried rabbinate. If a rabbi is dependent on his congregation for his livelihood, his freedom of action may be constrained.

We did not always need full-time rabbis. "The rabbi who can combine his leadership with another occupation may acquire an added dimension to his ministry," I said, "as well as much-needed independence." I wrote that I was not suggesting "the entire English rabbinate should become non-professional but simply that some of our rabbis might be recruited from among those who also hold other occupations. We have able men among us who have attended yeshivot and also hold leading positions in the professions or in business: their talents could well be harnessed for the benefit of the community, if only in a part-time capacity."

In early 2006 the Endowment turned that into a possibility when we launched a new part-time *semichah* programme. Students could continue working in their professions while twice a week receiving an intensive course of tuition. Not only would they study *halachah* but also broader practical skills such as counselling or public speaking to equip them for service in a modern community, as well as history and ethics. It was, of course, infused with the Western Sephardi ethos of synthesis and halachic moderation. While we required students to have an undergraduate degree and aptitude in Talmud, they could bring their experience of the wider world into their rabbinate; one of our first cadre was in finance, another in IT. I encouraged the students to go to the annual Limmud education conference to familiarise themselves with the wider Jewish community and one year at the conference, they ran a pop-up *beit midrash* ("house of learning"), where anyone could drop in at any time of the day and study with them.

The practicalities necessary to bring a project like this to fruition, such as arranging the contracts or scholarships for students, we left safely in Lucien's hands. For our principal lecturer, we were lucky enough to prevail on Dayan Amor – who also became head of our Beth Din – to come down from Manchester. We were helped by the willingness of Jonathan Sacks, to give his imprimatur to the course, which widened its appeal. Some in the United Synagogue would have preferred Jonathan to keep his distance from anything that was not under their control but I was delighted he came on board. He would sign the *semichah* with Dayan Ezra Basri, head of the Jerusalem Beth Din, Dayan Amor and myself.

"You know, Abraham, only you could get me to wear one of these," Jonathan said in his top hat at the first ceremony for the graduates of our programme at Bevis Marks in 2009.

In my address to the new rabbis, I recalled something that the Reverend Simeon Singer, the president of Jews' College, had said to young students 105 years earlier.

In no other profession was there a greater temptation to vanity, he warned them. They should always remember the respect their congregants showed them was not for them personally but the Torah they represented. And I retold the story he had quoted from the 19th-century Hebrew poet Yehuda Leib Gordon:

When King David decided to bring the Ark of the Covenant to Jerusalem, the King's men placed it in a cart and harnessed a couple of cows to it. The cows noticed that wherever they went, hundreds of Israelites came out in a jubilant mood to welcome back the Ark, rejoicing and bowing down before it.

Impressed with their reception, the cows said, "We must be very important. Look at the fuss they are making of us." But it was not them that the people were honouring, it was the Torah. The puffed-up cows did receive an honour – not one they would have sought, as they were offered up for sacrifices.

Since its inception, the London Montefiore Semicha programme has trained fifteen rabbis, with a third cohort of students currently on the course. They have gone on to various roles within the community; Rabbi Jeff Berger heads Rambam Synagogue, the first Sephardi congregation in Hertfordshire, Rabbi Dr Raphael Zarum is Dean of the London School of Jewish Studies, Rabbi Yaakov Finn manages the United Synagogue's community development fund. While the programme operates from Lauderdale Road, we later associated it with Jews' College (LSJS); the restoration of *semichah* would help to consolidate the college under Jonathan's presidency.

Late in 2016, we went one better by launching a part-time course in dayanut to train rabbinic judges, the first of its kind in the diaspora. It actually came about from a request made to the Endowment by Rabbi Joseph Dweck, my successor as senior rabbi of the Spanish and Portuguese Community. He had appointed Rabbi Daniel Kada as part-time minister of Wembley Sephardi Synagogue, who taught the rest of the week. "I would like to get a grant from the Endowment so that Rabbi Kada can give up his job as a teacher to learn to be a dayan," Rabbi Dweck asked me. "Yes," I told him, "but we are going to have to work out how to do it."

After Dayan Amor's death, we had turned to the Eretz Hemdah Institute of Advanced Jewish Studies in Jerusalem, to help with our *semichah* programme. Rabbi Ofer Livnat, the son-in-law of its principal Rabbi Yosef Carmel, was also using the internet for teaching dayanut in Israel so he was happy to help set up a distance learning course for us. The take-up delighted us. Our first eighteen students included not only a number of British rabbis, including Michael Harris, Cyril's son, of Hampstead Synagogue, Chaim Kanterovitz, the leader of one of the United Synagogue's largest communities, Borehamwood and Elstree, his predecessor Naftali Brawer, and Mendel Cohen of the Saatchi Shul, but also rabbis from Holland, Australia, Hong Kong and the USA. The fact that the Rabbinical Council of America, the country's professional body for mainstream Orthodoxy, was prepared to advertise the course enhanced its credibility. We were even able to recruit two rabbis who work in Stamford Hill.

The five-year part-time programme of study focuses on the areas of marriage, divorce and conversion. As Lucien Gubbay, who again was a linchpin in its organisation, has emphasised, it "follows Sephardi custom, approaching halachic decision-making with mildness and adopting the traditional view which stresses the middle way and avoids extremes". Nevertheless, some notable absences at the official opening suggested that not everyone subscribes to that ambition.

Through the Endowment, we have occasionally sponsored one-off events such as a public discussion one evening on the sensitive subject of organ donations. Although the Israeli Chief Rabbinate accepts the halachic validity of brain-stem death, the London Beth Din has so far resisted it. I regard it as a feather in our cap that dayanim not only from the London Beth Din but also from the Union of Orthodox Hebrew Congregations were prepared to come to us to debate the issues with Rabbi Avraham Steinberg from Israel, the foremost Orthodox expert on Jewish medical issues, who does accept brain-stem death. If there are two halachic views on a subject and people tend to be familiar with only the stricter one, I want to make sure they are aware of the alternative.

More recently, we hosted a panel debate on women in Jewish law which tackled such controversial subjects in the Orthodox world such as partnership minyanim and female ordination. Our line-up included Rabbi Professor Daniel Sperber, the British-born talmudic scholar from Israel's Bar-Ilan who has become the most prominent rabbinic supporter of partnership minyanim – Orthodox services which differ from the traditional format in that women are able to lead some of the prayers and can be called up and read from the Torah. We do not offer them in the Spanish and Portuguese Community and Chief Rabbi Mirvis has banned them in the United Synagogue but, despite that, a number of independent groups have followed precedents in Israel and North America and started them in the UK.

Rabbi Sperber's radicalism also extends to support of the ordination of Orthodox women at institutions such as Yeshivat Maharat in New Jersey – an innovation rejected by America's central Orthodox rabbinic establishment. Both partnership minyanim and women's ordination were opposed by Rabbi Sperber's fellow-panellists; Rabbanit Chana Henkin, founder of the Nishmat institute for advanced women's Torah study in Jerusalem, and Rabbi Dr Michael Rosensweig, yeshivah head at the rabbinic seminary of New York's Yeshiva University. But that we held such a debate at all, which attracted a full house in the hall of Lauderdale Road synagogue, is worth comment. Such is the sensitivity around the issues that mainstream synagogues, at least in the UK, have tended to shy away from openly addressing them. A few people told me they were surprised we were able even to assemble such a panel. We wanted to show it is possible to have intelligent discussion on areas of difference without it degenerating into angry polemic. I thanked the panellists, who had been models of respectful civility, for "having disagreed so nicely".

Another thing we did was to reprint Lady Montefiore's *Jewish Manual* from 1847, which is considered the first Anglo-Jewish cookbook. We once rounded off a dinner at Lauderdale Road to commemorate Sir Moses and Haham Gaster's contributions to Zionism by using her recipe for lemon cake as dessert.

The considerable funds that the Endowment now had at its disposal thanks to the book sale also enabled us to invest in another cause: the encouragement of young leadership. In 2013, we started a gap-year fellowship scheme, sponsoring five boys and five girls from the UK to spend a year in yeshivah or seminary in Israel. In keeping with the original intention of Sir Moses for Torah to be learned in his and his wife's name, I made it a condition of their participation that once a fortnight they would go to Mishkenot Sha'ananim and, in the little room where Sir Moses would pray during his visits, study some Torah. They have lectures from a variety of speakers, including a number of scholar ex-pats, which are arranged for them by Rabbi Asaf Mittleman, one of our Montefiore rabbis, and Rabbi Amram Nemeth, who also helps with our *semichah* programme.

Sir Moses had toyed with the idea of building his college in Jerusalem but decided against it on grounds of practicality, believing it was too far away. None the less, I remained keen that Mishkenot Sha'ananim, now an attractive conference centre, should be a place to remember his name. In 2013, we staged an international festival there to celebrate his legacy. In 2015, we took a group of outstanding Jewish graduates from various universities to Israel for an intensive summer seminar based at Mishkenot Sha'ananim. They included Yoseph (Joseph) Citron, who, as a baby had escaped serious injury when the IRA bombed Bevis Marks.

The seminar, which was organised by Dr Diana Lipton, a former reader in Bible at King's College, London, exposed its participants to leading modern Orthodox rabbis such as Meir

Soloveichik from New York or David Stav from Israel. We also introduced them to a broader spectrum of Jewish opinion, from Adina Bar-Shalom, the daughter of Rav Ovadia Yosef and principal of a Charedi women's college, to representatives of the non-Orthodox movements. One of our students, Hannah Goldstein, a former president of King's College Jewish society, reflected; "The programme taught me that there's more to leadership than power, prestige and money. Being a leader can be simple. All you have to do is act on what you know is right and, if you do it properly, everyone else will follow."

The latest initiative at Mishkenot Sha'ananim in which I have had a hand is the establishment there of a new centre to further UK–Israel relations which has been handsomely endowed in the name of the late Sir Naim Dangoor. I found this particularly fitting. Just as the leadership of the Spanish and Portuguese Community had passed to the children of the new immigrants from the Middle East, so the tradition of Sephardi Zionism which Sir Moses had established was being continued by the family of one of the most prominent Iraqi Jewish philanthropists. As Sir Moses would have said, *Lamaron Shevach*.

10

After the Pulpit

LET ME EXPLAIN how I came to buy an unexpurgated edition of *Lady Chatterley's Lover*. For many years I have been a collector of old books and have always enjoyed the search to add to my shelves. One day I happened to be in an auction house where most of the prospective buyers were browsing through the Judaica offerings up for sale. I wandered over to the more general lots and when I rummaged through one box, spotted something that caught my eye.

The two principal items were an edition of D.H. Lawrence's controversial novel, and an Amsterdam Haggadah printed in 1695. It was a classic Sephardi edition of the Haggadah, which was particularly noteworthy for containing the first printed map of the Land of Israel in Hebrew characters. When the auction started, it did not take me long to guess that the man bidding against me was probably after the *Chatterley*, while he must have worked out that I wanted the Haggadah. When I got the books, he asked me did I want all of them. I happily did a deal to sell him the *Chatterley* which helped defray the cost of the precious Haggadah.

My love of old books was kindled when I was as young as eight or nine by my Aunt Esther Maman, who was actually the sister-in-law of one of my aunts. When my aunt's husband died, Esther, who never married, was left with little so she moved into a house in City Mill Lane in Gibraltar which has been in Levy hands for 200 years. She remained loyal to us and we to her. Every so often she would present me with prayer books that had long been in her family, in each of which I carefully wrote my name as well as the date it was given to me. These beautiful old books imprinted a deep sense of tradition in me which I felt it my duty to honour and to guard.

Most of my acquisitions have a Sephardi connection. At auction I have bought a number of the little prayer books which Sir Moses Montefiore used to distribute to the children of our school, some containing his signature. One of my prize possessions is a prayer book from the late 17th century which is written entirely in Spanish. That is because most of the Marranos who left Spain did not know how to read Hebrew, so the books were published in their mother tongue. The prayer book, which is in unusually good condition with its metal clasp still intact, had once belonged to Sir John Simon, who in the 1840s had become the first Jew to practise at the common-law bar and to act in the role of a judge. It was bequeathed to me by a descendant of his who was also a barrister, Philip Rossdale, who had asked me to officiate at his funeral. Philip, whose father had been a vice-president of the United Synagogue, had grown up thoroughly anglicised but had become more attracted to Judaism through Rabbi Louis Jacobs and then went further to the religious right, ending up as a member of Munk's, the home of German Orthodoxy in Golders Green.

The pride of our collection must be *Thesorous dos Dinim*, "Treasures of the Laws", Manasseh ben Israel's abridged translation into Portuguese of the Shulchan Aruch, the Code of

Jewish Law. I had found the first fifteen pages in the home of one of my aunts in a box she used as a *genizah*, to store sacred writings which must be buried, and not destroyed (according to the biblical law prohibiting the erasure of God's name in Hebrew). Sadly, she had been buried before she had had the opportunity to bury the books. Even though I had only a fraction of the book, I could not part with it, it was too rare.

My cousin Momy Coriat in Paris had some old religious books he had little use for, so seeing I was a rabbi, he offered them to me. When I inspected them, I was amazed to discover the remaining pages of the *Thesorous*. I took the book to the British Museum to be restored; the spine was replaced but we retained the original covers. Inside Estelle wrote, "This book has been in the Levy family probably from the date of publication 5405" (1644).

Estelle and I also have a copy of the edition of *The Times* from 1840, which published the entire text of the Haggadah in English. Earlier that year, the medieval blood libel had been revived in Damascus when a group of Jews were accused of murdering a Christian priest to use his blood for a Passover rite. Sir Moses Montefiore set off for Alexandria in Egypt on his famous rescue mission on behalf of his endangered brethren and, to support him, *The Times* printed the Haggadah in order to demonstrate the utter absurdity of the libel. Estelle and I were visiting a shop which specialised in old copies of *The Times*. She remembered the date and, lo and behold, they had a copy of that very edition, which we bought at a snip for £5.

Another item with a link to Sir Moses is an antique Kiddush cup. I had been asked to say Kiddush at the *brit milah*, circumcision, of one of the Montefiores where they used a magnificent silver cup. One day I was on my way to a meeting of Jews' College at the office of Stanley Kalms in the West End when I passed Phillips' auction house; I popped in and there I saw an identical cup to the one I had used at the *brit*. "You must buy it," Estelle said. It was made in 1874, the year of his 90th birthday and is inscribed with a verse from the Song of Songs, "We will find your love more fragrant than wine – sincerely do they love you". A number of these cups were gifts either to or from Sir Moses; he received one from the first Chief Rabbis, Solomon Hirschell, while another he presented to the hazan of Bevis Marks, David de Sola.

Estelle and I also went to auctions for another reason. I had inherited some Georgian and Victorian silver cutlery engraved with my ancestors' initials but the set was incomplete so we used to go and see if we could pick up similar pieces. Other heirlooms embellish our home. On a wall hangs a *Shiviti*, an illustrated representation of Psalm 16 in the form of a seven-branched lamp, which is named after the opening Hebrew word of the verse, "I have placed God before me always", and is there as a reminder of the Divine Presence. When it came to us from a branch of my cousins, the Sequerras, in Portugal, it was in many fragments, which Estelle managed carefully to piece together.

If you were to enter our dining room, the first thing that would catch your eye is a brass candelabrum above the table, similar in style to the larger lamps suspended from the roof of Bevis Marks (which were replicas of those in the older Spanish and Portuguese Synagogue of Amsterdam: in fact, the Dutch community donated the largest of the seven candelabra, representing the Sabbath among the days of the week, to the London community). I first noticed it in the window of an antique shop that lay on my way to Jews' College in the West End. It was a bit expensive but after months of passing it by, I could resist no more and it has illuminated our meals for more than forty years. We have table mats which feature Belisario's famous etching of Bevis Marks in the early 19th century.

Our collection of antique *ketubo*t, marriage contracts, reveals a little slice of social history. The Ashkenazim had prohibited polygamy after the decree of Rabbenu Gershom in the 11th century but the Sephardim allowed it. Some of the *ketubot* we have from Gibraltar record adherence to the customs of the Jews of Castile, which stipulate that if a man wants to take a second wife, he may do so only with the permission of the first.

So, though I have lived most of my life outside Gibraltar, some of my Judaica remind me of my birthplace. My two brothers, however, remained there and became stalwarts of a Jewish community which managed to consolidate itself while other parts of the diaspora declined.

Solomon, or Momy as my elder brother was called, who sadly is no longer with us, always stood out from the crowd in his extravagant pinstripes and bowties. A captain in the Gibraltar Defence Force, he was its chief gunner, one of whose duties was to march to the top of the Rock on the Queen's Birthday and give the order to fire the guns in salute. But he had a problem because the Queen's Official Birthday was on a Saturday. So he consulted Rabbi Pacifici. "Do you actually fire the cannons yourself," the rabbi asked. "No," said Solomon, "I just give the command." "Well," said the rabbi, "I can't see any difficulty with that." Solomon established a flourishing estate business but he always heeded my father's instruction: "If ever you do any work for the Church, you are not to charge them."

While James gravitated more to the right-wing yeshivot of Gateshead and Mir, he kept both feet planted in this world. He took over our uncle Sir Joshua Hassan's law firm and has both the Chief Minister of Gibraltar and the Leader of Opposition among his partners. I felt if he had turned his hand to politics, he could have become Chief Minister himself.

My sister Loli moved in similar religious circles to James. Like her husband, Rabbi Ralph Berish, she was a teacher and for a time headed the secular studies department of Beis Rochel, the Satmar

Chasidic girls' school in Stamford Hill. Loli had been one of the first group of three girls who Rabbi Pacifici sent to seminary in Gateshead, something unheard of in Gibraltar at the time but which has since become routine for girls. Ralph has quietly helped many young people who went OTD, off the *derech* – in other words, who strayed from the path – to find their way back to the Orthodox community. He also used to arrange events for older singles in their mid-thirties, an age group that would find it hard to make a match in a community where people were commonly married by their early twenties; he invited me to be the speaker at his first event.

My other sister Nita's husband, Alan Corré, was, like me, a graduate of Jews' College. He served as a minister in London and Manchester and then as rabbi at America's second oldest synagogue, Mikveh Israel, in Philadelphia. A gifted linguist who had learned Esperanto by his barmitzvah, he eventually opted for academia and became professor of Jewish studies at Wisconsin University. Nita inherited my father's business acumen and built a complex of homes for the elderly for the Milwaukee Jewish community.

My mother would have been delighted by one thing above all about her family's progression. She always dreamed of having one rabbi in the family, but I was not to be the only one to have the title. She probably would have never believed that at the last count, she would have been able to muster a minyan of rabbis and rabbinical scholars among her descendants and their spouses.

I never tired of the rabbinate, despite the obstructions some lay leaders put in my way. My contract extended till the age of seventy-five which was unusual within mainstream British Jewry. The United Synagogue had lowered the retirement age from seventy to sixty-five. Jonathan Sacks himself showed no inclination to stay on; free of the shackles of office since he left it in 2013, he is as much in demand as a writer and lecturer as ever and, in a way, he has become Chief Rabbi to the English-speaking world and beyond.

The possibility even arose that I might become rabbi of a second congregation. Before he retired in 2000, Louis Jacobs, my teacher at Jews' College, called me and asked if I would be interested in succeeding him at the New London Synagogue. We had remained good friends despite any theological differences and he saw me as a kindred spirit. When he could not make it to a party held by my congregation in 2000 to thank me for my years of service, he wrote me a note in which he generously said that I had been "virtually a lone voice for tolerance, reason and humanity in the Anglo-Jewish community". Although the New London was a member of the Assembly of Masorti Synagogues, which had been founded in 1985, Louis' synagogue was basically Orthodox in practice and he was a traditionalist at heart with a soft spot for *Minhag Anglia*, the custom of the United Synagogue. He often told me he had never intended to start a new denomination.

I was ready to accept his offer but I had two conditions. Firstly, I would regularise any conversions carried out by the synagogue so that there would be no challenge to the Jewish status of its members. Secondly, I would remain as rabbi of Lauderdale Road. I thought it was an arrangement that could work; New London was less than a mile away from Lauderdale Road. Louis had no objections to either and recommended me to his lay leaders. However, they felt I could not ride two horses and insisted if I wanted to be their rabbi, I would have to give up Lauderdale Road. That was something I was simply unwilling to consider.

The year after I turned seventy, the Mahamad announced the search for my successor at the Spanish and Portuguese Community. Just as I had served a long apprenticeship under Haham Gaon, the idea was to find someone whom we could groom into the role who would be ready when I stepped down four years later. The Parnas Presidente, Edward Shaoul, told the *Jewish Chronicle*: "I can't imagine that Rabbi Levy will go until he knows the right person is in place."

Edward was no longer holding the reins when the Mahamad picked their man, Rabbi David Bassous, a Londoner of Indian-Iraqi origin who headed a Sephardi congregation in New Jersey. His brother Rabbi Aharon Bassous would have been a more familiar name to our congregation as he had remained in the United Kingdom and ran a synagogue in Golders Green, which was affiliated to the Charedi Union of Orthodox Hebrew Congregations. After a short visit to London to meet and speak to the congregation in late 2011, Rabbi David Bassous's name was put to a members' vote for approval as required by the *ascamot*, our regulations. While he secured the necessary two-thirds majority, it was by the narrowest possible margin, 268 votes to 134.

The whole process was thrown into crisis when a group of his opponents contested the result of the poll. They argued that one of two ballot papers declared invalid had actually recorded a vote against the candidate – which if it were ruled legitimate, would deprive Rabbi Bassous of his majority by a single vote. It was almost a replay of the acrimonious events of forty years earlier when a resolution to authorise the retirement of Haham Gaon had been carried only by the chairman's casting vote. As the rifts in the community deepened and there was talk of legal challenges, Rabbi Bassous did the honourable thing and withdrew his name.

The Mahamad, trying to pick up the pieces, wanted to make a fresh start. They decided it would help if I were to agree to go two years earlier than the expiry of my contract when I turned seventy-three in July 2012. It was not an option that had occurred to me but all I will say is the Mahamad might have acted more graciously. I remain ever grateful to David Price QC, whom I had taught as a barmitzvah boy and at whose wedding I had officiated.

He helped me negotiate my departure with the Mahamad and I took his advice to avoid a quarrel. With tensions already high in the community, I did not want to be the cause of more.

For the first couple of weeks, it felt strange to walk in and not take my seat beside the *hechal*. I was given a place at the front of the synagogue. But this was the community where I felt at home. I was still the same Abraham Levy who had come here to pray as a schoolboy more than sixty years before. I can't say I missed the preaching but I am glad still to be asked by families to help officiate at weddings. I feel a special sense of continuity when I stand under the *chuppah* with the children or grandchildren of couples I had married.

Happily, when our community next cast their votes for a new senior rabbi in 2013, there was almost unanimous approval. Rabbi Joseph Dweck, born in Los Angeles of Syrian-Jewish extraction, was a tall, imposing man in his mid-thirties who headed a community and school in New York. His wife, Margalit, was the granddaughter of no less than Rav Ovadia Yosef. On his "audition" in London, he instantly impressed as a speaker and his use of Facebook showed his rapport with young people.

Whereas we used to export spiritual leaders to America such as Rabbis David de Sola Pool, Henry Pereira Mendez, Sabato Morais and Haham Gaon, it was a sign of the times that we were now taking ours from across the Atlantic. In addition, given the composition of our membership today, it was appropriate that the new rabbi had a Middle-East background and I was reassured by the admiration Rabbi Dweck expressed for the western Sephardi ethos which, whatever other change he might usher in, remained at the core of our community.

I had a chance to celebrate that ethos elsewhere later the same year when I was invited to officiate at the induction of the new rabbi of America's oldest congregation, Shearith Israel in New York. Rabbi Meir Soloveichik was from an eminent rabbinic family, the grand-nephew of Rav Joseph Soloveitchik. He was an Ashkenazi, but then so had been Haham Gaster in London.

In my address, I said Rabbi Soloveichik reminded me "of the arrival in Spain of the Rosh, Rabbi Asher ben Yehiel, the 14th-century leader of German Jewry, who left Germany because of persecution. The whole Jewish world opened their arms to receive him as their rabbi but he chose to become rabbi of Toledo, an elegant, sophisticated community with many great intellectuals.

"Many of us have been to Toledo and seen the magnificent ancient synagogues of Santa Maria la Blanca and El Transito, national monuments today. The Rosh helped to fuse different views of Jewish scholarship in Spain. We pray that from this synagogue Rabbi Meir Soloveichik will similarly continue to influence for good Jewish life in this great city." I wished both him and Rabbi Dweck who was present, *hatzlachah*, success, in furthering "the great and noble traditions of our two communities".

Rabbi Dweck was so taken with the canonicals worn at the ceremony that he ordered them for his own induction at Bevis Marks the following year, in September 2014. The frictions over the elections two years earlier could be forgotten on a day when we looked forward, rather than back, when I welcomed my successor as an "exciting, learned and tolerant" new voice in British Jewry. In the ancient synagogue, different wings of the community were again able to come together in celebration.

If Immanuel Kant was right in his prescription for happiness, I could count myself happy, for indeed I had "something to do, someone to love, something to look forward to". When my portrait was duly unveiled alongside my predecessors in the Montefiore Hall, Sir Naim Dangoor sent me a letter apologising that he could not attend the occasion, adding: "You are too young to retire." The thought of retirement had never crossed my mind for I still had plenty to occupy me in my honorary roles as trustee of the Montefiore Endowment and, of course, as principal of

Naima Jewish Preparatory School. And here I must thank God. When I first started the school, it had been my original intention to transfer control to the congregation but the ambivalence I encountered towards it from within the community's leadership, in the early days, convinced me to keep it separate. I am glad that I did, for I am sure it has flourished all the more for its independence.

I entrusted the preservation of its ethos to a group I call the "Four Isaacs", each of whom is named after the wisest man and the most upright Jew I have known, my father Isaac. It comprises three of my nephews, Isaac Corré, a New York fund manager who runs a fund called Governor's Lane (Gibraltar), named after the birthplace of all my siblings; Momy's son, Isaac Levy, a financier and talmudic scholar who shares my passion for collecting old Judaica; and Rabbi Isaac Levy, who is also a lawyer in his father James's office; along with my son, Julian Isaac. If ever there were to be a problem related to the Jewish character of the school, it will be up to the Four Isaacs to resolve. I hope, just as my family have maintained the Abudarham Synagogue in Gibraltar for 200 years, so they will look after the welfare of the school.

We have been fortunate that there are still people ready to invest in Naima and its vision. When I took around the school one of the major donors to the new building project, Eliyahou Abraham, and his wife Joyce to show them what his gift would achieve, he remarked it was one of the happiest days of his life. The Moshal family have made sure it must be one of the best equipped schools for computers. Alan Howard, the leading hedge manager, who is of Adeni extraction, has been another generous donor. The school's supporters were rewarded when it received an "outstanding" classification from inspectors in 2015.

Julian, who successfully established himself in finance after qualifying as a chartered accountant but never wanting to work in that profession, has taken over the financial running of Naima

JPS from me, on a voluntary basis. Not only is he responsible for its annual budget, but he has also overseen the fundraising campaign for an extension on top of the Saatchi Synagogue.

The way Julian and his wife Sian have taken on the mantle of charitable work has been a source of pride to Estelle and me. While Julian is busy with Naima, Sian is working to upgrade the mikveh. She is also a *lavadora*, who performs the mitzvah of washing the dead before burial. Both she and Julian are staunch supporters of the Association for the Wellbeing of Israel's Soldiers, a charity raising money for religious and recreational facilities for Israeli servicemen. They have built two mobile synagogues for soldiers in Israel in honour of the bnei mitzvah of their two eldest sons. Julian and Sian live close by so we often get to see our four grandchildren – Avi (who, as is Sephardi custom, is named after me), Jamie, Rachel and Daniel.

Every so often Avi, who is a sixth-former at JFS, goes to spend Shabbat in Gateshead, where his cousin is studying. He once sent us a picture of himself sporting his cousin's wide-brimmed black hat. It goes to show that even though our family may span different shades of Orthodoxy, we get along together. If only that could be replicated on a grander scale.

Though an optimist by nature, I struggle to remain so when I survey the state of religion in Israel – not only because of the fault-lines between the religious and secular but also the lack of respect which different groups within Orthodoxy display towards one another. And when I hear the kind of inflammatory statements made recently by some Sephardi rabbis in Israel about non-Jews or non-Orthodox Jews, I shudder but am driven on to do what I still can to promote the Western Sephardi ethos. We must conserve its legacy on which future generations can draw.

Epilogue

THE SPANISH AND Portuguese Congregation in London which I entered in the 1950s was still pretty much the same as it was fifty years earlier when Dr David de Sola Pool left to become minister of America's oldest congregation, Shearith Israel in New York. Shearith Israel's current Emeritus Rabbi, Dr Marc Angel, wrote of Rabbi Dr Pool, that he was "always something of an outsider… to Ashkenazim, he was Sephardic. To Sephardim – most of whom came from Muslim lands – Dr Pool was a Western Sephardi, not really 'one of us'. To the Orthodox, he seemed a bit too refined, acculturated and universal. To the non-Orthodox, he was too Orthodox! To rabbis, Dr Pool was a scholar and gentleman. To scholars, Rabbi Pool was a rabbi, not an academic."

I recognise something of myself in that description, though I am not in any way trying to compare myself in stature to Rabbi de Sola Pool. I have never fitted neatly into any category. I was a "Rabbi Dr" – but not rabbinical enough for many rabbis and not scholar enough for academics. Although as the rabbi of the oldest community in British Jewry I might be considered at the heart of the Orthodox establishment, as the religious ground shifted, I came to occupy a lonelier position in the middle of the road.

In a career spanning four British Chief Rabbis, I lived through various changes. Grand cathedral synagogues have given way to house-based *steibls*. The orchestrated elegance of our worship I remain loyal to seems out of step with the current fashion for neo-Chasidic informality. High Anglo-Jewish traditionalism is in retreat before the passionate intensity of the religious right.

When Zionism is now a dirty word in many student unions and parts of the Labour party, our community feels under greater psychological pressure. Yet amid all the political fluctuations in the Middle East, our relationship with Israel is more complicated than it was in the years immediately after the Six Day War. I shared Professor Elie Kedourie's anxieties over Israel's capture of the West Bank and was never an advocate for settlement in Judea and Samaria. All I can say is that I doubt whether the Middle East in ten years will look the same as now.

However, there is one significant development I can only wholeheartedly applaud: the extraordinary rise of Jewish day school education. In the 1970s, around one in five Jewish children attended a Jewish school in Britain but the proportion has now grown to around two-thirds and the demand has not been satiated for there are still efforts to open new schools.

Not so long ago I was reading the novel *Conclave* by Robert Harris about the election of a Pope. Its subtitle has stuck in my mind, "The power of God, the ambition of men". Whatever mistakes I made in my rabbinate, I pray I never used God for personal gain or played politics with the *halachah*. Kashrut was meant to control our animalistic instincts, not to be used as a weapon of institutional power. I have never gone out of my way to court controversy but I did not duck conflict when pursuing what I felt was right. For all the projects in which I was involved

– the school, the mikveh, the rabbinic ordination programme – I had to overcome opposition.

I have tried not to deviate from the values I inherited from my parents and their family before them. We all remain sentimentally attached to the traditions we grew up with but I continue to espouse the classical Sephardi outlook out of conviction that it remains important in a polarised Jewish world. When there is friction not only between the religious left and right and the religious and secular but also among the different Orthodox camps, it is only the centre that can draw *Klal Yisrael*, all of Jewry, together. In that sense, we are the protectors of Jewish peoplehood. I remain a defiant centrist – despite Estelle thinking me over-optimistic.

I have tried to show respect to every section of Jewry, even though I may not share its views. I hope I have managed to communicate that to the 1,000 or so pupils who have come to our school. Our students still range from observant to secular. As principal, I continue to emphasise the importance of teaching Torah to children from less religious homes in a way that does not make them lose respect for their parents.

I visit the school once a week, though it is in my thoughts every day. There is nothing more heartwarming than seeing our first pupils as parents, bringing their own children through its gates. I enjoy that special sense of continuity which comes when we welcome to the school one of the new generation of a family. I buried the mother of Sir Naim Dangoor; one of her great-great grandchildren is a pupil at Naima JPS.

I continue to interview the parents of every prospective child. And when a child comes to school, I present them with his or her own little prayer book. Parents often tell me the prayer book is the first thing packed by their children when they go away. I was recently emailed a photo by some parents. It was a picture of their daughter on a plane bound for Israel holding her book and reciting her prayers. That, I told them, "makes it all worthwhile".

Glossary

adafina – Sabbath hotpot, cooked on Friday and kept warm for Shabbat

afikoman – a piece of matzah eaten to mark the conclusion of the Passover meal (traditionally it is hidden beforehand for the children to find)

agunah – a "chained" woman who is trapped in a dead marriage because her husband denies her a religious divorce

aliyah – (1) emigration from the diaspora to the land of Israel (2) the honour of being called to the public reading of the Torah in synagogue

berachah (pl: *berachot*) – a blessing to thank God, recited for example over food

Bnei Akiva – Orthodox Zionist youth movement

charoset – paste made of fruit, nuts, wine and spices eaten on Passover, symbolic of the mortar the Israelite slaves used in their hard labour in Egypt

Chillul Hashem – religious scandal ("profanation of the Divine Name")

Charedim – ultra-Orthodox (the "trembling" ones, as in God-fearing)

Chumash – the Pentateuch, the first five books of the Bible which constitute the written Torah. (The Soncino Chumash was for many years the standard edition used in mainstream Orthodox synagogues in Britain.)

chuppah – canopy under which Jewish wedding ceremony takes place

dayan – a religious judge in a rabbinic court

dayanut – programme leading to qualification as a dayan

finta – synagogue membership dues in the Spanish and Portuguese Jews' Congregation

Genizah – repository for storing sacred books no longer used (the most famous example is the Cairo *Genizah*, whose collection of medieval writings is now held at Cambridge and other universities)

haftarah – reading usually of the Prophets which follows the Torah reading in synagogue

Haham – religious head of the Spanish and Portuguese Community (literally, a "sage")

hakafot – formal procession of the scrolls around the synagogue on the festival of Simchat Torah (the "Rejoicing of the Law")

halachah – Jewish religious law

hatan – bridegroom

Hatan Torah/Bereshit – those respectively given the honour of completing the annual cycle of reading the Torah and of starting it anew on Simchat Torah

hazan – synagogue cantor

hazanut – the art of the hazan: singing like a cantor i.e. beautifully

hechal – ark in which the Torah scrolls are kept in synagogue
hora – Israeli folk dance

Kaddish – the mourners' prayer
Kal Nidre – the opening service on the evening of the fast of Yom Kippur
kasher – to make something kosher
kashrut – observance of kosher food laws
ketubah/ketubot – marriage contract/s
Kiddush – the prayer over wine recited at the start of a Sabbath or festival meal (meaning "sanctification")
Kiddush Hashem – an action which sanctifies God's name
kippah (pl: kippot) – skullcap worn by Jewish men
kollel – a gathering

Lamaron Shevach – May The All-High Be Praised

Mahamad – executive of Spanish and Portuguese synagogue Community
matzah – unleavened bread eaten on Passover
melaveh malkah – Saturday night gathering or meal after the conclusion of the Sabbath
Melech Hamashiach – King Messiah
mezuzah – a small scroll containing passages from the Torah, referring to the commandment of mezuzah, which is attached to the doorposts of Jewish homes
Midrash – rabbinic commentaries on the Bible which often take the form of legends amplifying the original text
mikveh – ritual bath, used for example in the rite of conversion or by married women after their menstruation
minyan – a religious quorum of ten Jewish men, the minimum necessary to recite certain public prayers
Musaf – additional Shabbat or festival service

parashah – weekly portion of the Torah reading

Parashat Korach – the weekly portion which recounts Korach's rebellion in the Book of Numbers

Parnas Presidente – chairman of a Spanish and Portuguese congregation

schnorrer – a beggar

Sefer Torah (pl: Sifrei Torah) – "Scroll of the Law", a parchment scroll containing the first five books of the Bible

semichah – rabbinic ordination

Shaare Tikvah – Gates of Hope

shaliach – an emissary, often an educator from Israel, who spends a year or two with a Jewish community in the diaspora

shamash – synagogue beadle

shechita – the kosher method of slaughtering animals for food

Shema – key prayer, "Hear, O Israel," recited morning and evening

shiur – (1) a religious class or lecture (2) term for a measurement in Jewish law

shivah – seven-day period of mourning observed by family immediately after a funeral

shochet – a religiously qualified slaughterer

shofar (pl: shofarot) – ram's horn blown on Rosh Hashanah, the New Year (the rabbis prescribed three different notes, tekiah, shevarim, teruah)

siddur – term for daily and Sabbath prayerbook used by Jews of central and East European origin. (The Singer's Siddur was the most common edition used in synagogues under the umbrella of the Chief Rabbi in the UK)

simchah (pl: *semachot*) – joyous occasion such as a wedding or barmitzvah.

Simchat Torah – a holiday which celebrates the end of the annual cycle of Torah readings

steibls – small synagogues

succah – hut with a roof of branches, which is used on the festival of Succot in memory of the booths in which the Israelites dwelt during their journey through the wilderness

tallit (pl: talletot) – prayer shawl worn by Jewish men

tebah (or bimah) – reading platform in a synagogue

tefillin – phylacteries, black boxes containing parchments with biblical passages referring to commandment of tefillin, worn by men at morning prayer

teshuvah – repentance (literally, "return"). The period between Rosh Hashanah and Yom Kippur is known as the *Aseret Yemai Teshuvah*, the Ten Days of Repentance

Tishah b'Av – fast commemorating the fall of the two Temples in Jerusalem

tzitzit – religious tassels worn by men daily as a reminder to observe the commandments – attached to a garment called a tallit katan, a small prayer shawl, although tzitzit is often used to refer to the garment itself

yahrzeit – anniversary of a person's death

Yehidim – members of the Spanish and Portuguese Jews' Congregation.

yeshivah (pl: yeshivot) – religious academy where boys go to learn Talmud

Yom Hashoah – Holocaust Remembrance Day (instituted in Israel and held on the anniversary of the Warsaw Ghetto Uprising)

Yom Tov – religious festival day

Zemirot – the opening section of the morning service

Acknowledgements

I am deeply grateful for the care and attention the publishers Martine and Peter Halban have given to this project. I officiated at Peter and Martine's marriage and, 34 years later shortly after the completion of this book earlier this year, I officiated at the marriage of their son Alexander at the same synagogue. Thanks are due to my nephew Isaac S Levy, author of *Don Moses De Isaac Levy*, for his advice; and to Lord Sacks for permission to quote from his correspondence. It has been a pleasure working with my collaborator Simon Rocker, who knows the idiosyncrasies of British Jewry better than most. All royalties from the sale of this book will go to Naima JPS.   *Abraham Levy*

The digital archive of the *Jewish Chronicle* has been an invaluable aid to retracing past events. Others sources have provided helpful background: *Carmel College in the Kopul Era*, Rabbi Dr Chaim Simons, Urim 2016; *Immanuel Jakobovits: a Prophet in Israel*, compiled and edited Meir Persoff, Vallentine Mitchell, 2002; *Sketches of Anglo-Jewish History*, revised and edited Israel Finestein, Soncino Press, revised edition (1956); *The Cousinhood*, Chaim Bermant, Eyre and Spottiswoode, 1971; *British Chief Rabbis, 1664-2006*, Derek Taylor, Vallentine Mitchell, 2007; *The Club: the Jews of Modern Britain,* Stephen Brook, Constable 1989; *Moses Montefiore: Jewish Liberator, Imperial Hero*, Abigail Green, Belknap Harvard, 2010; "The defence of shechita; Anglo-Jewry and the 'humane conditions' regulations of 1990", Geoffrey Alderman published in *New Community*, January 1995; Sir Moses Montefiore, *Segula – the Jewish Journal Through History*, 2013; Audio-interview with Rabbi Levy, Bea Lewkowicz, Sephardi Voices, 2012.   *Simon Rocker*